KUROZUMIKYŌ
AND THE
NEW RELIGIONS
OF JAPAN

KUROZUMIKYŌ

AND THE
NEW RELIGIONS
OF JAPAN

Helen Hardacre

Princeton University Press

Princeton, New Jersey

Copyright © 1986 by Princeton University Press

Published by Princeton University Press, 41 William Street, Princeton, New Jersey 08540
In the United Kingdom: Princeton University Press, Guildford, Surrey

All Rights Reserved

Library of Congress Cataloging in Publication Data will be found on the last printed page of this book

ISBN 0-691-06675-2

Publication of this book has been aided by the Whitney Darrow Fund of Princeton University Press

Clothbound editions of Princeton University Press books are printed on acid-free paper, and binding materials are chosen for strength and durability

Typeset in Hong Kong by Asco Trade Typesetting Ltd.

Printed in the United States of America by Princeton University Press, Princeton, New Jersey

Dedicated to the Fukumitsus of Okayama, Japan

Contents

Contents

Illustrations

Figures

Maps

Preface

While I was gathering data for this study, I lived in the Ōi Church of Kurozumikyō, 黒住教 in Okayama Prefecture, with its ministers, the Fukumitsus. Thinking that I might want time to myself occasionally, the Fukumitsus accorded me a rare privilege for their household: a room of my own. Luckily for me, as it turned out, that room did not become my private, cloistered world. There were doors on all four sides, and it soon became customary for any followers visiting the church to seek me out if I were not visible in the gathering room before the altar. One or several of my doors was quite liable to be flung open at any hour between 6 A.M. and midnight, as followers came to tell me stories of the many blessings they have received through Kurozumikyō and the Fukumitsus. They spoke of healings, powerful dreams, family problems solved, and the caring counsel of the church. They were eager to launch into their experiences, and often it was a struggle to keep up with them. I learned to keep notebook and tape recorder at the ready.

The ministers, especially Fukumitsu Katsue and Fukumitsu Sukeyasu, spared no effort to explain their beliefs and to share with me their hopes for the followers. Katsue's mother Hiroe took me with her all over western Japan and tirelessly explained to me Kurozumikyō doctrine and the inside stories of each of the many churches we visited. She wrote the story of her life for me, and I have translated this in chapter six. This document, and her daughter Katsue's sermon (translated in chapter three), vividly convey the joyful spirit and ethos of these "sun worshipers." The association I have come to enjoy through the Fukumitsus with Kurozumikyō followers includes many precious friendships, to say nothing of the data I obtained. Seeing the complete, unqualified dedication of the Fukumitsu ministers to their followers, I became aware of new depths of energy and power in the human spirit. Though I have written of Kurozumikyō as illustrative of broader issues, I am mindful of its uniqueness as well. No outside observer has a right to expect the riches that I received in my four-doored room (doorless, for all practical purposes), but I hope that every student of Japanese religions may have at least one such experience.

Acknowledgments

This study is based on research in Japan that was supported in part by a grant from Princeton University, for which I am very grateful. Professor Joseph Kitagawa of the University of Chicago, Professor George DeVos of the University of California, and Professor Byron Earhart of Western Michigan University read the manuscript and made extensive, substantive comments and suggestions that aided me greatly in revising it. I am also indebted to my parents, Paul and Gracia Hardacre, and to Suemoto Yōko for much editorial advice and encouragement. In Japan I benefited greatly from discussions with Professors Hirai Naofusa and Inoue Nobutaka of Kokugakuin University.

I am very much indebted to the Sixth Patriarch of Kurozumikyō, Kurozumi Muneharu, for granting permission for my study of Kurozumikyō and for facilitating innumerable opportunities for observation and interviews. I wish to thank the hundreds of Kurozumikyō followers who graciously and generously shared their time, their hopes, and their beliefs with me. Lastly, I wish to thank the editorial and design staff of the Princeton University Press, especially Miriam Brokaw, Cathie Brettschneider, and Laury Egan, for making this publication possible.

KUROZUMIKYŌ
AND THE
NEW RELIGIONS
OF JAPAN

CHAPTER ONE

The World View of The New Religions

The contemporary religious scene in Japan is commonly divided into the "established religions" (*kisei shūkyō* 既成宗教) and the "new religions" (*shinshūkyō* 新宗教 *shinkō shūkyō* 新興宗教). These categories are further divided into Buddhist-and Shintō-derived varieties of each as well as into further subcategories.[1] This study addresses the distinctive character of the new religions of contemporary Japan through a case study of Kurozumikyō 黒住教, a Shintō 神道 religion founded in 1814 by the Shintō priest Kurozumi Munetada 黒住宗忠 (1780–1850). With its headquarters in Okayama City, it is largely a rural group but also commands a significant urban following, amounting to about 20 percent of its total membership of 220,000. Founded by a priest of the "established" Shintō tradition, it is one of the oldest of the so-called new religions and seems to combine aspects of both new and established types.

THE NEW RELIGIONS OF JAPAN

The new religions and their members represent an important and distinctive sector of Japanese society. In spite of the great variety of their doctrines, new religions share a unity of aspiration and world view significantly different from those of secular society and from the so-called established religions. New religions constitute the most vital sector of Japanese religion today and include perhaps 30 percent of the nation's population in their membership.[2]

[1] Two much-used surveys of the new religions are H. Neil McFarland, *The Rush Hour of the Gods* (New York: Macmillan, 1967) and Harry Thomsen, *The New Religions of Japan* (Rutland, Vt.: Charles E. Tuttle, 1963).

[2] Ministry of Education, *Shūkyō nenkan* (Tokyo: Ministry of Education, 1982).

New religions have appeared in three waves in modern history, the first from roughly 1800 to 1860, the second during the 1920s, and the third in the postwar period. They have developed in relation to the established religions, and both have been powerfully shaped by the currents of Japanese and world history.[3] Neither can fruitfully be considered static, ahistorical categories. It is useful, however, to develop a systemic, comprehensive characterization of the new religions as they exist now in contemporary Japan. They display an orientation that shapes and channels the experience and behavior of a large proportion of the Japanese people. That orientation or world view in turn occupies a distinctive position in the history of Japanese religions.

Centering on temples and their clergy, established Buddhism maintains elaborate ecclesiastical hierarchies and ordains its priests in textually prescribed ceremonies. It upholds a strong distinction between priest and layman in which laymen sponsor temple rites but do not perform them. To a certain extent, the rewards awaiting the faithful are forthcoming after death, and to ensure their achievement, funerals and memorial rites should be performed by an ordained cleric. In Shrine Shintō (*jinja Shintō* 神社神道), another name for Shintō's established variety, the line between priest and layman is clearly drawn also. The priest's liturgical training and rigorous observance of purifications and abstinences entitle him to a proximity to deity impossible for the layman. The layman goes to the priest for ritual services, sometimes for special prayers to secure

---

Japanese scholars estimate that between 25 and 33 percent of the total population are members of new religions. Statistics for the new religions are notoriously unreliable and are subject to considerable inflation due to widespread practices such as counting members by households rather than by individuals. In recent years, however, the groups themselves have begun to feel a need for a more accurate count of their membership and so have in many cases begun counting members by dues actually received. Needless to say, this is a much more accurate measurement. Thus, problems with calculating the membership of the new religions are not so acute as in the past. If one calculates the number of members of new religious groups as reported in the *Shūkyō nenkan* and then subtracts as much as a third, the total is still in excess of 30 percent of the total population of Japan.

[3] Discussion of differences between "established" and "new" religions may be found readily in chapter 3 of Edward Norbeck, *Religion and Society in Modern Japan*, Rice University Studies, vol. 56, no. 1 (Houston: Rice University, 1970).

divine blessings here and now, such as safe childbirth, peace and safety in the home, or prosperity in business. Between established Buddhism and Shintō exists a division of labor most clearly observable in rites of passage: to Shrine Shintō are assigned the rites of birth and marriage while Buddhism retains title to rites of death and ancestor worship. In the established varieties of both Buddhism and Shintō are found ideas about the pollution of women, which have historically barred them from priestly roles. Both temples and shrines are generally passed from father to son, giving the priesthoods of both Buddhism and Shintō the character of hereditary occupations. The laity of the established religions is mainly recruited hereditarily on the basis of traditional family affiliations with temples and shrines. Both Buddhism and Shintō have established a number of sites as places of pilgrimage, to which local temples and shrines send the faithful. The validity of local practice is guaranteed in part by this continuing connection to venerable cult centers.

Among the doctrines of the new religions there is great variety, since doctrine frequently originates in revelations to a founder.[4] Most reserve a special place for ancestor worship, whether their main theological focus is Buddhist or Shintō. Often shamanistic practices resembling spirit possession have the aim of divining the ancestors' will or present condition. Founders tend to be charismatic individuals who attract a following through faith healing rather than through ordination and textual erudition. Many of the new religions' founders are women. The new religions tend to recruit their following through evangelistic proselytization and dramatic conversion, at least in the first generation. They promise followers "this-worldly-benefits" in the form of healing, solution of family problems, and material prosperity. In ethics they emphasize family solidarity and qualities of sincerity, frugality, harmony, diligence, and filial piety. Between laity and leaders there is only a vague dividing line, and for the most part, anyone may acquire leadership

---

[4] Historical studies and studies presenting trait lists of the new religions abound. A readily available combination of the two approaches is Murakami Shigeyoshi, *Japanese Religion in the Modern Period*, trans. Byron Earhart (Tokyo: Tokyo University Press, 1980), pp. 10–18, 48–51, 70–79, 82–91, 137–56.

credentials, including women. Frequently the new religions recognize no sacred centers but those of their own history. Although
the connection is not always acknowledged, the new religions have
grown out of the established and in many cases are not entirely
separate from them. For example, many new religions find it
difficult to overcome the attachment to established Buddhist
funeral and ancestral rites, producing the incongruous situation of
religions able to provide doctrine, ritual, and an organization
perfectly adequate for a human life span but forced at death to
return their believers to Buddhist temples for final disposition.
Funerals and ancestor worship commonly present difficult hurdles
in the process of a new religion establishing independence.

It is in world view rather than doctrine per se that the unity of the
new religions lies. The related term "cosmology" is widely used in
contemporary scholarship to refer to a world picture, a visual
image of various cosmic realms and their denizens: heavens, hells,
pure lands, demons, hungry ghosts, and the like.[5] The present
discussion, however, distinguishes cosmology from world view
and concentrates on the set of relations believed to link the self, the
body, the social order, and the universe as a whole.

Most writers on the new religions recognize a common orientation among the religions and have sought to articulate it. Two
approaches have dominated this endeavor. The first is to say that
the new religions represent reactions to the same social problems,
that they are reactions to a variety of "crises." I have written at
length on the problems of the "crisis explanation" and will not
recapitulate that argument here, since this study is not principally

[5] Recent studies that follow this usage are *Ancient Cosmologies*, ed. Carmen
Blacker and Michael Lowe (London: George Allen and Unwin, 1975) and Robert
Wessing, *Cosmology and Social Behavior in a West Javanese Settlement*, Ohio University Center for International Studies, Southeast Asia Series no. 47 (Athens: Ohio
University, 1978), pp. 22ff. Clifford Geertz makes a useful distinction between
"world view" and "ethos." "A people's ethos is the tone, character, and quality of
their life, its moral and aesthetic style and mood; it is the underlying attitude toward
themselves and their world that life reflects. Their world view is their picture of the
way things in sheer actuality are, their concept of nature, of self, of society. It
contains their most comprehensive ideas of order." See "Ethos, World View, and
the Analysis of Sacred Symbols," in *The Interpretation of Cultures* (New York: Basic
Books, 1973), p. 127.

6

historical in nature.[6] The second is the trait list identifying common elements. Many scholars have pointed out that the new religions typically include shamanic elements, ancestor worship, and faith healing. These trait lists have a certain utility in providing an index of features, but they fail to articulate the internal coherence of the separate items. Thus they fail to discover the most basic unity of religious orientation, of which the traits are expressions.[7]

I agree that the elements identified by the trait list approach are extremely significant. It is, however, precisely their particular combination, the relation among these various elements, that is most important, not their separate identities alone. The collection of elements that has been called constitutive of the new religions is in fact derived from a more basic source: world view. The goal of this work is to show how and why these elements fit together to make a coherent whole. In spite of the great diversity of doctrinal formulations of these groups, there is a unity among the new religions that is of a different order than a catalog of elements. The constituents of that unity may be shown through the example of Kurozumikyō.

THE WORLD VIEW OF THE NEW RELIGIONS

This discussion adopts the term *world view* for a characteristic conceptualization of the relation of the self to external levels of existence and stereotyped patterns of thought, action, and emotion based on that conceptualization. Thus to delineate a world view is

---

[6] Many earlier studies of the new religions tried to portray them as reactions to social crisis, broadly conceived. Although social change has been a catalyst in the founding of many new religions, this explanation is often too simplistic. The studies by McFarland and Thomsen, cited above, are two such examples, and there is considerable similar research by Japanese scholars. Typical of the type are Takagi Hirō, *Nihon no shinkō shūkyō* (Tokyo: Iwanami shoten, 1959) and Saki Akio, *Shinkō shūkyō* (Tokyo: Aoki shoten, 1960). For a useful bibliography on studies of the new religions, see Byron Earhart, *The New Religions of Japan: A Bibliography of Western-Language Materials*, Monumenta Nipponica (Tokyo: Sophia University, 1970). I have tried to detail the shortcomings of the crisis approach in *Lay Buddhism in Contemporary Japan: Reiyūkai Kyōdan* (Princeton: Princeton University Press, 1984).

[7] Thomsen, *The New Religions of Japan*, is a good example of this approach.

to specify how a group of people understands itself to be related to the physical body, to the social order, and to the universe, and to show how its members think, feel, and act on the basis of that understanding. This usage of world view represents an extension of the term's usual application. The following statement by E. M. Mendelson, a student of Robert Redfield, provides a fair summary of that usage.

> [World view] deals with the sum of ideas which an individual within a group and or that group have of the universe in and around them. It attempts to define those ideas from the point of view of the individuals holding them, from inside the culture rather than outside.... While emphasizing the cognitive aspect of ideas, beliefs, and attitudes, a world view cannot be clearly separated from its normative and affective aspects.[8]

It is apparent that world view treated in this way is a relatively static concept, emphasizing a general statement of ideas about the universe. If the world view of a people has any active meaning, any concrete utility in their lives, this must be specified in further characterizations of the term. Robin Horton discusses the predictive value of world view as follows:

> [World view] is designed to give foresight by spelling out the consequences of a variety of actions and happenings, and understanding by showing a great variety of phenomena as manifestations of a limited number of underlying principles related in a fairly simple way.[9]

Horton holds that world view also reflects human relations and establishes norms of behavior.[10]

It seems to me that the commonality so many writers on the new religions have identified is a matter of world view, not isolated traits. Much of the similarity I have observed, however, cannot be comprehended by a static usage such as Mendelson provides, or

---

[8] E. M. Mendelson, "World View," *International Encyclopedia of the Social Sciences*, 17 vols. (New York: Macmillan and The Free Press, 1968), 17:576.

[9] Robin Horton, "The Kalabari World-View: An Outline and Interpretation," *Africa* 32 (July 1962): 197–220.

[10] Ibid., p. 213.

even when the predictive and normative aspects discussed by Horton are also taken into account. In fieldwork and observation of a number of the new religions, I have found characteristic patterns of thought, action, and emotion directly linked to concepts of the self's relation to the body, the family, society, the state, and the cosmos. These patterns are described later in this chapter. Since they are inseparable from what is traditionally called "world view," I believe they should be integrated into the term. My aim is to shift from the static language of cosmology (a set image of the universe) to *action*, to examining the ways people *appropriate* religious ideas (each of which has of course a history of its own) and *use* them to achieve a variety of ends.

In the effort to develop this extended use of the term *world view* there is a continual interplay with the Japanese data that most immediately inform it. I have been struck in observing the new religions at how often they define and interpret problematic situations in ways that are structurally identical, even though doctrinally they are very different, one talking about *kami* 神, another about Buddhas and ancestors. The source of this unity is world view. World views must exist to define, interpret, and solve problems. Besides being "good to think," they are oriented to practice rather than existing as abstractions for their own sakes. They have a functional, operational reality. People act on them, think and feel in terms of them.

How does the analyst's rendition of world view relate to those held by members of specific new religions? The formalized conceptualization of self in relation to physical existence, the social order, and the cosmos plus associated behavior patterns that I call *world view* represents a considerable abstraction from observable reality. This abstraction involves extracting terminology specific to any certain group, finding language that is not uniquely the possession of any single one of them, correctly formulating relations among levels, and uncovering the most basic logic underlying observable behavior. The insider's world view is a "local version" of the analyst's abstract formulation. A local version is structurally identical to the analyst's model, but with all the terminology specific to the particular religion put back in. Unusually reflective persons may think through the entire local version, but no one

9

holds it entirely in consciousness all the time. Local world views are collective creations that become perceptible to an analyst only in their functional application. The analyst's presentation of world view is drawn up to solve an analytic problem: in this case, the question of how the new religions can be so alike in their patterns of behavior while on the surface—and especially doctrinally—they are so different. Believers ask truth questions about the constituent elements of local world views, but analysts ask utilitarian questions: is a particular analyst's formulation of world view an accurate rendering of the thought and behavior of the new religions? Does it help answer the question it was created to answer, or not?

World views themselves have histories, without a grasp of which they cannot be thoroughly understood. Tracing the history of the world view of the new religions is a task for a separate volume. The present study can deal with historical questions only in the case of Kurozumikyō, but it may be helpful to outline the historical context in which the world view of the new religions originally emerged.

I believe that the world view of the new religions first took shape in early nineteenth-century Japan in the context of a triangular relation among rural religious leaders, rural elites striving to shore up a perceived deterioration of the social order, and the state authority of the *han* 藩, the feudal domains governing rural society. At that time Neo-Confucian thought was extremely influential. After the Meiji Restoration of 1868, the state replaced the *han*, the rural elites became landlords and industrialists, and the religious groups began to exchange freedom from persecution for spreading government directives and the ideology later known as State Shintō. Thus the influence of the state upon the formation of the world view of the new religions was dominant, and present-day local versions of it reflect that influence in varying degree.

World views come into being in response to problems. They set in motion predictable chains of thought, emotion, and activity that lead people to act in roughly predictable ways. This is not to say that every aspect of their behavior down to the last detail is programmed, only that there is a high degree of regularity in the logic of their behavior. That regularity derives from the way a world view initially defines human problems. This contention rests on observation of many "redefinitions" of problems by leaders in counseling their followers. Sickness, familial strife, and economic misfortune are not raw situations but require structured definitions pointing to solutions.

Generally followers initially report a somewhat inchoate situation. Leaders then supply the links between its constituent elements and events, attach labels to incoherent emotions, and specify the correct as opposed to the presently disordered relation among the actors. In effect they *define* the situation in a way that is linked directly to its further analysis and to strategies of solution. Thus the original definition, directly based upon the conceptualization of the self in relation to the body, the social order, and the universe leads directly to a chain of thought, stereotyped emotions, and regular paths of action. These local paths of action include therapies in the case of sickness, reorientation and reaffirmation of social relations, and ritual directed to the local supernaturals. When the term *world view* is used in this manner, the way is opened to ask historical and anthropological questions about how and why people adopt certain religious ideas and themes (while passing over other options), why they interpret them in certain ways, and how they adapt them to society as presently constituted and to the shifting tastes and moods of their culture as they experience it.

World view is not a rigid grid but rather a consistent framework within which there is considerable variety. It is permeable, subject to coloration by cultural ideas and images. The world view of the new religions is continuous with Japanese culture as a whole, adopting Japanese cultural and religious patterns. It is different from "national character," describing a smaller subgroup of the Japanese, but it incorporates themes that are important hallmarks of the culture as a whole and reinterprets them or boosts them into heightened prominence. Thus to describe the world view of the new religions it is necessary to review ideas that have been gone over many times before in anthropological literature on Japan. World view is not articulated fully by the doctrinally centered expositions of any particular group.

The world view of the Japanese new religions conceives of the individual, society, nature, and the universe as an integrated system vitalized by a single principle. Every level represents the manifestation of that principle on a larger scale. The relations among the levels, however, are not static. They must be maintained in balance, harmony, and congruence. These qualities are manifested in conditions of happiness, health, social stability, abundant harvests, and regular succession of the seasons (free of such calamities as flood, drought, and major earthquakes). The opposite conditions (unhappiness, illness, social unrest, scarcity of food, and natural disasters) are symptomatic of a lack of harmony or congruence. Everything is interconnected so that a change in one dimension, no matter how small, eventually ripples out and affects other dimensions in a larger context. Religious practice is a striving for continuous integration of self with the body, society, nature, and the universe. This involves careful management of the most basic components: the self, the faculties of mind and emotion, and the personality.[11] See Figure 1.

Although a change in any area of the system eventually affects the whole, the self occupies a preeminent position. This is the area most susceptible to cultivation through acts of will. Sincere cultivation of virtue by an individual can produce important changes in health and can influence human relations for the better. Eventually these improvements will have an effect, however small, on the entire society. A qualitative improvement in social life affects the individual and contributes to cultivation of the self. The self and society, however, are related in such a way that one cannot expect action or ideology aimed at improving the quality of life to succeed unless the self is also engaged in cultivating virtue. There must be an awakening to the need for moral cultivation and a resolve to undertake it sincerely. If the self is awakened and resolutely so, sincerely striving for virtue and the conquest of egotism, then nothing is impossible.

Although the new religions inevitably adopt the system I have just described, they state it in different idioms. They may use Buddhist, Shintō, or colloquial terms for the self, calling it variously the *kokoro* 心 (heart-mind or heart), *konjō* (根性 guts), *reikon*

---

[11] A major study stressing the vitalistic character of the thought of the new religions is Tsushima Michihito et al., "Shinshūkyō ni okeru seimeishugiteki kyūsai kan," *Shisō* 665 (November 1979): 92–115.

(靈根 spirit), *tamashii* (魂 soul), and other terms. Similarly, they may name the principle vitalizing all existence by Shintō, Buddhist, or other terms: *kami*-nature, Buddha-nature, karma, *ki* 気, *yōki* 陽気, and so forth. They may predicate the existence of a variety of supernaturals who exist on a different plane than human beings, intervening in human affairs from time to time. These may be *kami*, Buddhas, Bodhisattvas, or ancestors. Alien to the system is the notion of a single deity standing outside the whole and manipulat-

Figure 1: The World View of the New Religions

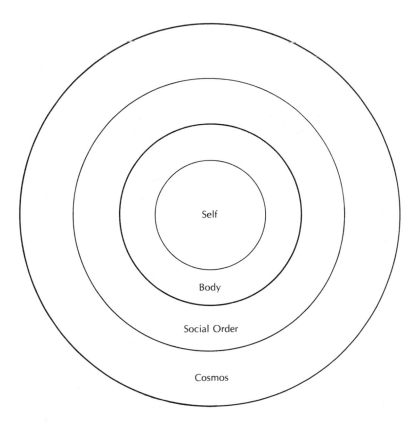

Self

Body

Social Order

Cosmos

ing it by means of an unknowable will. The supernaturals of the integrated system are subject to its rhythms and generally conform to its principles. The system is compatible with a variety of cosmological ideas and world pictures, including horizontal and vertical cosmologies seen in Japanese myths and in Buddhism's many-tiered realms of existence.

Because self-cultivation is the primary task of all, textual erudition, esoteric ritual, and the observance of abstinences are rejected or relegated to secondary significance. Lacking justification for a strong differentiation between the religious lives of priests and laity, the tendency to make the laity central is strong and pervasive. Since self-cultivation is the primary determiner of all human affairs, notions of fate or divine wrath (karma or *bachi* 罰, for example) are reinterpreted, ignored, or denied. In like manner, because of the primacy of self-cultivation, the concept of pollution cannot be fully credited, and this opens the door to greater participation by women than is the case in the established religions.

All problems can be traced to insufficient cultivation of self. Thus it is misguided to expect fundamental social change from political ideology. Instead, society can be improved only through collective moral improvement, the doctrine of meliorism. Similarly, attempting to cure disease simply by treating the body alone is useless. Healing can come about only through rededication to ethical values; hence medicine is effective only in a provisional way. Education and secular achievements apart from faith and cultivation of self are houses of cards, castles on sand. Accordingly, media-sponsored presentation of thoroughly secularized views of life are disapproved.

THE SELF

The centrality of self to world view is a matter requiring general exposition as well as separate treatment of the forms this idea takes in Japanese culture and more specifically in the new religions. A notion of self is a cultural universal, but in a given society or subgroup it is shaped and institutionalized in a particular way. Thus Western and Japanese notions of the self are very different. Notions

14

of self are not mere abstractions but instead "operate in the individual and in society as functional realities."[12] People act on the basis of a certain notion of self; they explain their actions to others in accord with it, and that construction of the self has a diagnostic function that comes into play when things go wrong and an explanation must be sought. The construction of self is the mainspring of world view. It organizes experience and structures the relation of the individual to that which is external. It establishes the conceptual boundaries of human possibility through linkage to concepts of control.

Andrew Lock shows how the self is inevitably conceptualized in terms of control. Control can be plotted on two axes: one represents ... loci of control (corresponding to internalized and externalized conceptions of the self), and a second of active versus passive orientation (or the degree to which the self is *in* control or *under* control). I reproduce his useful diagram in Figure 2.[13] Potential for action is enhanced by the extent to which the self is believed to be *in* control. A self *under* control is necessarily passive. One might fit the established religions of Japan, with few exceptions, on the right side of the diagram. The self is to some extent under the control of deities and is further limited in some cases by the temporal concept of *mappō* 末法, the Latter Days of the Dharma, according to which the conditions for achieving salvation are at the nadir. Folk cults of spirit possession would be grouped with externalized conceptions of the self under the control of possessing spirits. By contrast, the new religions belong to the lower left quadrant of the diagram. The self is emphatically not under control; control is located almost entirely within the individual, and the idea that responsibility for one's situation can be located in any external source is rejected. This is true even where the idea of karma is present, because that idea is interpreted to mean that the individual is responsible for all his karma, even that "in-

---

[12] David Bohm, "Human Nature as the Product of our Mental Models," in *The Limits of Human Nature*, ed. J. Benthall et al. (London: Allen Lane, 1973), p. 92.

[13] Andrew Lock, "Universals in Human Conception," in *Indigenous Psychologies: The Anthropology of the Self*, ed. Lock and Paul Heelas (London: Academic Press, 1982), pp. 19–36.

herited" from ancestors, since it is the individual's responsibility to transform karma to merit through ritual.

The conceptions of self found among the new religions represent accentuations and transformations of ideas found widely in Japan, but the new religions have created structured organizational forms and pathways of spiritual disciplines to imbue their concepts of self with religious significance and to underline the place of these in world view. The basic continuity seen in concepts of the self among

Figure 2: Conceptions of Self in Japanese Religions

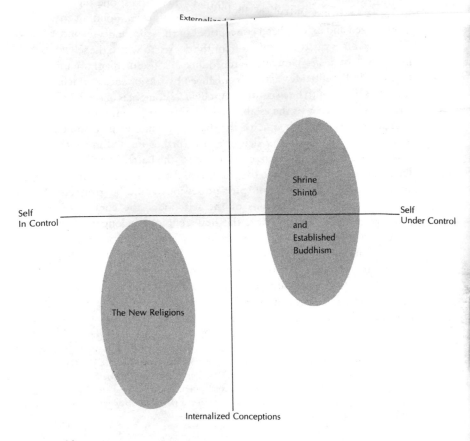

the new religions and in Japanese culture generally constitutes part of the permeability of the world view of the new religions and illustrates its symbiosis with Japanese culture as a whole. Furthermore, it is important to note that much of the terminology and general orientation of Japanese concepts of self derive from Neo-Confucian thought.

The historical chain of Neo-Confucianism's transmission to the founder of Kurozumikyō is treated in chapter two, but because the affinities between Neo-Confucian thought and the world view of the new religions are so strong, it seems appropriate to outline the notion of self found in Neo-Confucianism, a subject skillfully presented in the works of Tu Wei-ming. Attainment of sagehood is the goal of Neo-Confucian thought, and this goal entails a transformation of self through self-cultivation 修身 (Chinese: *hsiu-shen*; Japanese: *shūshin*). Becoming a sage is not achieving something external to the human being but attaining the highest fulfillment of human potential. The desired transformation of self may be equated with the attainment of sincerity 誠 (Chinese: *ch'eng*; Japanese: *makoto*), a quality that includes connotations of completion, actualization, and perfection as well as honesty and genuineness. Becoming sincere is not a simple matter but a "process of self-purification and self-authentication,"[14] which is equal to a thoroughgoing transformation of self, ridding it of all traces of egotism. The self is embedded in social relations, and it can be fully realized only by entering "into human relatedness in the spirit of reciprocity."[15] "Society is not conceived of as something out there that is imposed on the individual. It is in essence an extended self."[16] Thus the goal is not to escape from society, nor is the self thought to be trapped or fettered by society. Instead, society and human relations provide the only vehicle by which genuine self-transformation can take place.[17] In self-cultivation the self is "extended" in the sense that its genuine transformation inevitably entails the improvement of the physical body and the proper

[14] Tu Wei-ming, *Humanity and Self-Cultivation: Essays in Confucian Thought* (Berkeley: Asian Humanities Press, 1978), p. 95.

[15] Ibid., pp. 26–27.

[16] Ibid., p. 25.

[17] Ibid., p. 52.

regulation of family and the state, and it ultimately ensures the peace of the world.[18] Thus the self extends itself through the body to the family, state, and cosmos. It is blocked from attaining its proper fulfillment when it bounds itself off sharply into a narrow sphere and refuses relationship. This is egotism, the great enemy of self-cultivation. Selfish, egotistical desire rather than society is "the real threat to a genuine manifestation of the human self."[19] These remarks may be summarized as follows:

> There is an agreement among virtually all of the Neo-Confucianists: man is a moral being who through self-effort extends his human sensitivity to all the beings of the universe so as to realize himself in the midst of the world and as an integral part of it, in the sense that his self-perfection necessarily embodies the perfection of the universe as a whole.[20]

This complex of ideas about the self is found in the world view of the new religions stated in other idioms, using different terminology but identical in structure. This is not to say that the world view is historically derived whole in any direct way from Neo-Confucian thought, but the similarity in orientation is striking.

Let us turn to the terminology of the self as found generally in Japan and in the new religions. The ideas of *kokoro* and *ki* are the most important, and both are notoriously complex. The full range of meaning of these terms can become clear only in the context of their use, so here I simply sketch their outlines in relation to the world view as a whole and to related terms. Subsequent chapters will bring out the specific interpretation of these terms found in Kurozumikyō. The term I translate here as "self" is *kokoro*, and other glosses include "heart" or "heart-mind." It includes the faculties of mind, will, and emotion. The *kokoro* is not, however, the sum of these faculties in the abstract but differs in each person according to personality traits, dispositions, and aesthetic sensibilities. When Japanese make a distinction between "spirit" (*seishin* 精神) and flesh (*nikutai* 肉体), the *kokoro* is associated with the

[18] Ibid., p. 20.
[19] Ibid., p. 48.
[20] Ibid., p. 79.

spirit. The *kokoro* includes the soul (*tamashii*) but is not identical to it. After death the *tamashii* continues to exist, but the *kokoro* does not. The *kokoro* also includes *ware* and *ga* (both written 我), which mean the ego. *Ware* and *ga* are associated with a calculating attitude and selfish desire and carry a definitely negative nuance, whereas *kokoro* as a whole is positive unless otherwise qualified. In its primary meaning *kokoro* is possessed only by sentient beings, but one can also speak of the *kokoro* contained in a handknit sweater, a meal lovingly prepared, or in this book to the extent that the creators of these things "put their hearts into them" (*kokoro o komeru* 心を籠める). Revealing to others what one thinks in the *kokoro* presupposes a strong and usually longstanding relationship, and thus *kokoro* belongs to the "inside" (*ura* 裏), private realm for the most part, as opposed to outside (*omote* 表), public sphere. The *kokoro* however, is not so deeply hidden as the *hara* 腹, or *konjō*, the belly or guts.

The notion of *kokoro* is a hallmark of Japanese culture, and it is the central pillar of the world view of the new religions. The ideas above are shared by both. The difference in usage and interpretation is not a matter of a definite point of departure but of volume or intensity. Consider the following proverb, one that could be endorsed by the new religions and is a stock saying in secular society: *kurushimu mo tanoshimu mo kokoro no mochiyō* (苦しむも楽しむも心の持ちよう). A direct translation is, "Both suffering and happiness depend on how we bear the *kokoro*." We note first that *kokoro* is the object of the verb *motsu* 持つ, to bear, carry, have, possess, take firm hold of, grip, hold. That is, *kokoro* is borne or carried in a certain way, good or bad, and according to that we suffer or are happy. We are in control. An ordinary, nonreligious interpretation of this proverb would say that our attitude toward circumstances determines in large part whether we are happy or unhappy, or that an attitude of "positive thinking" can improve our experience of unfavorable situations even if the circumstances are not thereby altered.

An interpretation of the proverb among the new religions is likely to be much stronger, to hold that human beings certainly have the power to be happy, depending solely on the manner in which one bears *kokoro*. We need only exercise that power by self-cultivation. Moreover, the idea that circumstances can be changed by the power of diligently cultivated *kokoro* is pervasive. It is a question not only of a change of attitude but sometimes of radical material change, such as an improvement in economic situation or a miraculous healing. It is understood that the cultivated *kokoro* has the power also to change external persons and events, and that ultimately nothing is impossible. Exercising the full power of the *kokoro* is possible for anyone who practices self-cultivation through the spiritual disciplines of the particular religious group.[21]

Ki, "vital force," "material force," is the dynamic principle vitalizing all life, including the *kokoro*, and without which living things expire. Dead or inanimate things are such by virtue of lacking *ki*. *Ki* and *kokoro* are intimately related in that *kokoro* is kept living and vital by *ki*; without it *kokoro* cannot exist. In early Chinese thought *ch'i* (the Chinese pronunciation of *ki*) was considered to be a material substance, breath, or ether. In modern Japanese culture *ki* is nonsubstantial and closely related to the realm of affect. If the *ki* of two persons "meets" or "matches," it means that they get along (*ki ga au* 気が合う). To "apply" *ki* to something means to care or be concerned about it (*ki ni suru* 気にする). If one's *ki* is not applied to or is withdrawn from the sweater, the meal, or the book (*ki ga nuketa* 気が抜けに; *ki ga haitte inai* 気が入っていない), they will be poorly, sloppily done and lack any sense of vitality. The number of expressions involving *ki* in Japanese is virtually infinite, and they are used continually in completely secular settings as well as in religious circles. *Ki* can be of a *yang* 陽 nature, *yōki* 陽気, or it can be of a *yin* 陰 quality, *inki* 陰気. These general propositions apply equally to Japanese culture as a whole and to the new religions.

In the new religions whether *ki* is *yōki* or *inki* depends upon how it is cultivated. When it is cultivated well, it will be bright, ascendant, radiant, and powerful: *yōki*. When poorly cultivated, *ki* is *inki*, dark, sinking, dull, and weak. Part of the cultivation of *kokoro*, especially in the Shintō-derived new religions, is to be *yōki*. *Yōki-*

---

[21] For another exposition of this proverb's cultural meaning see Minami Hiroshi, *Nihonjin no shinri*, Iwanami shinsho 149 (Tokyo: Iwanami shoten, 1953; 37th printing, 1983), pp. 159–62.

gurashi 陽気ぐらし, "the *yōki* life," is an explicit ideal of such new religions as Tenrikyō 天理教.[22] If *yōki* and *inki* are used as adjectives, it is possible to speak of a *kokoro* that is *yōki*, *yōki na kokoro* 陽気な心, but this is redundant since a *yōki* bearing already implies that the *kokoro* is also *yōki*. To be *yōki* is to keep the self in alignment with the body and open to social relations in the family and beyond. To be *inki* is much the same as to "close the heart" (*kokoro o tojiru* 心を閉じる), connoting an attitude of morbid introspection, refusing to reciprocate, "hardening the heart," refusing to extend self beyond the narrowest limit. Extending *ki* through the body, to the family, through society, and ultimately to the whole universe keeps all these levels in harmony, which is the final goal of the world view.[23]

PATTERNS OF ACTION

While the terminology of the self is basic to understanding Japanese constructions of self, the patterns of action and affect in which these are embedded constitute the functioning of the world view of the new religions. Here I identify four such patterns: (1) the idea that "other people are mirrors," (2) the exchange of gratitude and repayment of favor, (3) the quest for sincerity, and (4) the adherence to paths of self-cultivation. Later chapters discuss in detail how these patterns take shape in Kurozumikyō. My goal in this chapter is to locate them in Japanese culture and to show in general how they are adapted by the new religions.

Each of these patterns represents an indispensable element of Japanese culture, and thus their implementation in Japanese religions is not unique. These patterns bridge secular culture and the new religions, initially easily recognized and accepted by the novice, later imbued with heightened force and intensity when the

[22] Tenrikyō is one of the oldest of the new religions. It was founded in 1838 by a peasant woman named Nakayama Miki 中山ミキ. One of its primary goals is to achieve *yōkigurashi*.

[23] There is a proverb concerning *ki* that is almost identical to the one about *kokoro* examined above: *Monogoto wa ki no mochiyō*, "Everything depends upon how we bear our *ki*."

novice becomes a seasoned stalwart. The difference between the new religions and the rest of society regarding these patterns lies in systematic exposition, organizational forms such as counseling groups that socialize members in the patterns, and rewards for their implementation.

"Other people are mirrors" is the idea that one's behavior is directly reflected in the attitudes of others. This pattern comes into play where one encounters a negative response of some kind from another person. If the other is the "mirror," the one who has been injured or rebuffed must search within his or her own *kokoro* for the reason why the offending party should have meted out that treatment. The victim is forced to share the blame.

In the new religions this idea receives consistent and sustained attention with organizational backup. Thus whereas in ordinary society the notion that other people are mirrors represents a tiresome truism much like the Biblical injunction to take the beam out of one's own eye before setting to work on the mote in someone else's, in the new religions it becomes a pattern of thinking, acting, and feeling in terms of which believers construct their behavior, feel certain emotions, and relate to other people. One situation in the new religions in which this pattern is activated is that in which one fails to proselytize a prospective convert. Failed proselytizers will inevitably be told that they have come face to face with their own faults when refused by a recalcitrant target convert. Because the proselytizers are also stubborn, say, it is natural that they encounter similar persons. They are our mirrors, held up to us by the ancestors, Buddhas, *kami*, or other local supernaturals. We should take the hint and weed that negative characteristic out of our *kokoro*.

In Buddhist groups such as Reiyūkai Kyōdan 霊友会教団, a believer who brings a personal problem to a leader is automatically commanded to repent, whether or not the believer was at fault. The idea that we bring suffering upon ourselves is deeply engrained and closely related to the idea that a properly cultivated *kokoro* is the unequaled preventative for all problems. Repentance becomes a formalized ritual act in many of the new religions, connecting them with a long history of Buddhist thought on repentance.

In chapter three a case study of Kurozumikyō healing is presented in which those followers who come seeking advice are made to accept blame for the problems facing their family. Indeed, in Kurozumikyō the idea that other people are mirrors (*tachi mukō hito wa kagami nari* 立ち向こう人は鏡なり) is one of the credal statements recited daily. Secular society sometimes puts teeth into this idea also, as in the now well-known "spiritual training" retreats furnished for company employees. Here, as in the new religions, repentance exercises become stereotyped patterns of action linked to other semi-religious ideas.[24]

The idea that other people are mirrors makes the individual totally responsible in all circumstances. Although the burden is heavy, there is also a tacit message that the self can control any situation. Placing blame and responsibility on the individual also denies the idea that "society" can be blamed for one's problems; hence concepts of exploitation and discrimination are ruled out of consideration. On the whole the new religions are uninterested in political action to improve society; to them it is a question of individuals improving themselves individually and collectively through self-cultivation.

The second item of Japanese personality that becomes a pattern of action in the new religions is gratitude and the repayment of favor. It is widely acknowledged in Japan that social relations are naturally hierarchical. Those in a higher position bestow favors or benefice (*on* 恩) on their subordinates, who incur a duty (*giri* 義理) to repay the favor (*hō-on* 報恩). The subordinate should feel gratitude (*kansha* 感謝 and other terms). In economic life this takes the form of paternalism in the workplace. An apprentice or younger worker submits to a long period of training for low recompense and becomes dependent upon a superior for training and for signs of approval. The boss, or "parent figure" (*oyabun* 親分), is not free to ignore the "child's" (*kobun* 子分) needs. Both parties are socialized to expect reciprocal gratification, the boss taking pleasure in his apprentice's maturation and growing skill. As DeVos writes,

[24] Dorinne K. Kondo, "Work, Family, and the Self: A Cultural Analysis of Japanese Family Enterprise" (Ph.D. dissertation, Harvard University, 1982), p. 52.

"The sense of order in precedence learned within familial relationships is transmitted into one's occupational role."[25] The language of parent and child does not come to an end when the apprenticeship is finished. In relation to the *oyabun* the apprentice remains forever subadult. Where an outsider might see a situation of gross exploitation, persons socialized in the ethic of paternalism see emotionally satisfying exchanges of nurturance and repayment. Furthermore, when the *kobun's* expectations are not met, the *kobun* does not automatically blame the *oyabun* but instead is more likely to "learn to ... distort his perception so that he will achieve fancied gratification from those in superior positions to him."[26] The ethic of paternalism makes people prefer to feel gratitude even when superiors do not deserve it, indicating what DeVos identifies as a strong need to experience gratitude and the repayment of favor, a "need to feel that someone has cared, ... [has] released his energies productively, and freed him from the necessity of feeling resentful toward an impersonal, ungiving world."[27] More intolerable than such distortion is facing a realization that people are "subject to a malevolent, impersonal, exploitative social system in which they are being used, broken, and cast away as rubbish."[28] Experiencing an insuperable block in this flow of gratitude is a source of great anger and frustration.

In the new religions, religious leaders and especially founders are cast in the role of superiors, and the organization as a whole becomes an object of gratitude. The tangible and intangible benefits of membership are most notably repaid by proselytization, thus bringing in new members. Opportunities for the experience and expression of gratitude are plentifully provided and surrounded with strong emotion, as when followers hear dramatic accounts of a founder's trials and hardships overcome in establishing the organization. Indeed, founders are often treated as apo-

---

[25] George DeVos, "Apprenticeship and Paternalism: Psychocultural Continuities Underlying Japanese Social Organization," in *Modern Japanese Organizations and Decision Making*, ed. Ezra Vogel (Berkeley: University of California Press, 1975), p. 216.
[26] Ibid., p. 219.
[27] Ibid., p. 220.
[28] Ibid., p. 221.

theosized parent figures, and in hearing their sufferings, followers are supposed to feel grateful and humble, as if the founder's hardships had been for their sakes alone. The "blessings" (*kudoku* 功徳), "compassion" (*jihi* 慈悲), of the founder, presented in highly charged, emotional language of a mother's suffering for her children, stimulates the believer to experience gratitude. By sustained socialization of this kind, presented in sermons, testimony, dramatic presentations, movies and video tapes, and extended to lesser leaders and the organization as a whole, gratitude and the repayment of favor become a series of ongoing exchanges.

Furthermore, gratitude takes on an almost material quality in its connection with the health of the body. When one is unable to or "forgets" to be grateful, the body as well as the emotions are blocked, and sickness is the result. A healing presented in the sermon in chapter three illustrates this theme in detail. As DeVos writes, "Japanese religions ... are ... effective when they redirect a sense of gratitude and obligation back to parental figures [who become] symbols and fictions, not actual people."[29] Not only are leaders and founders cloaked in the aura of the numinous, but followers come to mythologize their own pasts in order to demonstrate, for example, that sadistic bosses and mothers-in-law were actually loving, beneficent figures who were only, in their "compassion," trying to strengthen one's character.[30] The only attitude toward them can be a flow of gratitude. This theme is illustrated in the sermon in chapter three, in the treatment of counseling in chapter five, and in the life history presented in chapter six. The socialization of members in the pattern of gratitude and the repayment of favor are not limited to sermons, counseling testimony, and other means of "input." Followers are rewarded with rank, approval, and responsibility for implementing this pattern, and the converts of future generations will do the same, thus perpetuating both the pattern and the organization.

Thus the new religions make the general cultural idea of grati-

[29] George DeVos, "Afterword," in *The Quiet Therapies: Japanese Pathways to Personal Growth*, ed. David K. Reynolds (Honolulu: University of Hawaii Press, 1982), p. 126.

[30] Ibid, p. 130. See also Kondo, "Work, Family, and the Self," pp. 13–27, on the way this theme is expressed in workers' "spiritual training" retreats.

Chapter One

tude and repayment of favor a pattern of action by imbuing the
idea of gratitude with religious significance, linking it to concepts
of the body and its health, redirecting childhood experiences of
dependency and gratitude toward the organization and its leadership, helping members recast their own histories, redirecting anger
and frustration to repentance, seeking blame in oneself, and repaying the organization with proselytization and socialization of
novices. Socialization practices are directly linked to emotionally
satisfying rewards.

The third pattern is that of striving for sincerity. As discussed
above, sincerity implies actualization and completeness as well as
honesty and commitment. It is difficult to overstate the depth of
this ideal's appeal in Japanese culture.

If any single idiom can be taken as central to the many Japanese
vocabularies of growth, it is the notion of reaching out for
"sincerity" (makoto), of striving to act from motives that are
totally pure.[31]

Since the attainment of sincerity is a prime ideal of the Shintō
religion, the symbols of this theme are well known and prestigious.
Sincerity is inseparable from purity, an idea symbolized by the
color white, by venerable shrines, by the abstinences and purifications undergone by their priests, and by the minutiae of shrine
etiquette. These symbols are embodied not only by the Shintō
priest but by any person in whom there is no gap between action
and kokoro, in whom action is a genuine and spontaneous expression of the true self. That identity of self and behavior implies
complete commitment to one's role in society, an ideal pervasive in
East Asia and first enunciated by Confucius:

At fifteen I thought only of study; at thirty I began playing my
role; at forty I was sure of myself; at fifty I was conscious of my
position in the universe; at sixty I was no longer argumenta-
tive; and now at seventy I can follow my heart's desire without violating custom.

[31] David Plath, Long Engagements: Maturity in Modern Japan (Stanford: Stanford
University Press, 1980), p. 47.

26

As part of Japan's Confucian heritage, it is understood that the best way to reach a total commitment is to perform social roles and responsibilities—*as presently constituted*—wholeheartedly and sincerely. Chafing against the strictures of a role is a sign of immaturity.

The new religions, especially those of Shintō derivation, draw on the prestige of ancient purification ideas and practices, lending them organizational form and promulgating them through a program of spiritual disciplines linked to rewards. Sincerity becomes a result of purification through self-cultivation. By overcoming attachment to ego and selfish desire, one becomes "meek" (*sunao* 素直), one aspect of sincerity, and the opposite of which is *hinekureta* ひねくれた, twisted, sarcastic, sneaky, and suspicious of others' motives. Purification requires the removal of blockages (*ikizumari* 行詰) and arbitrariness (*muri* 無埋), as well as selfishness. The new religions turn the general quest for sincerity into patterns of action by providing role models of persons who have achieved it, by providing disciplines to supplement social roles, and by rewarding committed participation, thus motivating people to seek further gratification through the group. They systematically devalue or stigmatize those who participate in non-approved roles, especially women who work outside the home. By these various means the new religions socialize people to think that full participation in approved roles, mainly family-centered roles or roles established within the particular religious group, is the path to maturity, achievement, and full realization of sincerity.

Paths of self-cultivation, pursuit of which is the fourth pattern of action to be discussed, are available in great number in Japan. Traditional arts of pottery, flower arranging, tea ceremony, and calligraphy, as well as the martial arts, are all considered paths, *michi* 道, "Ways," toward maturity, depth of character, and fulfillment of self. Such practices of the established religions as sutra or prayer recitation, pilgrimage, chanting, and meditation are also considered elements of a *michi*. The paths of self-cultivation constructed by the new religions may prescribe different observances, but in essence their intent and import is the same as the *michi* of secular society. The major differences lie in greater organizational efficiency of channeling people through the path, counseling and other forms of socialization along the way, and systematic rewards for good performance. In many cases insiders refer to their religion simply as *O-michi* 御道, "The Way."

The new religions share with secular society some important presuppositions about paths of self-cultivation. This should be kept in mind in the discussion of specific paths in subsequent chapters. First is the idea that one progresses in a discipline by imitating those who are accomplished in it or by mastering set practices according to an invariable pattern. *Kata kara hairu* 型から入る, "entering through form," is a phrase expressing this idea. Entering through form represents a rejection of "entering" via explanation. Absorption in exposition of the way leads, it is believed, to egotism and the love of argument for its own sake (*rikutsu* 理屈). As DeVos points out, "Orderly exposition of thought is not traditionally regarded as an exemplary virtue, nor are diffuseness and obfuscation seen as contrary vices."[32]

Thus the new religions stress unquestioning performance of their established disciplines, fully aware that the demand for uncomprehending obedience (at least at the beginning) will cause the convert frustration. Also involved as a minor theme is the pedagogical principle that "physical action can be perceived as isomorphic with spiritual change."[33] Thus, for example, polishing floors can be assumed to "polish" the self. If one enters through form, eventually the *kokoro* will follow. The hardship entailed is not to be avoided; no one denies that it is punishing to polish floors by hand, recite sutras, or endure cold water ablutions. Hardship in itself is virtuous and confers compassion and maturity. All the new religions agree that a person's real potential cannot be fulfilled without suffering, and in this they share with secular society the suspicion about someone who has failed that perhaps *kurō ga tarinai* 苦労が足りな い, "the person hasn't suffered enough." That is, if one had endured sufficient trials before the present ordeal, one could have conquered this hardship. Accordingly it is important to establish how much leaders and founders have suffered in the course of their own self-cultivation.

[32] DeVos, "Afterword," p. 116.
[33] Kondo, "Work, Family, and the Self," p. 54.

THE LIMITS OF THE WORLD VIEW

This study uses Kurozumikyō to illustrate a world view characteristically held by the members of the new religions. Kurozumikyō serves as a felicitous example of this general pattern, but I do not wish to assert that the particular Shintō formulations seen at the level of doctrine are universal. Quite the contrary; these I take to be variable expressions in a changeable idiom.

In a single volume I cannot both explain fully the workings of the world view and substantiate the claim that it underlies the new religions as a whole. Faced with a choice of one of these options, I have chosen to provide as complete as possible an explication of the world view within a single group, but the reader is entitled to an account of the limits of the world view. In what groups is it not found? How does it work in Buddhist groups? Since some readers may feel that the account I have given so far utilizes a terminology that has more affinities with Shintō than with Buddhism, I believe it is important here to sketch briefly how the world view takes shape in a Buddhist idiom. For this purpose I provide the following outline of Reiyūkai Kyōdan and its local version of the world view.

Founded between 1919 and 1925 by Kotani Kimi 小谷喜美 (1901–1971) and Kubo Kakutarō 久保角太郎 (1892–1944), Reiyūkai Kyōdan, the Association of Friends of the Spirits, is one of the largest of the Japanese new religions, with a current membership of roughly three million. It is entirely a lay organization with no priesthood. Its central practice is ancestor worship utilizing an abridgment of the Lotus Sutra. Faith healing is an element of considerable importance. During World War II Reiyūkai escaped persecution by accepting government ideology, and it spread rapidly after 1945. Kotani succeeded Kubo after his death in 1944, and her leadership inaugurated a persistent trend for women to dominate grass-roots organization as counselors and healers.

After the war Reiyūkai began to call for a revival of the prewar family system and traditional morality. The group continued to expand until the early 1950s, when several schisms occurred. Nevertheless, in spite of being overshadowed in size by several organizations, it is a strong presence among the new religions, and the fact that most of its offshoots have generally perpetuated its ideas and practices suggests that these are elements of widespread appeal.[34]

Self-cultivation in Reiyūkai emphasizes *kokoro naoshi* 心直し, "curing the heart." In fact, some members speak of the group as a religion of *kokoro naoshi*. In explaining this idea, they say that the cause of all sickness, misfortune, and unhappiness lies in the *kokoro* and that to overcome these things one must cultivate self by performing spiritual disciplines, *shugyō* 修行. Disciplines of sutra recitation and proselytization are undertaken to "purify the heart" (*kokoro o kiyomeru* 心を清める), thus becoming sincere. We should be grateful to parents and ancestors from whom we have received life and health, and members should be grateful to the organization and its leaders. Proselytization partially repays members' debts to Reiyūkai, and it is a form of self-cultivation that brings home the message that "other people are mirrors." Rejections experienced in proselytization are warnings sent by the ancestors to alert us to our faults and to the need to persevere in self-cultivation.

When we cultivate the self through sutra recitation, ancestors receive a benefit: some of the negative karma they bear is transformed to merit, with the result that they move closer to salvation (*jōbutsu* 成仏, the attainment of Buddhahood) and will bless and protect their descendants. Thus the discipline of sutra recitation benefits both ancestor and descendant and sets in motion continuing exchanges of blessings, ritual service, and the transformation of karma to merit. In this way a reciprocity extending the self into the furthest conceptualized level of existence is effected by self-cultivation. Ultimately it is not simply a question of reciprocity between ancestor and descendant; because karma eventually links all sentient beings, individuals and their salvation are bound up with all other sentient beings and their salvation as well. The reason this is so is because of an understanding of karma (*innen* 因縁) that makes of it a quantity analogous to *ki* as discussed above.

Karma links human beings and eventually all sentient beings. Karma is inherited in the blood, and just as theoretically all human-

---

[34] On the founding and early history of Reiyūkai see Hardacre, *Lay Buddhism in Contemporary Japan*, chap. 1.

ity can, it is believed, be discovered to be related in some way by kinship; we are all connected by shared karma, whether or not we can establish each separate link in the chain.[35] Karma can be good (in which case it is called merit) or bad, depending on self-cultivation. In this way Reiyūkai can be seen to share the new religions' conceptualization of self in relation to physical existence, the social order, and the universe, and to combine it with typical patterns of thought, action, and emotion that maintain harmony among these levels. Its idiom is distinctive, but the structure of world view is identical to that outlined above.[36]

The new religions' world view is not found in the religion of Japan's Korean minority. The religious practices of this group represent a combination of shamanism and Buddhism in which individuals and their fate are ruled by a collection of Buddhist divinities such as Acala, ancestors, such functional deities as the toilet god, and star gods. Problems are diagnosed as due to offending one or another of these, and the solution is to hold large-scale rites employing religious professionals to discover the nature of the particular offense and the deities' requirements in the way of recompense. Participants know they should propitiate the local supernaturals regularly, but the chances for inadvertently giving offense to willful spirits are infinite, and there is little a person can do in many cases. We find no consistent construction of self in relation to other levels of existence nor consistent patterns of action save for more sponsoring of ritual. Thus although the minority has developed unique practices in Japan, in roughly the same amount of time as the younger of the new religions, at the level of world view the religion of the minority has nothing in common with the new religions. This conclusion strengthens the suspicion that the world

---

[35] In popular ideas about karma, as opposed to textual ideas and philosophy, the notion that karma is inherited is very widespread. On this phenomenon see Charles F. Keyes, "Introduction: The Study of Popular Ideas of Karma," and E. Valentine Daniel, "Conclusion: Karma, the Uses of an Idea," both in *Karma, An Anthropological Inquiry*, ed. Keyes and Daniel (Berkeley and Los Angeles: University of California Press, 1983).

[36] On Reiyūkai's ideas about karma, see my *Lay Buddhism in Contemporary Japan*, pp. 81–82, 127–30, 169–70, 196–97, 209–10.

view of the new religions is inseparable from Japanese ethnicity.[37]
The world view of the new religions to be described here does
not apply to Christian groups. It is limited essentially to those
groups founded in Japan by Japanese. Therefore, it does not apply
to such groups usually classified with the new religions as the
Korean Unification Church, Tōitsu Kyōkai 統一教会. Even among
the groups to which it is meant to apply, there have been periods in
their histories when the world view I will describe was overshadowed by other perspectives. For example, Ōmotokyō 大本教 in
its most millenarian phase was caught up in prophesies of the
millennium, and at that time the world view was dominated by
apocalyptic.[38]

I have adopted two strategies for explicating the world view of
the new religions through a case study of Kurozumikyō. The first,
employed in chapter two, is historical, exploring the matrix of
religious ideas from which new religions arose in the late Tokugawa period and examining the process by which Kurozumikyō
broke away from Shrine Shintō. The second strategy is systematically to consider each major area of Kurozumikyō's organization
and activity, showing how each reveals characteristic features of the
shared orientation of the new religions. This is the task of chapters
three through six. This endeavor will involve showing how the
nexus of ideas in which the new religions first arose is brought
forward into the present and adapted to contemporary circumstances. Further, examination of Kurozumikyō's ritual practices,
organizational structure, and interaction between ministers and
followers reveals areas in which the group seems to resemble the
older religious traditions more than the new. Those areas are
instructive in locating points at which new religions have difficulty

[37] On the religion of the Korean minority see Helen Hardacre, *The Religion of
Japan's Korean Minority: The Preservation of Ethnic Identity*, University of California
Institute of East Asian Studies Korean Studies Monograph Series 9 (Berkeley:
University of California, 1984).

[38] Founded in 1892 by Deguchi Nao, Ōmotokyō stands at the head of a number
of organizations, including Sekai Kyūseikyō 世界救世教 and others, that include a
marked strand of millenarianism. See Emily Ooms, "Deguchi Nao and Ōmotokyō: An Analysis of a Millenarian Cult in Meiji Japan" (M.A. thesis, University of
Chicago, 1982).

achieving independence from the old and in suggesting why this should be so.

Representing the oldest stratum of the new religions, Kurozumikyō is not in every aspect "typical" of all the groups in that category. In the ethical area, however, it is representative of a pervasive general outlook, and its organization illustrates patterns prevailing, with some variation, among many groups. Points of similarity and difference are indicated throughout the volume.

Both historically and typologically Kurozumikyō can be located at the threshhold dividing the new religions from the old and thus provides an apt case study for clarifying the distinctiveness of the new. Chapter two examines the process through which the Founder separated from Shrine Shintō and created an organization recognized at the time as a "new religion." We can document precisely the point at which the perception of his teaching as a "new religion" emerged, and this pinpointing enables us to identify what made Kurozumi's creation categorically different from Shrine Shintō in terms of doctrine, ritual, and organization.

A consideration of contemporary preaching and healing in chapter three shows how the Founder's doctrine is understood today. From the Founder's writings present-day ministers extract a doctrinal essence calling on all to cultivate their hearts (*kokoro*) in sincerity, optimism, joy, and perseverance. For both ministers and followers the emphasis on individual responsibility rather than the efficacy of rites or priestly ordination is the same. We can see an equalization of status fundamentally unlike the priest-layman relation of the established religions. Healing ritual is an area in which ministers and followers' status is clearly distinguished and that seems least in harmony with the otherwise generally accepted doctrine of individual ethical cultivation as the key determiner of all affairs. As healing is combined with counseling and explained in sermons, however, it is found inextricable from doctrine on cultivation of *kokoro*.

Chapter four considers the position of Kurozumikyō branch churches from a different angle, focusing not on the question of world view but the varieties of "old" and "new" in the churches' actual operations in particular locales. The typology "established religion" as opposed to "new religion" in Japan admits of a variety

33

of manifestations along a sliding scale; neither type is an exact summary of observable reality. Even within a single new religion, there are mixtures of elements associated with both new and old. A survey of the variety seen in Kurozumikyō can illustrate this phenomenon. Sometimes the church performs functions in association with a tutelary (*ujigami* 氏神) shrine, and Kurozumikyō ministers maintain close associations with shrine priests. Local people often are unaware of the distinction between Kurozumikyō churches and ordinary shrines and request the same rites from the churches as from a shrine. In addition, however, they also seek counseling on personal problems, a service not ordinarily performed by shrine priests. Women ministers play a major role in counseling, and their presence in that role is a factor conspicuously distinguishing Kurozumikyō as a new religion. The practice of hereditary succession leads to difficulties in staffing all 371 branch churches. This practice, derived from the established religions, profoundly affects the growth of the organization and the character of its ministry.

Returning to the focus on world view, the fifth chapter, "Ministers and Followers," examines the daily activities and organization of one Kurozumikyō branch church in detail. A consideration of ministers' counseling shows how doctrine about *kokoro* is implemented. Ministers tell followers that virtually all problems can be solved through cultivating the heart; in that the benefits proclaimed can be expected to occur in this life, they are properly called "this-worldly-benefits" (*genze riyaku* 現世利益). As that term has been used in studies of the new religions, however, it tends to carry a note of derogation, as if these benefits were only material ones. In a study of Kurozumikyō counseling, we can see that in fact the followers are called upon to reorient their entire lives before benefits are forthcoming. This evidence suggests a need to reinterpret the idea of "this-worldly-benefits."

There exists in Kurozumikyō's doctrine an explicit framework of ideas about life and the workings of the universe. At another level, Kurozumikyō has in addition implicit orientations in space and time that are particularly important in establishing the symbolic and aesthetic nuances of Kurozumikyō's local version of the overall world view. This is the subject of chapter six, which discusses concepts of space, time, and the human life cycle and shows that at this level Kurozumikyō sometimes chooses to suppress its identity as a "new religion" and to create in symbolic terms an image of itself as part of Shrine Shintō. Appendix A presents a translation of the prayer most used in Kurozumikyō, the Great Purification Prayer.

The most comprehensive study of Kurozumikyō is Charles Hepner's *The Kurozumi Sect of Shinto*, published in 1935 by the Meiji Japan Society. In the manner of studies at that time, a large part of the book is devoted to a general history of Japanese religions up until the time of Kurozumikyo's founding. The remainder of the volume is a study of Kurozumi's thought and does not treat the history, ritual, or organization of the group in any detail. As a philosophical study, Hepner's remains a useful work. The present study has a different task: using Kurozumikyō as an example of a pervasive orientation, it treats the historical development of Kurozumi's thought as the doctrine of the religious group he founded. It then turns to questions of organization, ritual, and world view and addresses the position of the group and its membership in contemporary Japan. These are questions Hepner did not consider, and thus there is little overlap between Hepner's work and this study; what overlap exists is confined to the outline of the Founder's life in the next chapter.

In Japanese scholarship several articles and chapters in larger works have discussed Kurozumikyō. These are listed in the bibliography. None of these works attempts a comprehensive study of it; generally these works are limited to a treatment of a specific aspect of Kurozumi's thought or to historical considerations of a section of the group's history. Their total volume is small, and no Japanese scholars are presently known to be engaged in a comprehensive study of the group.

This present study is based not only on the sources in the bibliography but also on the author's fieldwork in Kurozumikyō during the summers of 1980, 1981, and 1982, and during the year June 1983 to August 1984. The longest period of residence with group members was for two months during the summer of 1981. Because of contacts established during 1980, the author was very fortunate to be invited to reside in the Ōi Church of Kurozumikyō, located on the border of Okayama City. There I observed all the major rites of Kurozumikyō, some many times, and I was able to observe ministers counseling followers over an extended period of time. I came to know many followers in several areas of Japan; observed and interviewed at churches in Izumo, Kōchi, Osaka, Awajishima, Kobe, Kyoto, and Okayama; and frequently participated in headquarters activities. I was allowed complete freedom to interview, photograph, and record, and for this privilege I owe a great debt of gratitude to Kurozumikyō, the Sixth Patriarch, Kurozumi Muneharu 黒住宗晴, and to the Ōi Church, its ministers, and followers.

CHAPTER TWO

The Founding of Kurozumikyō

INTRODUCTION

This chapter considers the life of the Founder of Kurozumikyō, Kurozumi Munetada 黒住宗忠 (1780–1850), the development of his thought, and the early history of his religion. Following this introduction, the second section establishes the context of the later Tokugawa period (1600–1868) history, religious thought, and religious law governing the formation of religious associations. After briefly surveying the historical process of Kurozumikyō's formation, the chapter turns to a detailed study of Kurozumi's life and thought, divided into three stages. Changing perceptions of his following, first as an appendage of the Imamura Shrine where he served as a priest, and later as a full-fledged "new religion," are linked to changes in Kurozumi's thought and his relation to his shrine post.

THE HISTORICAL CONTEXT

The Founder was active during the closing days of the Tokugawa 徳川 era, and his thought is best seen against the background of contemporary history, religious thought, and religious law.[1] Tokugawa Japan was governed by a central administration called the *bakufu* (幕府 "tent government") and the local domains, or *han* 藩. The *shōgun* 将軍 headed the *bakufu* and ruled as the emperor's

---

[1] The following introduction is to serve as a background for nonspecialists. Accordingly, it passes over many aspects of contemporary scholarly controversy in favor of providing only a minimal coverage of basic social and political structures and the current of popular movements as these impinged on Kurozumi.

military deputy. The *shōgun* controlled lands amounting to about one-fourth of the whole, and other members of the Tokugawa family and their direct retainers (the *fudai daimyō* 譜代大名) held another 36 percent. A little less than 40 percent was held by about a hundred *tozama daimyō* 外様大名 (those who surrendered to the Tokugawa after 1600). The remainder was allocated to the imperial court and to a number of temples and shrines.[2]

The *han* or domains were ruled by *daimyō* 大名, and the *han's* revenue was measured in rice, by units called *koku* (石, about five bushels). A rice tax was collected from peasant cultivators and then redistributed by the *daimyō* for his own use and that of his retainers. A fixed system of classes ranked samurai, peasants, artisans, and merchants in a hierarchy. Samurai received fixed stipends in rice, which made them especially vulnerable to fluctuations in the market value of rice as a cash economy inexorably dominated the agrarian ideal.[3] In addition to the four classes, there were elaborate distinctions within each, representing in the case of samurai differences in stipends and ceremonial privileges in relation to the *daimyō*. As the period drew to a close, greater differences in mobility and status were to be seen in both commoner and samurai society.[4]

By 1800 Tokugawa society differed greatly from the situation in the seventeenth century. Mutual interest drew lower samurai and rich peasants together across class lines, and the realities of interest, influence, and power diverged widely from the traditional ideal. An important cause of these changes was fiscal mismanagement at the top. From 1750 on, the *bakufu's* expenditures rose while rice revenue fell, and the result was a growing annual deficit, which by

---

[2] William G. Beasley, *The Meiji Restoration* (Stanford: Stanford University Press, 1972), pp. 15–16.

[3] Ibid., pp. 14–15. Most samurai lived in castle-towns, not on the land; nor did most of them cultivate.

[4] On the political structure of Kurozumi's domain, Okayama, during the Tokugawa period, see John W. Hall, *Government and Local Power in Japan* (Princeton: Princeton University Press, 1966), chap. 12 and 13; see also Nagayama Usaburō, *Okayama-ken tsūshi*, 2 vols. (Okayama: Seibundō, 1930) and Taniguchi Sumio, *Okayama-han seishi no kenkyū* (Tokyo: Kōshobō, 1964).

1840 had reached half a million *ryō* 両 of gold.[5] To redress the deficit, the *bakufu* debased the currency and exacted forced loans from merchants, which predictably played havoc with the entire economy.[6] Simultaneously, it soberly lectured the people on the necessity of frugality, diligence, and thrift through sumptuary laws. The Tempō Reforms 天保改革 (1841–1843) represented a concerted effort to reduce the deficits, but they produced no lasting results.[7] Increasing numbers of people were under no direct control of an authority, and they were easily drawn into a rising tide of peasant unrest.[8]

Between the years 1813 and 1868, there were no less than 400 peasant revolts of varying scale. One of the most alarming to the *bakufu* was led by one of its own officials, Ōshio Heihachirō 大塩平八郎, in Osaka in 1837.[9] News of this uprising spread throughout Japan. No area of Japan was free of revolt, and the *bakufu* had reason to fear for its preservation and safety. Although these revolts were not "revolutionary" in the sense of seeking to replace the entire system with another, they clearly expressed the varied discontent of the people with their rulers.[10] Often the *bakufu* and *han* authorities responded to these uprisings with educational programs designed to raise village morale and secure allegiance to the status quo. Local authorities sponsored lecture tours by men representing a variety of creeds, incorporating Shintō, "national learning" (*kokugaku* 国学), and Shingaku (心学 Learning of the Heart-Mind; see below) concepts to convey to peasants a sense of place and purpose. Their theological differences aside, all espoused the values of filial piety, obedience to authority, thrift, and diligence, the so-called core values of the age.[11]

[5] Beasley, *The Meiji Restoration*, p. 51.

[6] Ibid., pp. 63–68.

[7] Hayashiya Tatsusaburō, "Bakumatsu-ki no bunkateki shihyō," in *Bakumatsu bunka no kenkyū*, ed. Hayashiya Tatsusaburō (Tokyo: Iwanami shoten, 1978), p. 10.

[8] Ibid., p. 29. These persons are called *sōmō* 草莽 in contemporary accounts.

[9] Beasley, *The Meiji Restoration*, p. 57.

[10] Ibid., pp. 57–59.

[11] Kamata Michitaka, "Ara-mura fukkō no nōmin undō," in *Bakumatsu bunka*, pp. 321–24. On "core values" see below. One such person who was a contemporary of Kurozumi and active in the same locale was Ōhara Yūgaku (1797–1858).

A popular movement that exerted great influence on the growth of new religions was Ise pilgrimage.[12] Because of the Grand Shrine's national status, it was easier for commoners to secure permission to travel there on pilgrimage than anywhere else, and by the end of the era there was a popular, explicit understanding that all persons, male or female, had a patriotic duty to make the pilgrimage at least once. In fact, pilgrimage became associated with coming of age rites and acquired an air of custom and duty rather than individual faith. Pilgrimage was surrounded by many secular amusements in the towns of Ise 伊勢 and Yamada 山田, which sported baths, hotels, brothels, and similar accoutrements of a "tourist trap."[13] An order of irregular priests, *oshi* 御師, attached to both Inner (*naikū* 内宮) and Outer (*gekū* 外宮) Shrines at Ise, maintained nationwide networks to funnel pilgrims through their lodging houses and to provide guide services. These facilities enabled pilgrims to procure protective talismans to take home to fellow villagers, an important goal of the pilgrimage.[14]

An outgrowth of the long-established custom of Ise pilgrimage was *okage mairi* 御陰参り ("thanks pilgrimage"), Ise pilgrimages on a wide scale occurring at intervals of roughly sixty years. No other movement of people in the entire Tokugawa period approaches the scale of Ise pilgrimage. On the pilgrimage route there was an element of sexual freedom and carnival unknown in village life, and the pilgrims often performed dances of abandon in transvestite attire. These dances sometimes gave way to destruction of headmen's houses and property, thus becoming a vehicle to express

[12] Improved transportation, greater safety of travel, and an increasingly widespread use of currency facilitated the popularization of pilgrimage. In the Tokugawa period use of palanquins and rental horses became economically possible for commoners. Shinjō Tsunezō, *Shaji to kōtsū*, Nihon rekishi shinsho (Tokyo: Chibundō, 1960), pp. 112–13.

[13] Ibid., pp. 120–23.

[14] Powerful *oshi* maintained "parishes" of 4,000 to 10,000 households to whom they annually distributed almanac-calendars and charms with the Great Purification Prayer inscribed. In villages they were received by confraternities formed to sponsor the pilgrimage, and almost every village had such a confraternity by the early nineteenth century. Each sent a number of its members on the pilgrimage annually. Ibid., pp. 125–27. See also Fujitani Toshio, *Shintō shinkō to minshū: Tennōsei* (Kyoto: Hōritsu bunkasha, 1980), pp. 69–70.

resentment of various kinds. Rich peasants, even *daimyō*, were so intimidated by the pilgrims passing through their lands that they willingly provided food and money to them, since these could so obviously be taken easily by force.

The pilgrimage played an important role in creating widespread, popular awareness of the entire nation in what was otherwise a highly localized society. Pilgrimage brought villagers into contact with the tastes, accents, and customs of inhabitants of other areas of Japan, and the Shrine became a symbolic vehicle for expressing a sense of common identity. Appropriately, the notion of Ise as the seat of the ancestral gods of the imperial house was superseded in popular consciousness by the idea of Ise as enshrining the highest gods of the Japanese people.[15] Thus Ise pilgrimage was instrumental in casting a growing sense of national identity in a Shintō idiom.

Tokugawa popular religions involved a Confucian conception of society as a hierarchy of complementary functions, regulated by proper conduct in the five relations.[16] As long as the relations of human society are in order, society will be harmonious, and the human world will be in accord with the cosmos. Humanity is the recipient of countless blessings (*on*) from superiors and beneficence from superordinate entities such as Heaven, the Buddhas, and the *kami*. These must be repaid, and the repayment of obligation (*hō-on*) became a primary religious action. In addition to (but not in competition with) superordinate entities was the idea of an underlying principle of the universe (Neo-Confucian *li*, the Buddhanature, *kami*-nature), and humanity must seek union with this principle. This idea is found in Confucian, Shintō, and Buddhist idioms, expressed as the quest to become a sage, to become a *kami*, or to attain Buddhahood. Toward this end, humanity must practice spiritual cultivation. The means to true cultivation was one of the enduring questions of the age, receiving a variety of answers from founders of new religions at the end of the period. Because egotism prevents unity with cosmic principle, moral cultivation is a sus-

[15] Ibid., pp. 72–78.
[16] That is, relations (1) between ruler and subject, (2) between husband and wife, (3) between brothers, (4) between parent and child, and (5) between friends.

tained struggle against selfish desire. Virtually all popular religions of the nineteenth and twentieth centuries originate in this matrix of ideas.[17]

Thirty years ago Robert Bellah wrote of the uniform commitment to "core values" (loyalty, filial piety, diligence, frugality, humility, and sincerity) as analogous to the Protestant ethic, a factor of Japanese society that facilitated its swift transition to an industrial society.[18] More recently Yasumaru Yoshio 安丸良夫 developed a similar notion of the "core values" (tsūzoku dōtoku 通俗道徳) as the key to Tokugawa religious thought.[19] He focuses on the pathos of a society entrapped in a narrow web of thought and emotion that legitimated and rendered invisible the most atrocious exploitation. The power held over the minds of the Japanese people by these values cannot be understood, he writes in criticism of Bellah, until one realizes that while they also *came down to* the people from their leaders (Bellah's emphasis), the *people themselves* were earnest advocates of them, eager architects of their own prisons. Yasumaru's work suggests the phrase "philosophy of the heart" (*kokoro no tetsugaku* 心の哲学) to distinguish the special characteristics of the popular religious movements arising at the end of the Tokugawa period.[20]

[17] See Robert Bellah, *Tokugawa Religion* (New York: The Free Press, 1956), on which the characterization in this paragraph relies heavily, especially chap. 3.

[18] Ibid., pp. 61–67. In a review of *Tokugawa Religion*, Maruyama Masao pointed out that whereas Bellah unqualifiedly linked these core values (especially loyalty) with economic rationalization (Max Weber's *Zweksrationalitat*), in fact each element of the core could be shown to have the opposite tendency as well; in addition, if followed to its consequences in the 1930s and 1940s, each value could be shown to lead to highly irrational results. Maruyama Masao, "R. N. Bellah, *Tokugawa Religion* no shōkai," *Kokka zasshi* 72 (April 1958): 437–58.

[19] Yasumaru Yoshio, *Nihon no kindaika to minshū shisō* (Tokyo: Aoki shoten, 1974).

[20] Utilization of the concept of core values requires significant qualification. Critics of Yasumaru's work point out that it is ahistorical, attributing to core values a changeless, monolithic character, as if once established they remained unchanged. Miyagi Kimiko makes this point in "Henkaku-ki no shisō" in *Kōza Nihonshi*, ed. Rekishigaku kenkyūkai, 10 vols. (Tokyo: Tokyo daigaku shuppankai, 1970–1971), 4:257–86. In fact, however, Japanese thought on these ethical concepts neither originated in the Tokugawa period, nor did it remain static during that time. Much

Kurozumi's thought revolved around the core values, and he never departed from them. He was not, however, preoccupied with them purely in the abstract, nor would he have understood them as independent of broader religious questions. Instead, he appropriated them through the channels of the Neo-Confucian tradition in Japan. The thought of Japanese Neo-Confucian thinkers differed considerably from Chu Hsi 朱子 and other Chinese figures of the school. Themes such as the quest for sagehood, however, remained vital in Japan, taking on a distinctly religious coloration and eventually influencing even such popular figures as Ishida Baigan 石田梅岩 and, indirectly, Kurozumi. What appears in Baigan and Kurozumi as a preoccupation with core values is, on closer inspection, an inheritance from the Neo-Confucian tradition.[21]

The cult of sagehood was a central religious ideal in Neo-Confucian thought, in Japan as well as in China. The aspect of sagehood most congenial to the Japanese was the sage neither as an ideal ruler nor as an original source of authority and orthodoxy, but

---

of the intellectual history of the period consisted of rival interpretations, and at the popular level, the doctrinal variety of the new religions is incomprehensible if we suppose that all derived from a single, unchanging source. Whatever the source of religious thought, it cannot be reduced to core values alone. Fukawa Kiyoshi makes a similar point in *Kinsei minshū no rinriteki enerugii* (Nagoya: Fūbaisha, 1976). While core values provided building blocks, they assumed many different forms depending on such factors as the emphasis of particular founders, the character of preexisting religious practice in a specific locale, and the mystical element of religious experience expressed differently in each group. Furthermore, no religion can be understood simply as a body of thought. However central its doctrine may be, ritual, symbol, and organizational structure are equally essential to the whole. Nevertheless, reflections upon a shared set of values provided an important component of the world view of Tokugawa new religious movements. In this sense Yasumaru's work enables us to perceive a unity of religious orientation amidst a variety of doctrinal formulations. In *Kinsei minshū shisō no kenkyū* (Tokyo: Kōshobo, 1979) Shōji Kichinosuke employs the idea of core values with similar qualifications to those introduced here. His work illustrates how different sectors of society appropriated core values, and how much variety existed in their interpretations.

[21] On Japanese Neo-Confucian thought, see William T. De Bary and Irene Bloom, eds., *Principle and Practicality* (New York: Columbia University Press, 1979).

instead as an individual perfected in self-cultivation.[22] Japanese thinkers such as Yamaga Sokō 山鹿素行 (1622–1685) recorded their self-cultivation in autobiographical works, and from these we learn what the central questions of the pursuit of sagehood are. There must first be an awakening to the need for self-cultivation and a resolution to pursue it.[23] But in what does self-cultivation consist? Is it to be attained through "quiet sitting"? Must the formal codes of behavior prescribed in Confucian writings be strictly followed? Is the object of these disciplines a repression of physical nature and a curbing of desire? Or should self-cultivation instead have the aim of nurturing the human spirit, originally one with the principle underlying the entire cosmos? All these are questions inevitably involved in the quest for sagehood as Japanese thinkers in the Tokugawa period understood that ideal.[24]

As appropriated by Japanese thinkers such as Yamazaki Ansai 山崎闇斎 (1611–1682),[25] Kaibara Ekken 貝原益軒 (1630–1714),[26] and Nakae Tōju 中江藤樹 (1608–1648),[27] Neo-Confucian thought took on a theistic emphasis that bore deep affinities with Shintō. Although each of these thinkers was quite different and founded a separate school of thought, they all believed in the perfectibility of human beings, a tenet that made the quest for sagehood plausible. Each saw in principle (li) a unity between humanity and the universe, and each idealized an experience of

[22] W. T. De Bary, "Sagehood as a Secular and Spiritual Ideal in Tokugawa Neo-Confucianism," in *Principle and Practicality*, pp. 127–88. See also Rodney L. Taylor, "The Cultivation of Sagehood as a Religious Goal in Neo-Confucianism: A Study of Selected Writings of Kao P'an-lung (1562–1626)" (Ph.D. dissertation, Columbia University, 1974).

[23] Though Confucians would not like the comparison, this idea is similar to the "aspiration for enlightenment" (*bodhicitta*) of Buddhist tradition and signals the moment when the aspirant becomes deeply serious about the quest.

[24] De Bary, "Sagehood," passim.

[25] On Ansai's view of the unity of Shintō and Confucianism, see Okada Takehiko, "Practical Learning in the Chu Hsi School: Yamazaki Ansai and Kaibara Ekken," in *Principle and Practicality*, p. 248.

[26] On Kaibara Ekken's view of the unity of Shintō and Confucianism, see ibid., p. 262.

[27] On the religious thought of Nakae Tōju, see Yamashita Ryūji, "Nakae Tōju's Religious Thought and Its Relation to Jitsugaku," in *Principle and Practicality*, pp. 307–35.

absolute oneness with the cosmos. It was on this last point in particular that they perceived a similar ethos in Shintō. In fact, it was shortly after a pilgrimage to the Ise Shrine that Nakae Tōju abandoned a formalistic insistence on observance of rites and codes of behavior. Instead he came to uphold the view that humanity is naturally in harmony with universal principle and must not be so preoccupied with observance of rites and rules that the spontaneity of the spirit is stifled.

> For a long time I have acted according to the formal codes of conduct. I have recently come to understand that such codes are wrong.... Abandon the ... desire which causes you to adhere to formal codes, have faith in your own essential mind, do not be attached to mere convention.[28]

The variety of Neo-Confucian thought that probably influenced Kurozumi most directly was the Shingaku ("Learning of the Heart-Mind") of Ishida Baigan (1685–1744).[29] While appropriating the notion of the heart-mind (the *kokoro*, *shin*) Baigan emphasized its ethical and affective dimensions, paying less attention to the rationalist side developed by other Japanese Neo-Confucians. Baigan's Shingaku was less a philosophical system than a "type and method of spirituality"[30] especially directed to townsmen and merchants. The basis of Shingaku was Mencius's concept of nature according to which the "innermost temperament" of humanity is originally good. Failure and misfortune result from lack of cultivation of *kokoro*, and it is the aim of Shingaku to "promote the recovery and cultivation of original, innate nature."[31] Daily cultivation consisted of introspection and self-examination in order to develop awareness of original nature.[32] Because selfish desire obstructs the individual's progress toward perfection and prevents the experience of all-pervading unity, another aim of self-cultivation is

[28] Ibid., p. 319.

[29] See Bellah, *Tokugawa Religion*, chap. 6.

[30] William T. De Bary, *Neo-Confucian Orthodoxy and the Learning of the Mind-and-Heart* (New York: Columbia University Press, 1981), pp. 206–10.

[31] Jennifer Robertson, "Rooting the Pine: Shingaku Methods of Organization," *Monumenta Nipponica* 34 (Autumn 1979): 313.

[32] Ibid., p. 320.

to be rid of egoism and to nurture a state of egolessness,[33] *ware nashi* 我なし. Although Kurozumi stated these ideas in a Shintō idiom, he incorporated the basic Shingaku framework virtually intact.

Tokugawa Religious Law

Formation of new religious bodies was not, however, solely a matter of belief. Religious organizations were strictly regulated by the state, and new groups had to reach an accommodation with the religious law of the day. Religious law of the Tokugawa period was penned in part to enforce the state proscription on Christianity.[34] As a method of surveillance, all subjects were required to become parishioners of a Buddhist temple. Some domains created the alternative possibility of becoming a parishioner of a shrine instead. Okayama under Ikeda Mitsumasa 池田光政 (1609–1682) was one of these. The temples then began the work of recording births, marriages, deaths, and other duties of a census-taking nature. Buddhist institutions were themselves governed by law codes (*hatto* 法度) requiring them to recognize the authority of a head temple (*honji* 本寺) of each sect and to rank subsidiary temples (*matsuji* 末寺) beneath.[35] Since Buddhism already had close-knit sectarian organization, it was relatively easy for the shogunate (though hardly painless for the Buddhist clergy) to utilize this infrastructure, streamline it, and make it serve the purposes of the state, which in this instance meant contributing to the maintenance of an orderly, stable rural populace.[36]

[33] Ibid.

[34] Throughout the period of disunity (1467–1600), Christianity had advanced steadily, and by the time of Tokugawa Ieyasu (circa 1600), there were some 600,000–700,000 Christians in Japan. The shogunate envisioned an intolerable future in which growing numbers of its retainers and those in their charge would pledge allegiance to a foreign religious overlord. Thus, a ban against Christianity was imposed.

[35] The conduct and qualifications of Buddhist clerics were duly codified by the shogunate, these representing for the most part a confirmation of existing sectarian practice.

[36] On Buddhist sectarian organization, see Ōkuwa Hitoshi, *Jidan no shisō*, Kyōikusha rekishi shinsho (Nihonshi) 177 (Tokyo: Kyōikusha, 1979), chap. 2. Shugendō was regulated through its connection with Buddhism.

Regulation of the Shintō side, however, required a different strategy, because of the amorphous character of *kami*-worship and because of the lack of institutional unity such as Buddhism had already developed. Large shrines, such as Ise, Kompira 金毘羅, Dazaifu 太宰府, and Kumano 熊野 Shrines had hereditary priesthoods and confraternities organized for pilgrimage.[37] In addition to pilgrimage sites, the cult of local tutelary deities (*ujigami*, *ubusunagami* 産土神, *chinjugami* 鎮守神) had become universal by the end of the seventeenth century.[38] Larger tutelary shrines, especially those connected with a *daimyō*, were often staffed with a hereditary priesthood, confirmed in their office by the *han*. In others, rites were performed by village residents, sometimes organized into parish guilds[39] called *miyaza* 宮座. By the mid-nineteenth century, these guilds were beginning to be replaced by territorial parish organizations called *ujiko* 氏子. A ritualist was chosen by lot or rotation to serve at spring, autumn, and other festivals after undergoing prescribed abstinences and purifications. He did not give up his secular occupation.[40] Seldom did small, rural tutelary shrines have a regular priest.

Since no common institution united all of Shintō, the *shōgun* in 1665 issued the *Shosha negi kannushi hatto* 諸社禰宜神主法度, a law code authorizing the Yoshida 吉田 house, descendants of the ancient ritualist clan, the Urabe, to grant rank to all shrines and

[37] Confraternities (*kō*, *kōshaku*) were led by representatives of the shrine in question. In the case of Ise, these representatives were called *oshi*. They cooperated with village headmen in assembling local villagers to pool their resources so that a number of members of the confraternity could make a pilgrimage and bring home protective talismans for the entire group. These representational confraternities (*daisan-kō* 代参講) were but one type of confraternity. For a comprehensive treatment of the development of various types of confraternities, see Sakurai Tokutarō, *Nihon minkan shinkōron*, rev. ed. (Tokyo: Kōbundō, 1970), part 2, chaps. 2–5.

[38] The development of this form of *kami*-worship is related to the formation of villages in which many unrelated households resided and conducted worship of a common territorial deity.

[39] These guilds were generally led by village headmen, officials, and prominent households of long residence in the village.

[40] Membership in the parish, coextensive with the local community, was obligatory and hereditary, not a matter of individual faith in the *kami* housed in the shrine.

priests.[41] Thus from 1665 the Yoshida house effectively controlled the organization of shrines. All priests had to apply to the Yoshida for permission to wear certain colors of vestments denoting subtleties of rank, and they had also to secure Yoshida approval for the use of honorific titles such as *reijin* 霊人 or *daimyōjin* 大明神 for local deities. Yoshida approval (often secured by heavy financial outlay) constituted a semi-official recognition that, in the case of the new religions of the period, was useful for avoiding persecution and suppression.[42]

Thus these twin codes of law regulating Buddhism and Shintō served as the nation's basic religious law from their inception in the mid-seventeenth century until the Meiji period (1868–1912). Implicit in these codes was the idea that the sects and shrines recognized at the time of the formulation of the law were the only ones to be countenanced. Heavy *bakufu* supervision was exercised over new construction of temples and shrines, and over their repair.[43]

THE FORMATION OF KUROZUMIKYŌ: OVERVIEW

The group presently known as Kurozumikyō became an independent religious organization by stages, and only the early ones have been treated in detail here. Nevertheless, it seems appropriate to outline the whole story to provide a framework of continuity into which the early stages may be fitted. The process by which this group became a new religion is linked to three periods in the career of its Founder, Kurozumi Munetada. After his revelation in 1814, the Founder collected numerous disciples by faith healing in his capacity as a shrine priest, and his teaching was not at first perceived as a "new religion." No matter that most followers had little if any prior connection with his shrine; as long as Kurozumi was a shrine priest, it was possible to consider his followers "parishioners." Kurozumi resigned from his hereditary office in 1843, and after that

---

[41] The Yoshida, however, did not control the small number of shrines directly attached to the imperial house. Those were put in charge of the Shirakawa house.

[42] On the regulation of Shintō, see Murakami Shigeyoshi, *Kokka Shintō*, Iwanami shinsho 770 (Tokyo: Iwanami shoten, 1970), pp. 52–60.

[43] Ibid.

the status of his followers became an issue. It was no longer possible to regard them as "parishioners"; their attachment to the man and not the shrine was too obvious, and he was no longer formally attending its deities.[44]

Thus began a period of limbo that did not end until 1876 when the Meiji government granted to a group now led by the Founder's disciples independent status as a "sect" of Shintō under newly established Meiji religious law. In 1846 Kurozumi adopted the name Kurozumi Kyōdan for his followers, but this was an informal designation carrying no legal status. During this period, the Founder died (in 1850), and his disciples began to proselytize in western Japan. Lacking any official legal standing, they were sometimes silenced by domain authorities, and swelling numbers made imperative the quest for official recognition and an end to patent vulnerability. Upon the High Disciple Akagi Tadaharu 赤木忠春 (1816–1867) fell the task of persuading the Yoshida house to grant the Founder posthumous apotheosis as *daimyōjin*, "great god," a mark of approval carrying the implication of legal recognition under *bakufu* law. In this he succeeded only after repeated rejection and renewed expense in the form of "contributions" to the Yoshida house. Meanwhile, the group encountered suppression in several areas.[45]

Akagi secured the desired *daimyōjin* title in 1856, but it proved insufficient to prevent localized repression. In 1863 the Okayama domain issued a proscription upon the religion as detrimental to the samurai spirit. Although this scarcely affected commoner participation, it was a slap in the face that glaringly demonstrated the group's insecurity. After the Meiji Restoration, Kurozumikyō cooperated enthusiastically in bureaucratic attempts to formulate a

---

[44] Kodera Motonoko, "Kurozumikyō no rekishiteki seikaku," *Okayama shigaku* 24 (September 1971): 39–64, distinguishes different epochs in the development of Kurozumi's thought. The periodization of the present study takes account of developments in organizations as well and thus departs significantly from Kodera's usage.

[45] On Akagi, see Kōmoto Kazunobu, *Akagi Tadaharu* (Okayama: Kurozumikyō Nisshinsha, 1980); Hirota Masaki, *Bunmei kaika to minshū ishiki* (Tokyo: Aoki shoten, 1980); Hirota M., *Bunmei kaika to zairai shisō* (Tokyo: Aoki shoten, 1980); Hirota M., "Bakumatsu ishin-ki no Kurozumikyō," *Okayama daigaku hōbungakubu jutsu kiyō* (Shigaku-hen) 35 (October 1974): 13–25.

state religion, but not even such a display could save it in some areas from suppression under a general ban on faith healing. Only when the newly created Bureau of Shintō Affairs made "Shintō Kurozumi-ha 神道黒住派" a Shintō sect in 1876 was universally recognized status attained, thus allowing proselytization and daily activities to go forward unimpeded.[46]

The search for independence proceeded by fits and starts, guided by an evolving desire for some organization independent of the Founder's shrine on the one hand, and by a need for recognition from central authority so as to escape suppression on the other. These changes in organization were paralleled by changing understandings of doctrinal questions. Only after some years did the Founder conclude that his message was not compatible with a confraternity attached to the domain shrine. He could not have envisioned a Shintō "sect," however, because religious law of his day did not provide for any such entity. The status of the group developed in tandem with social and legal change, influenced after the Meiji Restoration by Western concepts of religious law beyond the scope of this study.[47]

THE FOUNDER'S EARLY CAREER

Kurozumi Munetada was born on December 21, 1780, the third son of a low-ranking priest of the Imamura Shrine 今村神社, a tutelary shrine of the Okayama domain.[48] See Illustration 1. In secular matters, Kurozumi held the samurai rank.[49] As a child the Founder considered filial piety the highest good, and many inci-

[46] Oguri Junko, "Kindai shakai ni okeru kyōha Shintō no hatten," in *Ajia Bukkyō-shi.* 20 vols. (Tokyo: Kōsei shuppansha, 1972), vol. 19: *Kindai Bukkyō*, pp. 11–20.

[47] Ibid.

[48] Kurozumi's father's rank was *negi* 禰宜. A *negi* is an assistant in ritual, and the term may be used in addition to designate any priest of any shrine but Ise, where several grades of *negi* serve. When used as a term of rank, a *negi* falls below *kannushi* and above *hafuri*. Shimonaka Yasaburō, ed. *Shintō daijiten*, 3 vols. (Tokyo: Heibonsha, 1940), 3:99.

[49] He and his father held the rank *kachi* 徒. *Kachi* were low-ranking samurai who were originally in charge of security matters and supervision of the route of march on the *sankin kōtai*.

dents of his filial behavior are recorded. One that is often retold in contemporary Kurozumikyō churches has it that Gonkichi 権吉, as the child Kurozumi was called, was told by one parent to wear straw sandals and by the other to wear wooden clogs. Loathe to disobey either, he set out with a sandal on one foot and a clog on the other.[50] At the age of nineteen he resolved to honor his parents by becoming a *kami* in this life.[51]

Of the Founder's early education little is known, but there is no evidence to suggest that it surpassed that of the average priest of his day, which is to say that he knew such classical works as the *Kojiki* 古事記, the *Man'yōshū* 万葉集, the *Kokinshū* 古今集, the Chinese classics to a certain extent, and the writings attributed to Lao Tzu and Chuang Tzu. In addition, he studied divination by the hexagrams and had a knowledge of Chinese medicine. He was familiar with the Shingaku thought of Ishida Baigan, and he must have been acquainted with the *kokugaku* writers. Although he surely had some knowledge of Buddhism, it was probably limited.[52]

The Aspiration to Become a Kami

The young Kurozumi was first and foremost a Shintō priest, but his religious ideals were powerfully shaped by Neo-Confucianism. In his resolution to become a *kami* he was phrasing the sagehood

---

[50] Kurozumi Tadaaki, *Kurozumikyō kyōsoden*, 5th ed. (Okayama: Kurozumikyō nisshinsha, 1976), pp. 20–21.

[51] Ibid., pp. 24–27.

[52] Hepner, *The Kurozumi Sect*, p. 96. Hepner says Kurozumi did not know of *kokugaku*, but even if he had no direct acquaintance with works of Motoori and Hirata, their disciples were so active in Okayama that it is impossible that Kurozumi would not have known their views. On the general characteristics of the education of the Shintō priest in the Tokugawa period, see Kishimoto Yoshio, *Kinsei Shintō kyōikushi* (Tokyo: Ōbunsha, 1962), pp. 31 and 148ff. Judging from his later doctrines, Kurozumi's Confucian learning was in the Chen Tchsiu Neo-Confucian line, which came into Japan filtered through the strong spiritualist emphasis of the Korean scholar, Yi T'oegye. Kurozumi shows no interest in Confucian teachings for the ruler; instead he takes a theistic view of Heaven and later uses the term *ten* interchangeably with Amaterasu Ōmikami. On the theistic, religio-ethical strain of Neo-Confucian thought that most likely influenced Kurozumi, see De Bary, *Neo-Confucian Orthodoxy and the Learning of the Mind-and-Heart*, pp. 66ff.

ideal in a Shintō mode. He embarked on self-cultivation in the spirit of those seeking self-perfection, and the moment of his initial resolution marked the beginning of a quest in which he had to find answers to the same questions addressed by his forebears who had sought a rapprochement of Shintō and Neo-Confucian traditions.

Munetada grieved desperately when his parents died of dysentery within a week of each other in 1812. This sorrow probably contributed to his contraction of tuberculosis. He weakened until late in 1813, when the end was pronounced near. Believing he would not live to fulfill the dream of becoming a *kami* in this life, he vowed to heal the sickness of the living after passing into the other world, there to become a healing deity, or *reijin*.[53] He had his pallet carried to the verandah to worship the sun for the last time. This was the first of three occasions of sun worship, *nippai* 日拝, prior to his revelation.[54] The first took place around January 19, 1814. Two months later he had recovered enough to rise, bathe, and put on fresh clothes. Again he worshiped the sun, this time in gratitude for the restoration of health. This occurred around March 19, 1814.

By November he had completely recovered, and he worshiped the sun on November 19, the winter solstice (also his birthday) of his thirty-fifth year by the traditional method of counting age.[55] Facing the east at dawn, he inhaled the sun's rays deeply, and as he did so, the sun seemed to come down out of the sky, enter his mouth, and pervade his entire body, as if he had swallowed it. In this mystical experience he became one with the sun. This experience of unity with divinity, called the Direct Receipt of the Heavenly Mission (*tenmei jikiju* 天命直受), constituted the inspiration of the remainder of his life.[56]

[53] *Reijin* designates a *kami* believed to excel in communication between *kami* and human beings. *Shintō daijiten*, 3:429.

[54] *Nippai*, the custom of sun worship, was common in Okayama folk religion; it was not an invention by Kurozumi. Kōmoto Kazushi, *Kurozumikyō tokuhon* (Okayama: Kurozumikyō nisshinsha, 1961), p. 126.

[55] Traditional calculation counted a newborn baby as one year old. Thus by this method, Kurozumi was reckoned thirty-five in 1814, though by the Western custom, he would be thirty-four.

[56] Ibid., pp. 5–7. The term *tenmei* 天命 is of course the Mandate of Heaven in Confucian terms, and such a translation would not be entirely out of place in Kurozumi's case save for his lack of any political concern.

The Direct Receipt of the Heavenly Mission was an experience of absolute unity with the one god of the universe. Kurozumi referred to the deity both by the Sinified pronunciations Tenshō Daijin 天照大神 and Tenshōkōtaijin 天照皇大神, and by the Japanese readings Amaterasu or Amaterasu Ōmikami 天照大御神.[57] He believed Amaterasu Ōmikami to be the creator of all the universe and hence the parent of all living beings.[58] In their common origin, heaven and earth are one, and all the earth is governed by a single, divine rule. Amaterasu Ōmikami is the source of all life, and each separate life represents a portion of the life soul of the universe, a microcosm of that vital source, the "small soul" (*bunshin* 分心, *wake-mitama* 分霊).

Believing sickness to be a result of lack of harmony with deity, Munetada attributed his illness to excessive grief for his parents' loss. Filling his heart with sorrow, he had injured the small soul, depriving it of the joy (*yōki*) on which alone it can thrive. Thus the bright, joyous, vital character that is the natural state of humanity gave way to gloom and despair, sapping the small soul of its vital essence. Put in other terms, *yang* gave way to *yin*, and a state of purity degenerated to a state of pollution.

Kurozumi's Concept of Divinity

Kurozumi's view of Amaterasu Ōmikami amounts to henotheism in that the existence of myriad *kami* (*yaoyorozu no kami* 八百万神), the eight million gods, is accepted, and it is said that human beings are *kami* or become so upon death. But worship singling out particular gods only rarely played a part in Kurozumi's postrevelation

[57] Kōmoto, *Tokuhon*, p. 43. He also used the terms *ten* and *tenchi* 天地, "Heaven" and "Heaven and Earth," interchangeably with the above terms for deity. He sometimes used the term *ten*, however, in the sense of divine will, particularly when he spoke of entrusting all things to divine will (*ten ni makase* 天に任せ). See Kurozumikyō kyōhanhensan iinkai, *Kurozumikyō kyōtenshō* (Okayama: Kurozumikyō nisshinsha, 1981), pp. 60–61, 98, 110, 120, 129, 131, 134, 145.

[58] Needless to say, Kurozumi was not the first to speak of Amaterasu Ōmikami. She stands at the head of the Yamato pantheon in the *Kojiki* and *Nihon shoki*, and her cult at Ise received steadily increasing popular devotion during Kurozumi's lifetime. Contemporary Shintō scholars were intent on clarifying the significance of this deity to secular rule. Kōmoto, *Tokuhon*, pp. 24–48.

experience. This was unlike the Imamura Shrine where Kurozumi continued to serve, for there the deities Kasuga Myōjin 春日明神 and Hachiman 八幡 were enshrined in addition to Tenshō Daijin. Kurozumi saw all existence pervaded with a vital principle that he called yōki, "yang essence." As he used this term, it was equivalent to kami-nature, and it could also mean "joy" or "joyous." The world is pulsing with yōki, with divine life, and although it takes many forms, all depend upon a single source.[59] Alternately stressing the many forms or the unique origin, Kurozumi sought continual unity with divinity, the absence of any separation between human and divine will (shinjin fuji 神人不二). Because the grace of Amaterasu Ōmikami falls upon all without distinction, life united with her is open to all, without respect to social station. This note of equality was vastly different from the contemporary practice of established religion of any stripe, which underwrote existing social stratification.[60] Kurozumi's characteristic statements on the rewards of union with divinity include a doctrine of immortality. For example, "Those who dwell within the precincts of the shrine of Amaterasu [i.e., those with faith in Amaterasu] shall have eternal life," and "The heart of Amaterasu is our heart; when they are undivided, there is no death."[61]

Kurozumi's concept of divinity differed greatly from others of his day with which he was probably familiar. Conspicuous in its absence was any special link between Amaterasu Ōmikami and the imperial house. The theory holding that Amaterasu Ōmikami is the apical ancestress of the imperial line was prominent in the compilations of myth and in the Jinnō shōtōki 神皇正統記 of Kitabatake Chikafusa 北畠親房 (1293–1354). Kurozumi did not

[59] Ibid. Kurozumi's most characteristic statement along these lines is the short poem still used as a grace before meals: "How blessed it is that the grace of Amaterasu Ōmikami pervades all the universe, omitting nothing" (Amaterasu, kami no mitoku wa, ametsuchi ni michite, kakenaki megumi naru ka na!). Kurozumikyō, Kyōtenshō, p. 6.

[60] Both Buddhism and Shintō tended to accord high positions in parish organization to village headmen and others in positions of local authority. In other ways also they accepted the prevailing status order of society as inviolable.

[61] "Amaterasu, kami no miya ni sumu hito wa, kagiri shirarenu inochi naruran"; and "Amaterasu, kami no migokoro waga kokoro; Futatsu nakereba, shi suru mono nashi." Kurozumikyō, Kyōtenshō, p. 5.

explicitly deny this theory, but neither did he choose to incorporate it in his own teaching. Nor did he appropriate Motoori Norinaga's 本居宣長 (1730–1801) theory of Amaterasu as the sun or that of Hirata Atsutane 平田篤胤 (1776–1843) calling her the ruler of the sun. Kurozumi viewed the solar body as symbolic of Amaterasu but not identical with divinity.[62] Amaterasu is a superordinate entity whose vital essence, *yōki*, is the ground principle.

Healing

Soon after the Direct Receipt of the Heavenly Mission, Kurozumi began to preach, and his first converts were made by faith healing. Early in 1815 a maidservant in his household was seized with fierce abdominal pains, and Kurozumi cured her by applying his hand to her abdomen and blowing upon the area. This method of curing, called *majinai* 禁厭 or *toritsugi* 取次ぎ, was accompanied by recitation of the Great Purification Prayer. *Majinai* was believed to cure by inspiring the sick one with an abundance of *yōki*, directly transferred by hand and breath. That *yōki* in turn was acquired by Kurozumi through daily worship of the rising sun, inhaling its rays and reciting the prayer daily.[63]

Kurozumi unknowingly encroached on carefully guarded turf by healing. Physicians, *yamabushi* 山伏 (ascetics of the cult of sacred mountains), and Nichiren-school prayer-healers (*kitōshi* 祈禱師, *norikura* のりくら) stood to lose much from any new competition in the field of healing, and they were quick to protest. It is related in the *Tales of the Founder* (*Kyōsosama no oitsuwa* 教祖様の御逸話) that one morning Munetada awoke to find seven scars on his roof where an arsonist had tried to set it ablaze. The torch was found, and Munetada enshrined it upon his domestic altar, thinking it no ordinary event. Three weeks later the incendiary came forth and confessed, begging for forgiveness. He was a faith healer frustrated

[62] Kōmoto, *Tokuhon*, pp. 8–80, passim; Hepner, *The Kurozumi Sect*, pp. 105ff.
[63] Hara Keigo, *Kurozumi Munetada*, Jimbutsu Sōsho 42 (Tokyo: Yoshikawa kōbunkan, 1960), p. 12. Kurozumi also practiced curing by holy water and holy rice, and he developed a means of adminstering *majinai* by proxy to those too ill to visit him personally. The last means was called *kage no majinai* 陰の禁厭.

by loss of his erstwhile patients to Munetada.[64] The date of this event is not recorded, but in 1822 there were protests to domain authorities from Nichiren-school priests and from physicians complaining that Munetada was interfering with their practice of medicine.[65] These and similar incidents, which were repeated throughout Munetada's life, testify to the enmity with which he was regarded by physicians and healers.

Physicians, priests, and healers associated with the mountain cult Shugendō 修験道 all practiced medicine as a trade, holding customary title to a clearly defined group of people.[66] The news of Munetada's healing power spread rapidly, taking no account of the customary prerogatives of local healers, or of the economic loss his success spelled for them. The attraction of Munetada's healing was greater for the fact that he accepted no fees. He regarded healing as an expression of his mission and not as a trade.[67] Moreover, he made no distinction among those he healed regarding their social position or prior affiliation with his shrine.

Kurozumi's was an age in which medical treatment consisted of Chinese and native herbal medicine, moxa cautery, and massage, in combination with religious ritual, except in the case of those few secular physicians ministering to the upper strata of samurai society. Poor conditions of sanitation and the ravages of epidemic disease took a heavy toll. In these circumstances, a charismatic healer was no less than a living god, and many were drawn to Kurozumi precisely to be healed, inquiring only later into the content of his doctrine.[68]

Believing healing to be no more than the natural expression of

[64] Kōmoto Kazushi, Kyōsōsama no oitsuwa (Okayama: Kurozumikyō nisshinsha, 1976), pp. 1–4.

[65] Murakami Shigeyoshi, Seimei no oshie, Tōyō bunko 319 (Tokyo: Heibonsha, 1977), p. 338.

[66] Those Buddhist priests who practiced healing customarily enjoyed more or less exclusive rights to cure parishioners, whereas secular physicians mainly practiced among samurai. Yamabushi also had parish-like territories to which they could buy or sell title.

[67] Hara, Kurozumi Munetada, chap. 5.

[68] For a historical survey of Japanese religious techniques of healing, see my "Transformation of Healing in the Japanese New Religions," Journal of the History of Religions 20 (May 1982): 45–60.

unity with divinity, Kurozumi wrote as follows:

(1) The heart is the master, and the body the servant. When we awaken, the heart commands the body, but when we are confused, the body commands the heart.[69]

(2) The heart of Amaterasu is the heart of humanity, and when they are united, life is eternal.[70]

(3) The heart of the ancients had no form, nor has ours today. When we forget the body and dwell in the heart, now is the age of the gods; the age of the gods is now![71]

Healing and the Great Purification Prayer

The significance of Kurozumi's use of the Great Purification Prayer in healing is a complicated matter. At the most obvious level, use of the prayer in this context amounts to purification of pollution. If disease is considered a sort of pollution (*kegare* 穢), it makes sense that healing would consist of a purification. For Kurozumi, however, pollution was only symptomatic of the more general problem of inharmony with divinity.

The prayer's original use as specified in the *Engi Shiki* 延喜式 (927) was as a semi-annual rite of exorcism at the Heian capital on the last days of the sixth and twelfth months. Later, under Buddhist influence, the prayer in its several versions came to be recited much more frequently. In Kurozumi's shrine, priests probably recited this and other *norito* 祝詞 on prescribed occasions for a set fee. Kurozumi's innovations lay in frequent, daily repetition, in reciting the prayer for all and sundry regardless of whether they were parishioners, and in reciting it gratis. Furthermore, he urged followers to recite it as the nucleus of their self-cultivation, without

[69] This verse is found in the Founder's prayer, "Michi no kotowari": "Kokoro wa shujin nari. Katachi wa kerai nari. Satoreba, kokoro ga mi o tsukai; mayoeba, mi ga kokoro o tsukau."

[70] Kurozumikyō, *Kyōtenshō*, p. 3: "Amaterasu, kami no migokoro, hitogokoro. Hitotsu ni nareba, ikidōshi nari."

[71] From the prayer, "Michi no Kotowari": "Inishie no kokoro mo katachi nashi; ima no kokoro mo katachi nashi. Kokoro nomi ni shite, katachi o wasururu toki wa, ima mo kamiyo; jindai konnichi; konnichi jindai."

priestly mediation, and recitation by followers at their meetings became a central congregational observance. The prayer recounts the cosmogonic myth[72] (see Appendix A), and this use of creation mythology in healing is a general phenomenon in the history of religions. Mircea Eliade has explained this type of healing as follows:

> By making the patient symbolically "return to the past" he was rendered contemporary with Creation, he lived again in the initial plenitude of being. One does not *repair* a worn-out organism, it must be *remade*, the patient needs to be born again; he needs, as it were, to recover the whole energy and potency that a being has at the moment of its birth.... The cosmogonic myth is recited before him and for him; it is the sick man, who, by recollecting one after another the episodes of the myth, re-lives them, and therefore becomes contemporary with them. The function [is] ... to transport the patient to *where that event is in process of accomplishment*—namely to the dawn of Time, to the commencement.[73]

The mythic character of the Great Purification Prayer also lay in the background of Kurozumi's therapeutic use of it.

EARLY FOLLOWERS

In 1847 the High Disciple Tokio Katsutarō 時尾克太郎 (1817–1862), began compiling a register of members from 1815, and for the years 1815–1825, a total of seventy-nine names are recorded,[74] all from Bizen 備前 or adjacent Bitchū 備中. This fact seems to be contradicted by the information that beginning in 1825 a group of

---

[72] More precisely, the *Kojiki* and *Nihon shoki* contain Sinified cosmogonies, but the myth of origin recounted in the Great Purification Prayer serves in popular conception as a primal myth.

[73] Mircea Eliade, *Myths, Dreams, and Mysteries: The Encounter between Contemporary Faiths and Archaic Rites*, trans. Philip Mairet (New York: Harper and Row, 1960), p. 48.

[74] Taniguchi Sumio, "Bakumatsu ni okeru Kurozumikyō ni tsuite no ichikōsatsu," *Okayama daigaku kyōikubu kenkyū shūroku* 6 (March 1968): 70.

disciples (the beginning of the group's ministry) was kept busy day and night in many locales, holding meetings for preaching and healing. It seems likely that, in line with later practice, only those who received a personal certificate of fellowship (*jinmon* 神文) in Kurozumi's hand were actually recorded, whereas in fact many more attended meetings. Most members of the inner circle were samurai and members of their families who resided in the castletown of the domain. Kurozumi wrote regularly to samurai followers[75] while they were in Edo for the obligatory period of alternate attendance (*sankin kōtai* 参勤交代).[76]

At first, Kurozumi's followers were a confraternity of the Imamura Shrine. Kurozumi continued to serve as a priest there, but his relation to the shrine was severely strained by his new activities. A document of 1816 from the head priest directed him to cease healing and distributing talismans of the shrine to all and sundry. He was told to send those who came for healing to other shrine priests for performance of rites. Healing by charisma was beyond the scope of a priest's duties in traditional conception, and distribution of charms suggested that the shrine endorsed Kurozumi's activities.[77]

THE MIDDLE PHASE

Seclusion

The second major period of Kurozumi's career (1825–1843) alternated between proselytization and strict seclusion. This "seclusion" meant primarily sleeping at the shrine; it did not mean that he

[75] Ibid., p. 72. Kurozumi's correspondence has been edited and compiled in a critical edition by Murakami Shigeyoshi in *Minshū shūkyō no shisō*, Nihon shisō taikei 67 (Tokyo: Iwanami shoten, 2d printing, 1973), pp. 44–177. In roughly half of the approximately 200 letters the addressee is known, and most of the letters are to samurai followers. In his letters, Kurozumi commented on the health of family left behind, and in many cases he tendered spiritual counsel, sometimes in poetic form.

[76] *Daimyō* were required to spend half their time in Edo; thus they alternated between Edo and their home domains.

[77] Kurozumi Tadaaki, *Kyōsoden*, pp. 67–68. The shrine's complaint is reproduced in full on these pages.

never left the shrine. He confined himself to the Imamura Shrine for a total of a thousand days and nights during the period September 1825 to May 1828. This seclusion was a traditional discipline called *sanrō* 参籠 or *okomori* 御籠 り. While in seclusion Kurozumi practiced sexual abstinence, recited prayers in astronomical numbers, and gave a course of lectures on the Ise Shrine. He continued to receive those seeking healing, to conduct meetings, and to distribute tens of thousands of talismans.[78] Here Kurozumi was experimenting with purification and abstinence as a type of self-cultivation. He had vowed, however, to remain in much stricter seclusion than he actually practiced, and he gave up these disciplines before the time he originally set for himself.

Seclusion, purification, and abstinence are traditional forms of self-discipline and cultivation in Shrine Shintō. These are the disciplines of the professional priest that set him apart from the layman and give him a greater religious authority.[79] In rejecting these disciplines, Kurozumi asserted that self-cultivation is not incompatible with the lay life.

Rejecting Shintō's traditional purifications and abstinences, Kurozumi established a unique form of self-cultivation. Still pursuing the goal of becoming a *kami*, he practiced worship of the sun (*nippai*) daily. As in his original healing, he worshiped by kneeling, facing the east, and opening his mouth wide, breathing in deeply, and swallowing the sun's *yōki*. *Nippai* was accompanied by recitation of the Great Purification Prayer. These observances were made the nucleus of daily individual self-cultivation as well as the core of group ritual. In addition, Kurozumi recommended a spirit of egolessness (*ware nashi, ware o hanareru* 我を離れる, and other terms) and cultivation of an attitude of joy (*yōki*). When these attitudes become pervasive, the spirit of joy and gratitude expresses unity with divinity.

Even in seclusion Kurozumi was active in proselytization

[78] Hepner, *The Kurozumi Sect*, p. 75; Taniguchi, "Bakumatsu ni okeru Kurozumikyō," p. 66. Unfortunately, no texts of these lectures remain.

[79] Seclusion was practiced by other founders of new religions at the end of the Tokugawa period. For example, Kawate Bunjirō 川手文治郎, founder of Konkōkyō, remained in seclusion for most of his life. See Murakami Shigeyoshi, *Konkō daijin no shōgai* (Tokyo: Kōdansha, 1972).

throughout Bizen and Bitchū while his disciples proselytized further afield. Between 1828 and 1833, some two hundred merchants were converted, and Kurozumi apparently paid them special attention.[80] He also frequently lent money to samurai followers or acted as guarantor of their loans. Okayama samurai, like their fellows all over Japan, were living ever more meagerly in the final years of the shogunate.[81] (See Map 1.)

Throughout his life Kurozumi practiced divination[82] by the hexagrams, based on the *I Ching* 易経. At first glance this practice seems to be at odds with the doctrine of individual responsibility and the dependence of all things on *kokoro*. As subsequent chapters will show, there is a division among the contemporary ministry as well regarding divination and other practices that suggest that the course of events is determined by forces other than human effort and will. It would be mistaken, however, to think that Kurozumi sought deterministic prognostication from the hexagrams. It is more likely that he used divination to know the general direction of change so that he could prepare himself and be in harmony with it.[83]

Meetings of the Followers

Nominally a confraternity of the Imamura Shrine, Kurozumi's followers met in *kōshaku* 講釈, a term applied both to meetings held in Kurozumi's house and to meetings hosted by believers in their own homes. Meeting days (*kaijitsu* 会日) were held six times monthly at Kurozumi's home, and the followers, called *michizure*

---

[80] His solicitous treatment of merchant followers may have been prompted by his own financial circumstances, which were bad. A poor manager of money, Kurozumi was often hounded by creditors. As often as not, he secured loans for a third party and then had to bear the moneylender's wrath when that person failed to repay. See ibid., p. 77, and Kōmoto, *Kyōsosama no oitsuwa*, pp. 7–12.

[81] Taniguchi, "Bakumatsu ni okeru Kurozumikyō," p. 75.

[82] Hepner, *The Kurozumi Sect*, pp. 65–71, discusses instances recorded of Kurozumi's divinations.

[83] Hellmut Wilhelm, *Change, Eight Lectures on the I Ching*, trans. Cary F. Baynes, Bollingen Series 62 (Princeton: Princeton University Press, 1960), p. 19. Wilhelm discusses nondeterministic uses of hexagram divination.

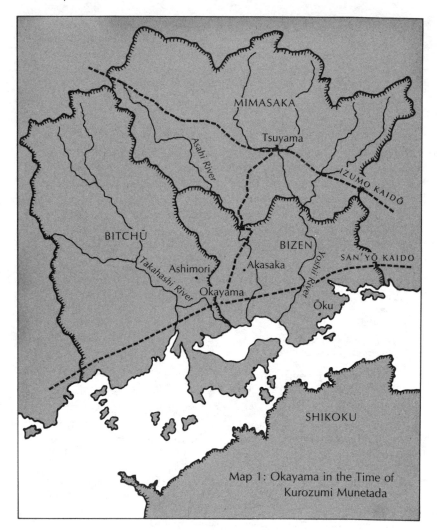

Map 1: Okayama in the Time of Kurozumi Munetada

道連, assembled to hear Kurozumi preach, to recite the Great Purification Prayer together, and to receive healing rites. Kurozumi spoke without notes of any kind, and the meetings lasted as long as eight hours.

Followers themselves hosted periodic meetings on a rotating

basis, called *kōseki* 講席, beginning in 1815.[84] Most were in Bizen or Bitchū. For example, there was one meeting hosted by seven samurai but also including merchant members, and when they held a meeting, Kurozumi would attend, conduct recitation of the Great Purification Prayer, preach a sermon, and perform *majinai* for those seeking healing. Various *kōseki* were named, generally after the locale, or in the case of merchants, after the shop where they held meetings.[85]

Proselytization Through Village Headmen

Kurozumi and his disciples developed the important practice of using the mediation of *shōya* 庄屋, village headmen, to gain access to new followers.[86] Village headmen held a pivotal position in Tokugawa society. They represented the lowest rank of domain control and were commoners, not samurai. Except for serious crime, they held the "powers of justice and police," and they collected the rice tax. They represented the pinnacle of village organization and were the best spokesmen of local, rural interests.[87] *Kōseki* were held in temples, shrines, and houses of village headmen. Meetings were advertised with the call for all the sick to come and be healed.[88]

Why should village headmen have been willing, even eager, to have Kurozumi preach to peasants in their charge? In spite of the hierarchy of the four classes and the assumption that class status acquired at birth was unchangeable, there was by the end of the

[84] Once a month is a rate that appears frequently, but we do not know whether this was an invariable standard.

[85] Kurozumi Tadaaki, *Kyōsoden*, pp. 65–66. For example, a predominantly samurai confraternity in the castle-town was called Kometsuki-kai, and a merchant assembly was called Shichijima-ya 七島屋, after the main convenor's place of business. See also Kōmoto, *Kyōsosama no oitsuwa*, pp. 215–16.

[86] Headmen attended meetings and contributed to the group under the rubric of *hatsuho* 初穂, "first fruits." Taniguchi, "Bakumatsu ni okeru Kurozumikyō," p. 79.

[87] Marius B. Jansen, *Sakamoto Ryōma and the Meiji Restoration* (Princeton: Princeton University Press, 1961), pp. 30–31.

[88] Kurozumi Tadaaki, *Kyōsoden*, p. 66. The *Tales of the Founder* describes a meeting held in a temple, much to the displeasure of the priest, who was not informed in advance; see Kōmoto, *Kyōsosama no oitsuwa*, pp. 61–63.

Tokugawa period considerable mobility in the lower strata of the peasant class.[89] Their mobility weakened the authority of village headmen, putting the latter in the position of trying to defend and strengthen the normative order. This was particularly true of the "rich peasant" group, gōnō 豪農.[90] In the defence of traditional prerogatives, the interests of the gōnō and of domain authorities were identical insofar as both strove to maintain a peaceful, orderly peasantry. The threat of peasant revolt and uprising was an ever-present spectre at the end of the period, and education in traditional values was seen as one preventative measure.

Long a leader in education, the Okayama domain had an impressive institution for gōnō and headmen's education, the Shizutani Gakkō 閑谷学校 (est. 1675).[91] Attached to it was a less formal school for commoners, staffed mainly by gōnō and samurai teachers, called the Tenshinkō 天心講 (est. 1782).[92] Actually, the school was modeled on a religious confraternity (kō) and was convened periodically for study of the Classic of Filial Piety and other Confucian writings. During the eighteenth century, the fortunes of Okayama's commoner schools established by the domain rose and fell, but by the century's end, the Tenshinkō was flourishing and continued to do so until Meiji.[93]

Contemporary reports by the headmen to the domain voice the fear that the peasants have departed from the ways of their fathers, are worshiping strange gods, and are using these observances as an excuse to take holidays. Whereas previously village officials had complete authority over religious holidays and the work schedule, by 1780 their control was crumbling, and they sought to employ the Tenshinkō to bring their charges back to tradition by preaching

---

[89] Sasaki Junnosuke, *Bakumatsu shakairon* (Tokyo: Kōshobō, 1969), pp. 147–48.

[90] Ibid., p. 263. When new agricultural technologies spread to rural areas in the seventeenth century, production increased, and village headmen became wealthy peasants: gōnō.

[91] Shibata Hajime, *Kinsei gōnō no gakumon to shisō*, ed. Negishi Yōichi (Tokyo: Shinseisha, 1966), p. 150.

[92] The Tenshinkō was established for ordinary peasants, komae byakushō.

[93] Ibid., pp. 157–60. When Yokoi Shōnan visited it in 1851, instructors were holding sessions six times monthly in a number of locations.

the values of obedience and filial piety.[94] By the end of the eighteenth century, there were men and women students, including both *gōnō* and ordinary peasants.[95]

Throughout the latter days of the Tokugawa period, village officials tried to instruct the peasantry in values congenial to the traditional order, and their efforts included sponsoring both religious and secular preachers. The Shingaku thought of Ishida Baigan was viewed as a popular version of Confucian thought, the official orthodoxy, and Shingaku preachers were frequently invited to address the peasantry.[96] Shingaku eventually came to be proselytized through a network of "colleges," confraternities, and preaching halls.[97] Later on, the Hōtoku 報徳 movement, which propounded Ninomiya Sontoku's 二宮尊徳 version of ethics, was employed in Meiji Japan in much the same way.[98]

When Kurozumi's disciples approached village headmen in Okayama, they followed in the footsteps of Tenshinkō lecturers and Shingaku preachers. In fact, one word for Kurozumikyō Laymen's Meetings used throughout Okayama today is *Tenshinkō* 天心講. Although Kurozumi's doctrines represented to him the path to sagehood, they doubtless appeared to local leaders anxious to shore up their own authority a serendipitous recommendation to preserve the status quo.[99]

[94] Ibid., pp. 186–89.

[95] Ibid., p. 200.

[96] Shoji Kichinosuke, *Kinsei minshū shisō no kenkyū*, p. 101. Matsudaira Sadanobu built a hall for the propagation of Shingaku thought, the Nisshinkan.

[97] There were more than 180 "colleges" in forty-four provinces. See Jennifer Robertson, "Rooting the Pine," pp. 311–32.

[98] Shingaku was used in this way in many areas of Japan. After the Kansei Reforms of 1775, sixteen *han* in the northeast accepted it, and *gōnō* were avid in its propagation. See Shōji Kichinosuke, *Kinsei minshū shisō no kenkyū*, pp. 172ff. See also Richard P. Dore, *Education in Tokugawa Japan* (Berkeley: University of California Press, 1965), pp. 236–37, and Inoue Nobutaka, "Hamamatsu ni okeru Kurozumikyō no juyō to tenkai," in *Toshi shakai no shūkyō*, ed. Tamaru Noriyoshi (Tokyo: Tokyo daigaku shūkyōgaku kenkyūshitsu, 1981), pp. 204–16. Inoue shows how closely related was the propagation of Hōtoku and Kurozumikyō in Hamamatsu.

[99] Dore, *Education in Tokugawa Japan*, pp. 237–41. Dore shows how the preachers of a variety of creeds were adapted to promote core values and maintenance of the status quo, and how these harmonized with Confucian orthodoxy.

The High Disciples

Kurozumi's closest disciples are known as the High Disciples. There were seven in all, of whom three became significant leaders during Kurozumi's lifetime.[100] Furuta Masanaga 古田正長 was a high-ranking samurai of the Okayama *han*, who received a *jinmon* in 1819 and thereafter continued to promote Kurozumi's teaching.[101] In 1821 Ishio Kansuke 石尾乾介 (1775–1859), originally a parishioner of the Imamura Shrine, joined Kurozumi and held *kōseki* at his home; he wrote frequently to Kurozumi when he was in Edo for alternate attendance. About one-quarter of Kurozumi's total correspondence is addressed to Ishio, who promoted Kurozumi's teaching by proselytizing on the road to Edo. Of the early High Disciples, Ishio was the most active in proselytization.[102] An important figure, though not counted among the High Disciples, Hishikawa Ginzaburō 菱川銀三郎, better known as Ginjibē 銀治兵衛, was the son of a Buddhist priest who converted to Kurozumi's teaching. He was Kurozumi's personal attendant, following him everywhere, but not becoming active in proselytization.[103] The third High Disciple was Kawakami Tadaaki 河上忠晶 (1795–1862), a Wang Yang Ming 王陽明 scholar in the employ of the Bizen domain who joined in 1822. He wrote a book in Chinese on Kurozumi's teaching, apparently intending it to be used in proselytization. The conversion of a scholar of Chinese thought seems an unlikely event, and in fact it was precipitated by rather extraordinary circumstances. Kawakami's mother was cured by Kurozumi of an eye ailment, and she persuaded her son to join. Later Kurozumi was joined by others numbered among the High

---

[100] As mentioned above, Akagi Tadaharu eventually became even more important than Munetada's successor, but this occurred after the Founder's death.

[101] Murakami, *Seimei no oshie*, p. 338. Furuta had a stipend of 550 *koku*. As late as the mid-1840s, Furuta is recorded as a regular at *kōshaku*; see p. 47.

[102] Kurozumi Tadaaki, *Kyōsoden*, p. 72. Ishio's stipend was 140 *koku*. His correspondence with Kurozumi is one of the richest sources on early practices of Kurozumi's followers. Ishio apparently proselytized in Edo using calligraphic scrolls (*sansha taku sen* 三社託宣) in Kurozumi's hand. These bore the names of Tenshō Daijin, Hachiman, and Kasuga Myōjin. While Ishio was in Edo his father hosted the *kōseki* back in Okayama. These activities were known to the *han*.

[103] Ibid.

Disciples, most notably by Akagi Tadaharu and Tokio Katsutarō, mentioned above. Upon Munetada's death, the high disciples divided proselytization territories among themselves to advance the group in Western Japan.[104]

It should also be noted that there were important women disciples from an early date, including Kawakami Tsuyako 河上艶子 (1816–1857), mother of Kawakami Tadaaki. After her healing, she was constantly at the Kurozumi house to assist in meetings. She was close to Kurozumi's wife, Iku, who must also be counted an important disciple. Although convention did not permit samurai women to preach and proselytize, they were influential in spreading knowledge of Kurozumi's teaching through contacts with other women.[105]

The presence of one high-ranking samurai among the High Disciples, Furuta, and at least two others of relative consequence, Kawakami and Ishio, probably accounts for the Imamura Shrine's tolerance of Kurozumi's flagrant violation of the 1816 order to stop healing and using the shrine as a base from which to launch a religious association. Had Kurozumi not had this protection, the shrine could easily have forced him to its will.

The formation of the Seven Household Principles was the most important event of Kurozumi's middle period. What follows are Kurozumi's prescriptions for correct self-cultivation:

(1) Born in the Land of the Gods, you shall not fail to cultivate faith.
(2) You shall neither become angry nor do harm.
(3) You shall not give way to conceit nor look down upon others.
(4) You shall not fix upon another's evil while increasing the evil in your own heart.
(5) You shall not malinger in the work of your house except in illness.
(6) While pledged to the Way of Sincerity, you shall not lack sincerity in your own heart.
(7) You must never stray from the spirit of gratitude.

---

[104] Ibid., pp. 53–72. See also Hepner, *The Kurozumi Sect*, p. 186.
[105] Ibid. Apparently there were no female ministers until the Meiji period.

These rules must never be forgotten. The hearts of all you encounter shall be as mirrors to you, reflecting the face you have presented to them.[106]

The Principles stress faith (1), and harmony with other people (3, 4) and with the existing social order so that there is no interior resistance to full absorption in duty (2, 5), resulting in total commitment (6, 7).

THE LATE PHASE

In the last phase of Kurozumi's career (1843–1850), his movement made the most strides to independence. In 1843 he retired from his post as *negi* of the Imamura Shrine and passed it on to his first son, Munenobu 宗信. We can see from the registry of followers that numbers increased rapidly after this time, particularly of commoners, whereas samurai stopped joining after 1846. This shift is due to a perception of Kurozumi and his followers as constituting a new religion and hence a phenomenon unsuited to samurai involvement.[107]

In relinquishing the post of *negi*, Kurozumi cast off the limitations the job imposed on his activities and freed himself to devote his life entirely to proselytization. It was, however, no longer

---

[106] Kurozumi Tadaaki, *Kyōsoden*, p. 101. The Principles are known as the *Shichi-ka-jō* 七ケ條, or as *Nichinichi kanai kokoroe no koto* 日々家内心得の事. The original is as follows:

(1) Shinkoku no hito ni umare, tsune ni shinshin naki koto.
(2) Hara o tate, mono o ku ni suru koto.
(3) Ono ga manshin ni te, hito o mikudasu koto.
(4) Hito no aku o mite, onore ni akushin o masu koto.
(5) Mubyō no toki, kagyō okotari no koto.
(6) Makoto no michi ni irinagara, kokoro ni makoto naki koto.
(7) Nichi-nichi arigataki koto o torihazusu koto.
　　Migi no jōjō tsune ni wasurubekarazu.
　　Osorubeshi, osorubeshi.
　　Tachi mukō hito no kokoro wa kagami nari.
　　Onore ga sugata o utsushite yamin.

[107] Kodera, "Kurozumikyō no rekishiteki seikaku," pp. 46–50.

possible to regard the group as a confraternity of the shrine. In 1846 a document called the Rules of 1846 (*Kōka sannen goteisho* 弘化三年御定書), drafted by disciples and authorized by Kurozumi, established the independent status of Kurozumi Kyōdan 黒住教団, the Kurozumi Church.[108] As a *kyōdan* 教団 had no legal status, its members were in effect "outside the law." The six articles of the Rules grant authority to Kurozumi's disciples to minister in his stead and to perform all rites in his name.

The ceremony of joining the ranks of the followers had until that time consisted of making a personal vow to Kurozumi to uphold the Seven Household Principles, and thus membership had been directly linked to the person of the Founder. When the group expanded to further regions, however, a new method had to be found. Delegating authority to the disciples made it possible to perpetuate the group after the Founder's death. The Rules specify that certificates, talismans, and healing of ministers carry the same validity as if given by the Founder. Followers were urged to regard ministers' words as the Founder's, and the Rules were promulgated to all followers by the ministers.[109]

The Membership Register by 1835 contained 1,117 names by date of entry and place of residence. Of these 317 (28.4 percent) were from Bizen, and Mimasaka 美作 accounted for 503 (45 percent). There was a large influx of commoners from Akasaka 赤坂 and Ōku 邑久 counties in Bizen from 1840 to 1850, and these had mostly been recruited by village headmen of the area. The Akasaka headman was particularly devout and had Kurozumi come and preach there twice monthly, a distance of twenty-five kilometers each way.[110]

---

[108] Kurozumi Tadaaki, *Kyōsoden*, p. 126.

[109] Ibid., pp. 125–27.

[110] Taniguchi, "Bakumatsu ni okeru Kurozumikyō," p. 77. In addition to village headmen, there was a great variety among Kurozumi's commoner followers. *The Tales of the Founder* includes stories about the following sorts of people: *ōjōya* 大庄屋, of Akasaka in Bizen (pp. 25, 66); the *ōjōya* of Ōku county, Nakayama Tsunejirō 中山常二郎 (pp. 160ff.); a Bitchū doctor (p. 41); a Sakushū Shintō priest (p. 136); a Mimasaka doctor (p. 151); an Ōku cotton merchant (p. 140); a drug manufacturer (p. 47); a dyer (p. 155); a stone mason (p. 194); a tile maker (p. 196); and a Bizen potter (p. 205). The presence of a significant number of artisans is notable.

Most samurai who joined Kurozumi did so between 1836 and 1846. Until the promulgation of the Rules of 1846 and the Membership Register in 1847, there was no particular significance attached by domain authorities to samurai receiving a certificate of membership from Kurozumi or to their pledge to obey the innocuous Household Principles. Residence in the castle-town made many parishioners of the Imamura Shrine, and under this umbrella they could attend Kurozumi's meetings without attracting domain attention. The matter was put on a different footing, however, with the publication of these documents and Kurozumi's retirement from the shrine. Their leader was no longer acting as a priest but as a private individual. A listing in the Membership Register thereafter identified a person as a follower of Kurozumi, not in his capacity as shrine priest, but as the author of an independent creed—in short, as the founder of a new religion.

Moreover, the presence of one's name upon the Register implied acceptance of the Rules. This meant a possible subordination of samurai to the ministers, not all of whom were of samurai rank, to say nothing of the further niceties of rank within the samurai category. In brief, then, a samurai who followed Kurozumi after 1846 stood open to charges that he might put his allegiance to Kurozumi Kyōdan before his allegiance to the lord, and that he was willing to countenance a person of lesser secular rank being above him in religious matters. None of this harmonized with the prevailing status ethic, and as a result we find that samurai ceased to join after this time, though there is no evidence of a formal proscription originating with the *han*.[111]

Evidence from the Membership Register concerning the rank and rice stipends of samurai followers suggests that most were of middle rank or below, although several powerful figures, such as Furuta Masanaga, also appear. Of the forty-five samurai whose ranks are known, twenty-four were *hirazamurai* 平侍 (*heishi* 兵士), nineteen were below that rank, and three were above.[112]

Another tangible proof of the independence of Kurozumi

---

[111] Taniguchi, "Bakumatsu ni okeru Kurozumikyō," p. 75; Kodera, "Kurozumikyō no rekishiteki seikaku," pp. 46–49.
[112] Taniguchi, "Bakumatsu ni okeru Kurozumikyō," p. 75.

Kyōdan was the creation of preaching halls, *sekkyōsho* 説教所. That is, in addition to occasional meetings, we now find structures that had no function but to accommodate meetings and that had no connection with temples or shrines.[113]

A treatment of the last phase of Kurozumi's career is appropriately concluded with a contemporary account of meetings as they were held in the late 1840s and as perceived by a commoner follower.

> The *kaijitsu* on the twenty-seventh were very well attended. We nearly always went, but there were others who came from even greater distances, only to return on the same day. In those days there was a sword-rack in the entry way, and there were many swords placed there. Everything was quite dignified, and as we left our umbrellas there and entered the house, there was a great crowd come to worship. Among them were such distinguished samurai as Lord Ishida, Lord Furuta, and others. They didn't receive seats of honor, however, just because they were samurai while farmers sat in the back. There were no such distinctions. Merchants, artisans, whoever came first, sat in the front. Some prominent people had to kneel on the ground all day while low-born women and children took the best seats. Even though those were days when the samurai held high status, they could neither see [to the front of the room] nor move about.
>
> Once the *kōshaku* began, there was silence. The only sound was an occasional clap.[114] No one so much as moved—not even the women and children. You might suppose that a stiff air of formality prevailed, but it wasn't that. Our Founder's voice seemed to penetrate into our very bones, and quite naturally our heads became heavy, and we knew nothing but the sense of gratitude. Once the meeting was over, I forgot entirely what had been said. I have such a good memory for other things that I have been called a "living calendar," and until I turned sixty or so I could remember events of the past

[113] Kodera, "Kurozumikyō no rekishiteki seikaku," p. 46.

[114] Not applause, but a *kashiwade* 拍手, a clap indicating agreement, as someone in a Christian church might say "Amen" in the middle of a sermon.

down to the hour they happened. But I have never been able to recall the content of a sermon. I never tried to—I was simply grateful.

After the sermon, people requested healing, also in the order of first-come-first-served. There were some who had been carried in to receive healing. After these healings, we took supper, and it was about [ten at night] when the meeting broke up.

All the followers were kind and treated each other warmly, taking special care of the sick. Thus, wherever we met fellow followers, it was like meeting a relative, and we had an unaccountable affection for each other. Once when I was returning home from a meeting, I chanced to meet five or six samurai ahead of me on the road. I was following along behind when they asked me politely how far I was going. When I replied that I was going to Shimo Yamada 下山田 in Ōku county [about twenty kilometers away], they apologized for detaining me when I had so far to go and bid me go on before them. When they stood aside and let me pass, I knew they had acted this way because they were followers, and I was filled with gratitude.[115]

Believing that all humanity are children of Amaterasu Ōmikami, possessing small souls that mirror her own, Kurozumi countenanced no class distinctions. Although he did not denounce the pervasive obsession with hierarchy, his own conduct and that of the group constituted an implicit denial. Similarly, in relations between the sexes, he recommended a spirit of "mutual reverence," ogami-ai 拝み合い. Incidents from his life describing his love for his wife are numerous and are often retold today.[116] The theme of human equality evoked a strong, positive response from commoner followers.

Kurozumi developed a distinctive form of self-cultivation, centering on daily sun worship and recitation of the Great Purification Prayer. These practices also became major congregational observances. The incompatibility of Kurozumi's doctrine with Shrine

---

[115] Kurozumi Tadaaki, Kyōsoden, pp. 62–64.
[116] Kōmoto, Kyōsosama no oitsuwa, pp. 63–66.

Shintō was signaled in the founding of a separate organization. Kurozumi and his followers found support and a means of access to the peasantry by proselytizing among village headmen. By the time of the Founder's death, the ministry had achieved a secure position and was able to consolidate doctrine and ritual. The ways in which that doctrine and ritual are perpetuated in contemporary Japan is the subject of subsequent chapters.

CHAPTER THREE

Preaching and Healing

This chapter discusses two phenomena central to virtually every new religion: preaching and healing. Both are directly linked to the centrality of the laity, and both serve to socialize members in the characteristic conceptualization of self and regular behavioral patterns discussed in chapter one. The most intimate and sustained contact between leaders and followers takes place through preaching and healing, and themes of gratitude, sincerity, "other people are mirrors," and the power of self-cultivation are expounded repeatedly in these contexts, explicit and implicitly. In Kurozumikyō the leaders' most direct and concentrated teaching occurs through sermons, in which they demonstrate the Founder's timeless relevance by juxtaposing events from his life with examples drawn from a particular church's followers, illuminating the present with the past. By various techniques of speech, posture, as well as by clapping once, loudly (the *kashiwade* 拍手), at crucial passages, the leaders underline the most important parts of what they have to say. Though in Kurozumikyō the preacher is seated upon a raised dais, the intimacy of the subject matter and the manner of its exposition draw leaders and followers closer together rather than differentiating their status in soteriological terms. One can generalize rather widely about this feature of preaching in the new religions on the basis of Kurozumikyō's example. In healing we can see how gratitude becomes almost substantial. When gratitude cannot flow from the self through the body, to other people, and to the local supernaturals, the reciprocity of benefice is interrupted. The self is prevented from extending to other levels, and thus it cannot attain its full realization. When the self is most narrowly circumscribed, the body in which it dwells becomes ill. Healing then becomes a matter of reiterating and implementing the principles of world view to recover reciprocity and harmony. Though

74

local terminology varies widely, etiologies of disease as well as therapies bear a structurally identical relation to world view across the new religions, as well as showing remarkable similarities with such indigenous therapies as Naikan and Morita therapy.[1]

PREACHING

Although no treatment of Kurozumikyō would be complete without a consideration of its Founder, it is also true that contemporary followers' knowledge of the Founder is devotional rather than historical in any strict sense. The Founder and his teaching are mainly known to them through preaching and through books and magazines published by Kurozumikyō.

Kurozumikyō uses its Founder's writings as its holy writ. Other than these and a prayer book, there are no scriptural writings. An official biography of the Founder and other devotional literature are distributed by the headquarters. In addition, followers generally subscribe to the monthly magazines *Omichizure* お道連 and *Nisshin* 日新, and most followers own other devotional works as well. *Tales of the Founder* (*Kyōsosama no oitsuwa*), owned by most followers, is a collection of anecdotes illustrating the Founder's filial piety, love for his wife, and perseverance in the face of opposition. These episodes, especially those related in the second chapter and others presented in the sermon below, are the ones best known by contemporary followers. Although a majority of followers own copies of *Tales of the Founder*, their most immediate source of Kurozumikyō doctrine is ministers' sermons. Retelling the same episodes many times, ministers stress the present-day application of the morals presented by these stories. Contemporary ministers do not continue the Founder's interest in the hexagrams, in horoscopic lore, or in a doctrine of immortality. Although they may respond to a direct request for horoscopic information, ministers do not

---

[1] On Naikan, Morita, and other indigenous Japanese therapies see Takie S. Lebra, "Self-Reconstruction in Japanese Psychotherapy," in *Cultural Perceptions of Mental Health and Therapies*, ed. A. Marsella and G. White (Dordrecht, Holland: D. Reidel, 1982), and David K. Reynolds, *Morita Psychotherapy* (Berkeley and Los Angeles: University of California Press, 1976).

initiate conversation in that vein. In other words, the present-day ministry has abandoned the more occult elements of Kurozumi's thought.

Sermons perform a vital function in teaching followers approved ideas and attitudes. Whereas in newer Buddhist groups there are regimented programs for educating a new member, in Kurozumikyō there is no program for religious education except for those training for the ministry.[2] In relying upon ministers' sermons to accomplish the task of religious education, Kurozumikyō reflects the religious habits of the period of its founding. In those days public lectures and sermons were the primary medium for conveying newly established creeds.[3] In contemporary Kurozumikyō, sermons heard at branch church meetings are usually a member's only formal instruction.

Through every sermon runs a thread of doctrine about *kokoro* and its power to improve any circumstances. Key attitudes are gratitude (*kansha, arigatai kimochi* 有難い気持), sincerity (*makoto*), optimism and joy (*yōki*), and perseverance (*gaman* 我慢). The contrary attitudes of ingratitude, insincerity, pessimism, and laziness cause problems. People become pessimists and ingrates because of pride (*manshin* 慢心 and other terms), which makes them inattentive to spiritual cultivation.

Ministers phrase these ideas also in a symbolic idiom. The soul of each human being (*bunshin, wake-mitama*) mirrors the soul of God. Originally entirely united with Amaterasu Ōmikami, we are healthy, happy, and prosperous in our natural state. The blessings (*okage* 御陰) that flow from unity with divinity are limitless. Knowing this and rejoicing in our good fortune, we should be grateful. So long as we preserve this spirit of gratitude and joy, we are pure (*junsui* 純粋 and other terms), but when our mindfulness slackens, we become impure (*kegare*).

Kokoro clouded by insincerity and pessimism is not in harmony with divinity. Stated another way, it is impure and in need of

[2.] For the experienced member there are correspondence courses, but these are not for novices, nor are they automatically taken by a majority of members.

[3] During the *bakumatsu* era, the new religions appropriated many of the proselytization techniques used in Shingaku. See Robertson, "Rooting the Pine," pp. 311–32.

purification (*harae* 祓). In this state, it is only to be expected that the flow of blessings from Amaterasu Ōmikami will cease. Applied diagnostically, this framework of ideas sees in sickness, misfortune, and domestic inharmony signs of division from deity. Thus a particular illness or problem is but a symptom of this more general problem. The ultimate solution to any problem is to change *kokoro*, to restore its harmony with deity, and the means to that end is in all cases renewed cultivation of core values.

Endless possibilities for illustrating these ideas exist in the problems followers bring daily to their ministers. When ministers illustrate the Founder's teachings through a recent event at that branch church, it gives followers a sense of immediacy and renders vivid the point that the teaching (*omichi* 御道, *mioshie* 御教え) is a timeless ethic for life.

Sermons are delivered at branch church meetings held two, three, or four times monthly, depending on each church's schedule. See Illustration 2. They last from twenty minutes to an hour or so. The minister generally begins with a quotation from the Founder and may interject these throughout the sermon. Followers can recognize these because they are in semi-classical Japanese. When the Founder is quoted, or when a particularly impressive event is recounted, the followers strike a *kashiwade*, clapping once or twice, as when saluting the *kami*. Ministers speak without prepared text of any kind. They may speak without attempting to arouse the emotions of the audience, but more often they use voice, gesture, and a fan held in one hand to create an emotional involvement in the audience.

The following sermon was given in the Ōi Church of Ōi Town in Okayama Prefecture on June 30, 1981 by Minister Fukumitsu Katsue. The Ōi Church and its ministry are the subject of chapter five. The sermon begins with a quotation from the Founder.[4]

"The Way consists most fundamentally in abandoning rationalization and dwelling continually in the blessings of each day, never departing from this spirit in the slightest. When we live in this manner, our present existence here and now is the High Fields of

---

[4] Kurozumikyō, *Kyōtenshō*, pp. 110–11 (nos. 162, 87).

Heaven. Yet looking around us we see rich and poor alike sunk in despair. Greatly relieved are those who have entered my Way! Regarding everything in the world with joy may be called the greatest blessing of this floating world. All things depend upon the heart. As I have said countless times, there is nothing but *kokoro*. And furthermore, those who live by the heart are wise, while those who die are fools.[5] Surely God, [*kamisama*, i.e., Amaterasu Ōmikami, Tenshō Daijin] will sustain us ever more strongly." [*kashiwade*]

(the sermon continues)

Today, June 30, 1981, on this day of our thankful meeting, this is a moment, right now, which in all our lives we can only experience once. Just now Mitsumori Masako (a follower of the Ōi Church) told us how she received a great blessing from God, how God saved her when it seemed her life was lost. As she gave thanks before the altar, all of us here received a blessing as well.[6]

We all imagine that our lives are in our own hands, but as our Founder has said in a poem, "That which we call our own is entirely Heaven's work. Who causes us to breathe in sleep, we ourselves or God?" We have been granted life by God, and moreover we are alive today because there is a need for us. Our Founder has said that the Way of Tenshō Daijin is to love light and to spurn darkness.

Once, while the Founder was still alive, a man who had leprosy came to see this man called Kurozumi Munetada. It was a disease that everyone abhors. Then, that samurai from Okayama who was afflicted with the disease, this leprosy, went to the Founder's house. He said, "Sensei [Teacher], my disease can never be cured!" What do you think the Founder said? He said to the leper, "Have no fear. You will surely receive a blessing. In this teaching, however, there is nothing except gratitude. The most important thing is the word "grateful" (*arigatai*). Please, starting today, I want you to say it—

---

[5] A reference to his doctrine of immortality through perfecting *kokoro*. Perfection of the heart-mind dwelling in joy could, Kurozumi believed, result in immortality.
[6] This sermon was preceded by the testimony of the woman named here.

"Thank you," "I am grateful." Say over and over again, one hundred times a day, "Arigatai, arigatai, arigatai, arigatai." Recite this word "arigatai" one hundred times.

The leper went away, taking with him the words received from this man Kurozumi, and soon a week had passed. Every day he continued to say, "Arigatai" one hundred times, over and over: Arigatai, arigatai, arigatai, arigatai. When a week had passed, he went again to this man Kurozumi and said, "Reverend Kurozumi, I still haven't been able to feel grateful. What should I do in order to experience gratitude?"

The Founder replied, "From now on, I want you to recite "arigatai" one thousand times a day for a week." That's what the leper was told. Being an obedient person, the leper went away and did as he was told, reciting "arigatai" one thousand times a day: arigatai, arigatai, arigatai, arigatai. A week went by. The leper's disease, however, was not cured. At the beginning of the third week, the leper went again to the Founder. He said, "Sensei, even though I say it one thousand times a day, I don't feel the least bit grateful."

The Founder said, "Is that so? In that case, starting now, I want you to recite the word 'arigatai' ten thousand times a day for a week." So the leper went away again, and in order to say "arigatai" ten thousand times a day, he had to say it almost constantly, about everything, like this: arigatai, arigatai, arigatai, arigatai, arigatai. And still he hadn't completed the ten thousand. So he kept at it. And finally, just as he was finishing the ten thousandth time, he broke out in a high fever. His throat was dry, and he coughed violently. In the midst of his fever, he sneezed continually and expelled much phlegm. Then he began to cough up blood, and, finally, when he had coughed up a great clot of blood, for the first time since his illness began he was able to sleep soundly through the night, and when he awoke, what do you think had happened? His leprosy was healed! [kashiwade]

Let me tell you, everyone, there is nothing so precious as the heart. I know that you have many reasons for coming before this altar today. There are those who have come with spiritual anxieties, and then there are others with any number of worries. Still others are tormented day and night by sickness, while some have come in joy to give thanks for blessings they have received. Truly, we are all sustained by each other, and all of us entrust ourselves entirely to God when we sleep. When we are asleep, it is just like babies sleeping peacefully together unawares, the way we entrust ourselves entirely to God in sleep.

But when we open our eyes, when we can see with our eyes, hear with our ears, and are affected by things outside ourselves, then we feel all the emotions in the world. Then our hearts can become clouded. Our hearts can become like those of demons.

The Founder spoke these words: "When the heart becomes one with God's, then we also become God. And when the heart becomes one with Buddha, we become Buddhas. When the heart becomes like a viper, we can even become vipers."[7] That is, according to the way we train our hearts, we can become either demons, or we may have the hearts of gods or Buddhas. According to the great virtue of Tenshō Daijin, each and every one of us can become a manifestation of God, and thus here and now our meeting is an assembly of the 800 million gods.

But in spite of that, why is it that we must neglect ourselves? Why must we give ourselves pain? Why must we be in anguish? That is because we gradually lose our way and stray from the heart of Tenshō Daijin. Tenshō Daijin tries again and again to sustain us. As it says in the prayer "Michi no Kotowari, 道のことわり": "Nothing is more precious than the breath of life we receive continually, night and day. We live within the vast heart of God. We dwell here in the heavenly land."[8]

But regrettably, we inflate our egos (ga o hari 我を張り) and go along day after day, believing that as long as we ourselves are not inconvenienced, let the devil take the hindermost. So we spoil the soul we have received from Tenshō Daijin. We become angry and do harm. When we pile up these sins, they take the form of sickness. Eventually, we become ill. Besides that, any number of disasters and misfortune will come to us.

[7] Kurozumikyō, Kyōtenshō, p. 78 (no. 71).
[8] This passage is not a direct quotation from the prayer "Michi no Kotowari." The prayer, however, conveys similar sentiments.

The Founder, however, has repeatedly proclaimed that no matter how much we train ourselves, misfortune and sickness cannot be defeated by the body. Our spiritual training is to reject misfortune. Though we may suffer, afterwards we will be filled with joy. That is our religion, and there is nothing to our religion without this. That's what the Founder said. So we have a choice. Either we shrink and narrow our hearts, or we open them wide. In life we have to choose one path or the other. If every day we say "arigatai" and constantly sustain our hearts in this spirit, then we need never think of death. Everything will be cared for and sustained for us.

But in spite of this, our hearts gradually regress, and we start to pity ourselves and think, "Nobody's as bad off as I am. Nobody suffers like I do." And let me tell you, everybody, when you've spent ten years thinking like that, it comes true. Help each other never to lose your grip on the arigatai spirit! We should be grateful for the gift of life—for the very fact that we are alive today! Just as the Founder said, "Those who die are fools," so we must remind each other once again what a precious thing it is that we can come together today—right now—before the altar. This moment, here and now, here together just as we are, is a blessing to us all. We must be grateful for the blessings we receive.

This is not a religion for healing sickness; ours is a religion for healing the heart. The Founder said so emphatically. Le me tell you what I'm thinking now, everybody. When our families live harmoniously, when we are in harmony together, that moment is the Dance of the Gods (kami kagura 神神楽), laughing together in the High Fields of Heaven. This is as great and precious as the gods laughing together in the High Fields of Heaven. But when we look about us, from one family to another, aren't we losing even the greetings of courtesy like "Good morning," or "Good night"?

The other day three followers came to the church. One of them, the husband, is a twenty-nine-year-old man I'll call A-san. Let me tell you what he does, everybody. He works for a concrete construction firm. He heats up the metal reinforcement and then pours in the concrete, but in an unfortunate accident, a little spur flew into his eye. On top of the pain, everyone could see that he'd really been injured, so they carried him to the doctor. Well, to tell you the

81

result of the doctor's examination, it was that it looked like bacteria had got way back in the eyeball. Worse yet, it looked like he would probably lose the eye, the doctor said.

When they heard the diagnosis, the wife and her mother, who were by A-san's side, came straight to the altar here. So then the Vice Chief Minister knelt here at the altar of our forefathers and prayed for them the Great Purification Prayer.[9]

She told them, "Listen, A-san, and this goes for your wife and mother, too. You've got to bring the sun into your hearts right now. The minute you let a fog fall over your hearts and start thinking about blindness, you're going to have a blind man on your hands! Now listen to me. You've come here to the altar, and the Founder will save you. Starting right now I want you to start working on your hearts. A-san will absolutely be saved from blindness!"

That's how strongly she encouraged them. So the man and the wife both drank holy water and said in tears to the Vice Chief Minister, "Sensei, can he really be saved? If he goes blind, our whole family will be wiped out."

So the Vice Chief Minister said to them, "You've got to go home and face that surgery with faith and hope!" Receiving these words, they went home, and what do you think happened, everybody? On the second of this month, he was so much better that they came to give thanks! [kashiwade] That was the man the doctors decided was ninety-nine point nine percent sure to be blind!

When at last the doctors unwrapped his bandages, when the cloth was taken from his eyes, the doctors said to A-san's wife, "All right now, prepare yourself. He may be blind. We've done everything medically possible, but he may be a blind man." His wife braced herself and calmed her heart. She thought to herself, "God has saved him. The Founder surely has saved him!"

When they took the bandages off, the doctors asked him, "Can

[9] Use of the title Vice Chief Minister sounds in Japanese as in English like a circumlocution. Although the speaker is referring to her own mother, ministers avoid terms that indicate kinship relations in sermons, probably to remove the sense of personal reference as much as possible.

you see this light?" And what do you think happened, everybody? He could see it! [*kashiwade*] Receiving this vast blessing, the three of them came to give thanks.

Helen was right here, too, gathering data, when they came. She thought this was a thanksgiving visit and was taking it all down. I was here and so was my husband. We were all sitting right here in this room, talking about the teaching. We were saying that the younger a person is, the greater the need for the Founder's teaching. The reason is that, while the Founder was alive, there was never a happier husband and wife than he and his wife, nor was there ever a more considerate husband. One time the Founder was at his desk making a scroll with "Tenshō Daijin" written upon it. He noticed that his wife seemed to be a long time in the toilet. He laid down his brush, put aside the scroll, and went to the toilet and called out, "Iku, are you all right?"

I'm here to tell you, everybody, he did that many times during his life. Then another time, he came home from preaching, and, knowing that he must be tired, his wife brought him a cup of tea. When the Founder saw her coming to him carrying that hot cup of tea, he joined his palms in prayer just as he would to God and said, "Thank you!" He worshiped her.

One of the disciples who was there said to the Founder, "Sensei, why do you join your hands before your wife?" How do you think the Founder answered him? He replied, "She is my wife, but she has received a small soul from Tenshō Daijin, and that means she is a child of God. She is one of the eight million gods. When I think that this god should consider my comfort and bring me a hot cup of tea, how could I *not* join my hands?" The disciple who had doubted the Founder was greatly moved. That's the story that has come down to us. That is how the Founder regarded his wife.

When at last his wife Iku died, he went to the grave and couldn't bear to leave her. That's the kind of consideration he had for her—in life and in death. And for us who are alive today, it is precisely because of a connection formed by God that we women come to marry our husbands or that men come to marry their wives. That connection formed by God is what marriage is all about.

And who is it that can best see how a wife and husband treat each

83

other in daily life? It's their children. So starting today, let your homes be a picture of the Dance of the Gods, a spectacle of the High Fields of Heaven. Starting today, lead a happier life! [*kashiwade*]

Well, when I had said that to A-san and his family, his wife who was sitting there said, "Sensei, let me tell you about *me*. I've got a worthless life (*akirame no jinsei* 諦めの人生)."

Surprised, we asked her, "Why? Why is your life worthless?" Then the mother-in-law [wife's mother] opened her mouth to speak. "You just can't get close to this man, Sensei. This man has already got two children in primary school. He's been blessed with two children, and they're going to school, but it's got to the point where they make fun of him."

Then the wife started in. "Sensei, if he'd only talk to us a little! But no, he never says a word, never compliments my cooking. In his coming and going, his mouth seems to be glued shut! Well, I really got mad. Every day I call up my mother here and give her an earful of what I have to put up with."

Well, everybody, here they were, going back and forth, giving that poor man a real tongue-lashing. There he was, sitting between them, the man who had been told it was ninety-nine point nine percent sure he was going to lose an eye, and who had received a blessing and been saved. Back and forth went the wife and her mother. As soon as one finished a sentence, the other had something even worse to say. The husband sat silent, listening to them. Just then I suddenly recalled the time fifteen years earlier when they got married right here in this church, before this very altar. So I said to them, "You've come here today in this frame of mind, but think back fifteen years ago. Didn't you two celebrate your marriage in front of this very altar fifteen years ago? Was it January? Think back to the ceremony. Here in front of the altar of Amaterasu Ōmikami, the eight million gods, and the Founder, what was it you promised here in front of God's altar?

"Beginning on this auspicious day, we both have begun a pure, new, shining life through our solemn marriage ceremony here before the altar of God. We vow in the presence of God that we will always honor with joy in our hearts the sacred tie that God has bound between us. With sincerity we will deepen our understanding of each other and will love and respect each other. Becoming one in heart and body, we will encourage each other in our work in sorrow as in joy, founding a peaceful family to repay the blessings of the ancestors. Together we solemnly promise to uphold this vow." [10]

Isn't that what you promised fifteen years ago in this church on this very spot? Was that promise a lie? And I can tell you something else. No matter how much a couple wants children, children come at the bidding of the ancestors and the gods. Just take a moment to think about that. Isn't it true that you've been blessed with two children who are now in primary school? Have you ever thought about what that means? There are plenty of people in the world who spend lonesome days because they can't have children. When you are so blessed as you are, don't you feel grateful today for the blessing you've received? I want you both to think back to the promise you made fifteen years ago!

They were listening. The husband was still silent, but he was listening. In spite of his wife and her mother sitting there criticizing him right here in front of us, he just sat there listening.

So we said to the wife, "Have you ever thought about your husband's good points? You won't find a more upright and fine man than he is. He doesn't gamble. He doesn't chase women. He doesn't waste money, and hasn't he come here before the altar with you today?

And I'll tell you something else. If your husband *had* lost his sight, you really *would* have a worthless life. But he was saved by the virtue of the Founder, and by the blessing of Tenshō Daijin he was delivered from a life of blindness, wasn't he? What are you dissatisfied about? What have *you* got to complain about, anyhow?

Right here in front of the altar, by the power of holy water, I want you to tell me one more time what it was you promised. But you don't need holy water any more. I want you to think back to the thrill of fifteen years ago—experience that again. Then I want you to make a promise at the altar in front of God. I want you to apologize to your husband and mother—just a word. Then we

[10] This is a quotation from the Kurozumikyō marriage vows as given in Kurozumikyō Kyōgaku kyoku, ed., *Nichiyō norito shū* (Okayama: Kurozumikyō nisshinsha, 1978), p. 51.

said, "Please, just a word—apologize to your husband and shake hands." I know it took a lot of courage, everybody. But even though she hesitated at first, the wife bowed once before the altar and said, "I apologize for the way I've been up to now. Please, let's make a new start." Then she moved to take her husband's hand. [*kashiwade*] He grasped her hand firmly and shook it. Her mother sitting there began to cry.

Then that man, who up until that moment had swallowed his tears, cried out in a loud voice and broke into tears. The rest of us were deeply moved, and we were crying, too. Because the Founder sustained them so much, their "worthless life" was turned around on that day, on the second of June, right here.

Truly, everybody, I want you to think together about what that means! Think about the people in the world who, when they get to be sixty, seventy, or eighty, look back on their lives and say to themselves, "How happy my life has been!" Then there are the people who look back and feel they've led worthless lives. And how about the ones whose only pleasure is looking forward to their pension checks? Those people are hated by the young. Will they go to the next world with a heart like that, everybody?

The Founder has said that both pain and joy depend upon the heart. You can be happy or sad, just as you like. The Founder tells us this depends on whether we close our hearts or open them up.

Please, go forward encouraging each other to be arigatai. As it says in the Seven Household Principles, "The hearts of all you encounter shall be as a mirror to you, reflecting the face you have presented to them." And then as our Founder has written in a poem, "If you go through life regarding everything as a cause for gratitude, it will turn out to be so in reality." [11] [*kashiwade*]

And if you face every event saying, "Arigatai, arigatai," then *whatever* it is will truly turn out to be arigatai.

I think this is the most important part of our religion. I think it is important to begin the day with the thought, "Another day! Again today God gives me life so that I may work for humanity and for the world!" [*kashiwade*] Then, after worshiping the sun, say "Good morning," and at night say "Good night." These little things are

[11] Kurozumikyō, *Kyōtenshō*, p. 94 (no. 143).

truly an important part of life! I know you have come here today in many frames of mind, but I'll tell you something the Founder said. There was a man who came to the Founder for *majinai*, to be cured of lung disease. The Founder said, "As long as you remain sunk in gloom, there is no hope for you. I want you to start laughing—today." But the sick man protested, "But Sensei, how can I laugh when nothing's funny?" The Founder replied, "Precisely! The reason I want you to laugh is because nothing's funny." [laugh] So start laughing like this: Ha ha ha, ha ha ha." So the man went home thinking, "It's *still* not funny," but nevertheless, he laughed as he had been told: ha ha ha. He thought, "This isn't the least bit funny. It's idiotic!" But in spite of that he continued to laugh, "Ha ha ha," as he had been told.

In those days they didn't have electricity like we do now. Instead, they had oil lamps. The light cast the shadow of his face upon the wall. He had been so ill for so long that he was terribly emaciated, and his shadow looked just like a skeleton. When he saw that shadow, laughing with that huge mouth wide open, he couldn't help breaking into guffaws. He bellowed with laughter, and finally it was so funny he couldn't stand it, so he laughed and laughed.

While he was laughing so loud, the neighbors started wondering, "What's *he* laughing about?" So they went over for a look, and there was the man looking at his shadow and laughing to beat the band! Ha ha ha, ha ha ha, ha ha ha! Well, seeing that, the neighbors broke out laughing, too. All of them went on and on laughing. The sick man who had been constipated for so long finally got some relief, and he felt like eating. That night for the first time in years, he ate a big meal. He had not been able to sleep soundly during his illness, but now for the first time in a long time, he slept deeply. And what do you think happened, everybody? That man was healed! [*kashiwade*]

That just goes to prove what the Founder said: everything depends on the heart! Please! Those of you who are sunk in gloom, go home and clean up your houses. Let the sun shine in from the east, and let its power inside. Start greeting your family each day by saying "Good morning." When you meet a neighbor, say hello. Then at night in your homes, talk with each other and enjoy each other's company. Say "Good night" to each other. I want you to

87

live joyously, joyously, so that every day is the embodiment of joy in this world. Even if you make some mistake, take it to the Founder in prayer, and don't lose the spirit of joy. Clap your hands before the altar, and live each day so that the Founder will be glad, too! Thank you! [*kashiwade*]

(end of sermon)

Although the doctrinal content of this sermon is representative of Kurozumikyō sermons in general, it is unusual in the intensity of its delivery and in the degree of the followers' involvement. It illustrates vividly the combination of action patterns discussed in chapter one, including the idea that other people are mirrors, the notion of the goal of religion being a "curing of the heart" (*kokoro naoshi*), and the emphasis on gratitude. By the sermon's end, there was literally not a dry eye in the house, and several people who knew I had recorded it asked for copies of the tape. This heightened atmosphere in sermons is found where there is a deep and long-standing personal involvement between minister and follower, as is true of the Ōi Church. It is also due to the exceptional talent of this minister to evoke a sense of contemporaneity, adopting a semi-classical Japanese to relate events of the Founder's day, switching to the modern style and the accent of Okayama when relating the story of A-san.

HEALING

As in many sermons, the subject of this one is healing. Healing represents the direct implementation of world view in solving a concrete problem. In Kurozumikyō medicine is not proscribed, but its effectiveness is believed limited and shallow. Because the cause of all disease is in *kokoro*, only treatment of that source can produce a real cure. Although medicine can alleviate symptoms, it is power-less to strike at disease's core. Thus Kurozumikyō does not eschew doctors and medicine entirely, but it also does not expect lasting health of the whole being to result from medical therapies alone.

Healing is a major activity of all the new religions, and in their understanding of illness they share a general similarity of outlook. They accept the existence of an order in the world whose outlines have been revealed by a founder and expressed in an idiom that is dominantly either Buddhist or Shintō. In that order, the continued vitality of the cosmos is guaranteed by an impersonal principle or superordinate entity, and health is a natural expression of harmony with that principle or correct reciprocity with superordinate entities.

This idea is subject to a variety of formulations depending on the group's doctrine. In Kurozumikyō the central idea is that each human life is a microcosm of deity, based upon the small soul (*bunshin, wake-mitama*). Harmony must exist at two levels. First, moderation in diet and in daily activity is essential. Second, the family must maintain harmonious relations based on the observance of the five relations, calling most of all for respect for elders (manifest in filial piety and ancestor worship) and a distinction in hierarchical status between men and women (expressed in public deference by women to men in a variety of forms, whatever their actual balance of power). Disharmony at either level results in or manifests itself as disease or misfortune. Conversely, when disease or misfortune occurs, its cause is analyzed and its treatment prescribed according to this understanding of illness and its cause.

This general scheme may be phrased in either a Shintō or a Buddhist idiom; theologically the ancestors and the idea of karma as well as *kami*, Buddhas, and Bodhisattvas readily find a place in it. The similarity among the new religions in their ideas on illness and healing has no single point of origin or any founder. Instead, it is part of contemporary religion's heritage from the Tokugawa period. A salient feature of religion in the latter part of the Tokugawa period was its high premium on individual religious experience. Followers of a plethora of creeds were exhorted to believe that they, not fate, determined the quality of their own lives by the extent to which they disciplined themselves in core values. Under the impetus of this new activism, healings provided vivid testimony to the power of the individual to wrest life from the jaws of death, proof like no other of virtue's triumph. Thus in Kurozumikyō as in many other groups, healings continue in great number, thriving quite independently of progress in medical science.

The cure of A-san related in the sermon above required a major readjustment in the social relations of the patient and his family. This case began early in 1981. Ogawa Shōzō [the name is fictitious], of the Ōi Church, received an injury to his eye, which became so infected that his doctor feared he would lose it. At the same time he sought medical help; Ogawa, his wife, and her mother came to the church; they requested prayer and applied holy water to the eye; and Ogawa drank holy water regularly. After surgery, Ogawa recovered most of his sight, and this was judged a true healing. The three of them came to the church on June 2, 1981 to give thanks. There was no attempt to distinguish between faith and surgery as being more efficacious in the cure. They were received at the church by ministers Fukumitsu Katsue and her husband Sukeyasu.[12] Although Shōzō was well enough to give thanks, he had not fully recovered his sight, and the cure was as yet incomplete. Thus thanksgiving rapidly gave way to counseling.

The ministers addressed the relation between husband and wife. Because the wife was hanging her head and looking generally depressed, Sukeyasu spoke to her for four or five minutes, telling her it was wrong to be pessimistic (*inki*). Katsue joined in and told the wife she should build up the husband's confidence in himself and not slip into the belief that theirs is a boring, dead-end relationship. Sukeyasu urged the husband to love and cherish his wife, repeating the episodes from the life of the Founder included in the sermon.

The couple remained silent, and it was clear that their affection for each other was stifled by a variety of problems. The wife's mother seemed to take her daughter's part in any dispute, and their opposition to Shōzō was communicated to the children. In order to draw the couple out and help them air their differences, the ministers began to relate experiences from the early days of their marriage when they also were struggling to determine and accommodate the needs of the other. They stressed above all the couple's need to renew their love for each other. Sukeyasu told the

[12] Subsequent to this event, Katsue's husband changed his name, becoming Fukumitsu Sukeyasu. He gave up his given name, Yamamoto Kōichi, when he was thus adopted into his wife's family.

husband that he must thank his wife for keeping their home while he is at work, and Katsue added that women set quite a store by being thanked and need to know that they are loved. Thus encouraged, the three began to smile, and the ministers sent out for Chinese noodles to celebrate.

Over this repast, the wife's mother admitted her contribution to the couple's problems. The ministers advised the couple to worship the sun daily and to cultivate the spirit of gratitude, and they particularly urged that the husband's illness not be considered a form of punishment from heaven (tenbatsu 天罰). Instead, all should avoid closing their hearts (kokoro o tojiru) and should be grateful for what they have, believing that all will turn out for the best.

Through the grumbling dwelled upon in the sermon, the wife was finally able to express her feelings. She said she felt an all-inclusive dissatisfaction, as if hemmed in on all sides (happō fusagari 八方塞り). Her husband remains so silent that she cannot guess his real feelings, and being so withdrawn, he fails to set a strong example for their children. Both ministers introduced the notion that marriage is a form of spiritual training (shugyō), something given to humanity to enable it to develop spiritually. In fact, the idea of marriage as a form of spiritual discipline is found quite widely in the new religions, regardless of whether they derive from Buddhism or Shintō. Thus it is to be expected that problems will arise, and that shared faith will play a central role in their solution. The sermon echoed this theme by recapitulating the marriage vows of Kurozumikyō.

The problem in the couple's relationship was not only integral to the healing of the husband's injury; in fact, the injury was reinterpreted as one manifestation of the problem in the family. The breach between husband and wife was attributed to a lack of mutual love and gratitude, linked to a misconception of the nature of marriage. The cure of the physical ailment is thus seen to be completed only by a rededication to the proper ethic in marriage, including a reaffirmation of the ideal hierarchy in the domestic group.

There are interesting parallels to be drawn between the cures related in the sermon and the counseling given to the Ogawas, on the one hand, and between the sermon's healing and the general attitudes recommended in daily life, on the other. Superficially, leprosy, an eye injury, and lung disease have nothing in common, but the three separate cures are structurally similar. All resulted from reversing a condition of clogging, retention, or bottling up. Intense recitation of "arigatai" leading to the leper's expulsion of fluids and clotted blood restored him to health. Forced laughter facilitated long-awaited intestinal movement in the lung patient, enabling him to eat heartily, sleep deeply, and get well. Ogawa's release of long pent-up emotions completed the healing of his eye. Linking physical ailments with a pent-up state of some kind grows directly out of classical Sino-Japanese therapeutic traditions.

> The classics state that diseases become manifest when the body gets out of balance and the *ch'i* [J: *ki*] does not circulate properly ....[13] Internal causes were attributed to an imbalance of one's emotional state .... Theoretically, therefore, sickness in this model is seen not so much in terms of an intruding agent, although this aspect of disease causation is acknowledged, but rather as due to a pattern of causes leading to disharmony. These causes can be at the environmental, the social, the psychological, or the physiological level ....[14]

In this view disease results when *ki* is blocked. Normally the body maintains an internal balance through the circulation of *ki* and bodily fluids, and within its environment balance is achieved through a constant interchange of food, water, air, and social relations.[15] The Kurozumikyō contribution to this scheme is the idea that daily worship of the sun draws into the body the *ki* of the sun that is also the principle guaranteeing the continued vitality of

---

[13] *Ki*, or "vital essence," "the breath," is a universal principle believed in this tradition to underlie and vitalize all existence. Here it is basically identical to *yōki* in Kurozumi's terminology.

[14] Margaret Lock, *East Asian Medicine in Urban Japan*, ed. Charles Leslie, Comparative Studies of Health Systems and Medical Care, no. 4 (Berkeley: University of California Press, 1980), pp. 37–38.

[15] Ibid., chap. 3, passim.

the cosmos.[16] In addition to the Chinese philosophy represented in theories of *ch'i*, the Japanese mythic compilations contain a complementary view of disease as one type of pollution. Pollution is to be treated by expulsion or exorcism, accompanied by therapies of a similar character: sudorifics, purgatives, or emetics. "The medicine was required to be strong and to produce a visible and perhaps violent reaction inside the body, resulting in some form of expulsion."[17]

Counseling and preaching consistently include injunctions against closing or shrinking the heart (*kokoro o semaku suru* 心を 狭くする, *kokoro o tojiru*) and instead recommend expanding or opening the heart (*kokoro o ōkiku suru* 心を大きくする, *kokoro o hiraku* 心を開く). When the heart is contracted, then emotionally and physiologically the result is a bottling-up or retention of that which should be released to the outside, summed up in the phrase used by Ogawa's wife to describe her own dissatisfaction: *happō fusagari* (all roads blocked). Clearly such a phrase also aptly describes Ogawa's own inability to express emotion.

His wife most earnestly desired him to overcome this evident blocking of emotion, but in counseling the ministers took a different tack: forcing her to accept a definition of the problem as (1) communal, involving the entire family, and (2) as one in which she bore a major burden of the blame. Forced to apologize to her husband, she tacitly confirmed her acquiescence in their hierarchical status relation, and it was this action that triggered the violent release of his pent-up emotions. Thus, in this healing, factors that cosmopolitan medicine would distinguish as physiological, emotional, and social are treated as equivalent in their necessity to the cure.

The *kokoro* is maintained on a daily basis by cultivating the spirit of gratitude, remaining constantly aware of the blessings of deity. Thus to be *arigatai* is therapeutic in a mild way, and hence to recommend recitation of the word itself when an acute problem

---

[16] Here Kurozumikyō unifies in the figure of Amaterasu Ōmikami the idea of an impersonal principle or ground of being and a personalized superordinate entity.

[17] Lock, *East Asian Medicine*, p. 25.

becomes manifest is but an extension of this therapy. Much the same might be said of laughing as an expression of happiness or amusement, and laughing as therapy. The audience to the sermon is urged to apply similar therapies in their relations with each other and in their families through attention to correct expression of greeting.[18]

In these ways followers are counseled to take an active role in the management of their physical and emotional lives, treating the body and mind as a unified whole. This focus on the present quality of life, "right here, right now" (konnichi tadaima 今日只今), yields in its most intense formulation the idea that the present existence is heaven[19] and that a happy family mirrors a colloquy of the gods.[20] This idea so prominent in the sermon is expressed in the chant-like ending of the Michi no Kotowari prayer; here the ultimate result is the attainment of divinity: "Now is the age of the gods. The age of the gods is now .... When the heart becomes kami, then we become kami."[21]

MAJINAI

Combined with counsel of this kind, Kurozumikyō healing utilizes the rite called majinai. Performed only by ministers, this rite is in a sense an inversion of daily worship of the sun: nippai. In nippai one sits facing the rising sun and opens the mouth wide to inhale its yang essence: yōki. After inhaling, one swallows the breath and forces it deep into the lungs. Nippai daily recapitulates the Founder's sun worship that resulted in his healing, and it is practiced daily by ministers and followers after recitation of the Great Purification Prayer.[22]

[18] The concern with correct greetings is a seemingly minor point but one asserted pervasively in the new religions. Correct greetings are seen as a sine qua non of correct human relations in Reiyūkai, for example, as well.

[19] Konnichi tadaima ga takama no hara.

[20] Kami kagura.

[21] "Ima mo jindai, jindai konnichi, konnichi jindai .... Kokoro ga kami ni nareba, sunawachi kami nari."

[22] Nippai may be followed by singing Kurozumikyō songs in which the Founder's poetry is set to music.

When used in healing, a minister administers *majinai* by blowing upon that area of the body affected by disease or injury, simultaneously rubbing it with one or both hands. In this way the *yōki* inspired in *nippai* is transferred to the follower through the minister's hands and breath. This direct application of *yōki* imparts the essence of divinity symbolized by the sun. *Majinai* is intended to be used in combination with the reorientation of ethical life. It is not a substitute for that reorientation. See Illustration 3.

Ministers will perform *majinai* for any follower who requests it. At branch church meetings after the sermon is finished, all followers generally request it, whether or not they are ill. There is a general perception that in addition to its curative potential, it is useful in strengthening the spirit against the pride and gloom that invite disease. Thus it is apotropaic as well as curative. A person who is ill receives *majinai* often and may also drink holy water or attach a packet of specially blessed rice (*senmai* 洗米) to the afflicted area. Furthermore, followers experiencing a problem of human relations are regularly given *majinai* to strengthen them in their trials. Thus *majinai* has many uses.

During my field work I heard literally hundreds of tales of healing. Followers are eager to relate how they have proved the truth of the teaching in their own lives, and many can relate numerous stories of the times they have been cured through Kurozumikyō's various therapies. This is true of the followers of virtually any branch church. Followers universally believe that they can be cured through the ethical reorientation prescribed by ministers in sermons and counseling, and they utilize *majinai*, holy water, and holy rice to strengthen their resolve.

This examination above allows us to summarize Kurozumikyō healing as follows. *Kokoro* is identified as the center of all mental-physical existence, and it determines the health of the whole. *Kokoro* may be strengthened by self-cultivation and by the concentrated application of *yōki* in *majinai*. Healing is a restoration of balance within the body and in family relations, and of the unity with divinity experienced to perfection by the Founder. Healings are described in an idiom of expulsion, expurgation, and purification, the main elements of the traditional Shintō concept of *harae*. Thus Kurozumikyō chants in its prayers, *Harae tamae, kiyome tamae*

祓給え, 清め給え, "Cleanse and purify." Healing regularly involves changes in relationships with other people, calling on them to adopt Kurozumikyō's world view. Kurozumikyō's understanding of health and illness is inevitably at odds with cosmopolitan medicine. Instead of therapies focused upon manifest symptoms in order to bring the organism to full functioning capacity, Kurozumikyō insists upon a reorientation within the social environment under the command of *kokoro* unified with divinity.

CONCLUSION

Preaching and healing reveal the contemporary interpretation of the Founder's teaching. Horoscopy, divination by the hexagrams, and the promise of immortality are for the most part ignored. Ministers explain their conspicuous omission by saying that such elements tend to distract followers from the preeminent need for cultivation of *kokoro*. Because the hexagrams and the like embody a fatalistic attitude and suggest that human life is determined by forces other than individual responsibility, they are not in harmony with the view that *kokoro* can triumph over all adversity, and it is that idea that is now regarded as the essence of the Founder's thought.

Contemporary ministers have also systematized the variety of ritual practices seen in the Founder's works. Most important, they use worship of the sun, *nippai*, and healing rites, *majinai*, as complementary inversions of each other, closely integrated with doctrine about *kokoro* and with the desire to recapitulate the Founder's experience of unity with divinity. The continued use of holy water and holy rice, by contrast, is not so smoothly connected with the doctrine centering on *kokoro*.

The organization of Kurozumikyō as reflected in preaching and healing retains the egalitarian tenor set by the Founder.[23] Ministers'

---

[23] The Founder's heightened awareness of his samurai followers finds a dim reflection in followers' consciousness of status differences among themselves, but this matter is better considered in the following two chapters where questions of followers' social relations are addressed more directly.

status in Kurozumikyō is not vastly different from that of the followers. The ideal daily practice of ministers and followers is the same self-cultivation. Followers regard ministers as qualified advisers and counselors because of their greater experience in those activities, and as qualified healers because of their more intense self-cultivation.

Much of that which distinguishes the new from the old in Japanese new religions is epitomized in the phrase *lay centrality*, a tendency to narrow the gap between leaders and followers. The tendency is relative, more marked in some groups than in others. It can be observed in several aspects of Kurozumikyō preaching and healing. Contemporary Kurozumikyō doctrine asserts no essential difference between ministers and followers, either as regards the certainty of salvation or the nature of the religious life. The central responsibility of both is to orient life around the core values, and this duty falls equally upon both ministers and followers. The special prerogatives of the ministry are preaching, healing, and conducting group ritual. Followers may give testimony or assist in ritual, but they do not perform *majinai*.[24] Although no esoteric part of the doctrine is withheld from the laity, the followers are not charged to grapple with it intellectually or to appropriate it on that level. Sermons provide the major vehicle of religious education.

Counseling and healing are intimately related. When ministers counsel their followers, they commonly discuss their own personal lives quite intimately, forging a bond quite unlike the priest-parishioner relation in Shrine Shintō, in which the exchange of services for money or produce is conspicuous. In Kurozumikyō followers donate whatever they wish for services, and there is a general understanding of acceptable amounts; but ministers will perform rites upon request, whether or not a fee is forthcoming and regardless of the amount. Counseling is given gratis over long periods of time. It regularly involves the hierarchical principles of the traditional joint-stem family, the *ie* 家. In general the norms of

---

[24] One exception to this general rule is *kage majinai*, "substitute *majinai*." In this practice a follower who cannot receive *majinai* directly from a minister receives it from a spouse or relative who has been specially authorized by the minister to perform *majinai* on this occasion only.

the prewar family system provide an assumed framework of orientation for all the new religions.

Healing is a political act in the broadest sense. It requires not only a recapitulation of the principles of the world view but also a reaffirmation of them. On the one hand, a physical ailment may provide the occasion to discuss problems of an intimate, social nature, revelation of which is normally tabooed in Japanese society.[25] Few who have read the literature stereotyping the Japanese as reserved, never revealing emotion, and never discussing a personal problem, can fail to be surprised by the frankness and candor with which exactly the opposite characteristics are seen within the churches and meeting houses of the new religions. Consensus and suppression of individual inclination in favor of the needs of the group are relative matters achieved by many through precisely the sort of counseling seen in Kurozumikyō healing. On the other hand, though the solutions to problems understood as successful healings unquestionably result in many people becoming much happier and better adjusted to their social situations, it would be naive to ignore the fact that their cures have required them to accept relations of power and authority that are often profoundly exploitative. These relations in the family are linked to analogous structures in the public domain that function, among other things, to exclude women or relegate them to subordinate positions and to keep the young in positions of dependence for extended periods.

[25] Lock, *East Asian Medicine*, pp. 221–24.

CHAPTER FOUR

Branch Churches in
Kurozumikyō

In a consideration of the world view of the new religions, it is necessary to bear in mind that world view is linked to a typology of "new religions" versus "established religions." A general characterization of the new and the old was provided in chapter one. Types by their nature are idealized and abstracted from the data of observable reality. This being the case, observed data do not exactly conform to the type but range along a continuum, clustering around the type but with significant variation. The operation of Kurozumikyō branch churches displays mixtures of the old and the new. In part this mingling is a factor of the group's history, founded by making a break with Shrine Shintō but retaining rites and ideas derived from it. In part it originates in localized relations with other religious institutions, especially Shintō shrines. The result is a variety of styles. This chapter presents a sampling of that variety in order to illustrate further the spectrum of old and new even within a single new religion and to establish the range within which the Ōi Church, subject of chapter five, is situated.

The conduct of life in the branch churches of Kurozumikyō challenges the stereotype of the new religions derived from the large, urban groups that come most readily to mind when the topic of new religions is raised. Having been in existence now for about 170 years, Kurozumikyō has experienced many of the same types of routinization as characterized the established religions of the period of its founding. In many ways functioning in rural society like a village tutelary shrine of Shrine Shintō, Kurozumikyō has come to rely upon the habit of hereditary affiliation to recruit its members rather than on proselytization and conversion. The performance of customary rites derived from Shrine Shintō, such as House Purification, *yabarai* 家祓, and Grounds Purification, *jichinsai* 地鎮祭, becomes the entrée for ministers to form a pastoral relationship with followers. Often the occasion of such rites facilitates a reticent follower's request for counseling in problems of a personal nature. Here Kurozumikyō distinguishes itself from the customary practice of Shrine Shintō in that its ministers, especially women, actively counsel the followers. A priest of Shrine Shintō would be unlikely to counsel a parishioner.

This chapter considers the branch church system, describing rural and urban churches to illustrate their variety and the ways in which they have sunk deep roots in local communities. The activities of Kurozumikyō churches resemble those of Shrine Shintō in many respects but combine these elements with others more often associated with the new religions. Counseling is the church function to which followers are most strongly drawn and one that sets Kurozumikyō apart from Shrine Shintō. The role of women in providing counseling is so important that without their participation a church stands empty.

A branch church generally has attached to it a number of Laymen's Meetings, initiated and sponsored by the laity, which meet periodically for worship and fellowship. Examination of these associations reveals important information about the social composition of the followers and about the nature of Kurozumikyō's appeal to them. Insofar as possible, Kurozumikyō branch churches are managed by families and passed on from parent to child, much as shrines are passed on from father to son. Although it does not limit inheritance of church headship to the male line, Kurozumikyō maintains the practice of hereditary succession. While underwriting the Church's staffing this practice also limits its potential for growth.

ORGANIZATION

The branch churches are organized according to wards (*kyōku* 教区), growing out of the original High Disciples' division, after the death of the Founder, of proselytization areas. The wards are each administered by a Ward Director and serve to facilitate communication among branch churches. Since followers are most numerous in Okayama Prefecture, there are three wards there, indicating a concentration of branch churches. The next most numerous are Hiroshima, Tottori, and Shimane Prefectures, followed by the three prefectures of Shikoku, and then Hyōgo, Nara, Osaka, and Kyoto Prefectures, and Hokkaidō, Kyūshū, and Tokyo. The bulk of the membership is concentrated in western Japan, though the group maintains no statistics that permit a more detailed regional distribution to be formulated.

In all there are 371 branch churches and preaching stations, divided into twenty wards. The churches are ranked as Great (-*dai* 大), Middle (-*chū* 中), and Small (-*shō* 小), of which there are fourteen, thirty-four, and 307, respectively. Many of the small churches are entirely inactive, but no one is sure precisely how many. In addition there are sixteen Preaching Halls (*fukyōsho* 布教所), of even smaller size than the Small Churches. There are also two shrines, one in Okayama City and one in Kyoto. The headquarters judges that the followers number 220,000, but this figure is admittedly a rough estimate.[1] The whole Church is presided over by a Patriarch, the first son of each generation of Munetada's line. The present Patriarch, Muneharu, is the sixth.

Roughly 80 percent of the churches are in rural areas, and this proportion parallels the generally rural composition of the followers, of whom perhaps an equal ratio live in rural areas. There is no statistical evidence, but observation suggests that the families of most rural followers farm, cultivating small holdings in rice land with a vegetable garden for home consumption. In Shikoku and the Izumo area there are some followers who farm larger tracts of rice land, whereas in Tottori Prefecture fruit orchards provide a greater income than rice lands. In some Okayama areas peaches, grapes, and melons are grown for cash income.

In domestic arrangements the three-generational, co-resident *ie* pattern is the conceptual norm, though more and more young couples elect to establish a separate domicile for themselves and

---

[1] This information was collected by consulting the headquarters staff of Kurozumikyō, the annual government publication on religious organizations *Shūkyō nenkan*, and the Kurozumikyō publication *Nisshin*. The January issue of *Nisshin* lists all the churches, their addresses, and the names of the minister in charge.

their children, even if it is on the same plot of land as the house of the husband's parents. In these three-generational arrangements most often the young couple both work at salaried jobs while the older generation farms and cares for young children. There is also a marked tendency to supplement farm income with cottage industry by middle-aged women and their daughters-in-law, an example being the small-scale manufacture of work clothes in or near the home.

Followers of any age have generally completed compulsory education (now nine years), and among the younger generations perhaps 30 percent have received further education in public high school or vocational schools. A smaller proportion still has attended college or junior college. Urban followers show little occupational homogeneity, though there is a concentration in white-collar jobs of the tertiary sector, in small-scale sales and service. One does not find so marked a concentration among owner-operators of family enterprises or the self-employed as is evident among the larger Buddhist new religions. There are few members of large corporations, and urban female followers tend not to work outside the home. Income is difficult to estimate, though in those terms the vast majority is middle class; ministers report no followers living either in poverty or in affluence, nor have I observed either extreme.[2]

It is difficult to achieve a confident grasp of the ministry of Kurozumikyō. In about 80 percent of the 371 churches a man is listed as the official Head Minister of the church, but upon observation of the actual operation of a church, women ministers are found more frequently than men. The headquarters maintains no statistics that clarify the matter. Although the tendency is to appoint a man as titular head and thus as the official representative of the church to the public, observation suggests that in most cases a man is assisted by his wife trained in the ministry and often by other female family members as well.

Recent seminary classes have been about half female. There are

---

[2] Information in this paragraph is based on consultation with headquarters' staff, observation at various churches, interviews with members, and a small survey carried out among Laymens' Meetings in Okayama.

no clear records of the age distribution or educational background of the ministry, but observation suggests that the oldest generation completed compulsory education; among those ministers now in their thirties there is a contingent of perhaps 30 percent who attended college or junior college. Most recent seminary graduates will succeed their parents in the operation of a branch church, and only a minority have experienced work in the labor force outside the Church.

Headquarters claims 3,184 ministers in all (probably a considerably inflated number),[3] which suggests a very low ratio of ministers to followers, on the order of 2 percent at most.[4] Women are listed as heading a church in forty-four cases, one woman heading three churches. There are fourteen cases in which a man is listed as head of more than one church, never more than three. It seems reasonable to assume that for all practical purposes a minister can give full attention to only one church, though another family member may in fact have charge of daily operations. Seventeen churches are presently without a minister and can be assumed to have fallen into disuse. Headquarters says that a significant number of churches are staffed but actually have no activity—they also have lost all vitality.[5]

Attached to the churches are Laymen's Meetings, rotating assemblies of the followers convened periodically and attended by ministers for recitation of the Great Purification Prayer, sermons,

---

[3] This number probably includes all those qualified as ministers through correspondence courses as well as those actually in charge of a church.

[4] The statistics Kurozumikyō provided the government in 1983 show 2,142 male ministers and 1,042 female, a total of 3,184 ministers and 220,193 followers. These statistics would require us to assume an average of about nine ministers per church, but nowhere did I observe more than three or four, usually only one or two. I believe these statistics may represent the number of people who have ever taken formal ministerial training, whether at the seminary or by correspondence courses. It is not the case that such a number are currently active in the ministry. It is also true that some are active in the ministry without having been formally trained for it, and it is this factor that most likely accounts for the fact that observation at most branch churches (especially rural ones) indicates that 40 to 50 percent of the ministers are women; see Ministry of Education, *Shūkyō nenkan* (1980), pp. 60–61.

[5] *Nisshin* 70 (January 1980): 46–55.

healing, and a common meal. A large rural church may have attached to it as many as fifty Laymen's Meetings, a middle rural church ten to fifteen, and most urban churches seem to have none.[6]

Churches and Shrines

The combination of churches (*kyōkai* 教会) and shrines (*jinja* 神社) in Kurozumikyō calls for explanation. In the first place, I should explain that glossing *kyōkai* as "church" is intended to distinguish the pastoral activities of ministers from the purely liturgical functions of shrine priests. The *kyōkai* of Kurozumikyō have no connection with Christianity. The Kaguraoka Munetada Jinja in Kyoto was founded in 1858 while the affairs of the group were nominally controlled by the Yoshida house in Kyoto. Permission was given to establish an object of worship representing the spirit of Munetada, and later the spirit of Akagi Tadaharu was similarly enshrined.

At present there is a branch church of Kurozumikyō adjacent to the shrine, which is entirely supported by the group. The landscaping, however, is such that someone unaware of the existence of the church would easily mistake it for the dwelling of the shrine priest. The real head priest of the shrine, the *Gūji* 宮司, is traditionally a younger brother of the incumbent Patriarch, but this is a nominal appointment, and in fact that individual is not in residence. It is the minister of the church who actually tends the shrine. The shrine itself receives visits and contributions from a number of local residents, and those who are also members of the church will worship at its altar after worshiping at the shrine. The church occupies two rooms in the minister's house, but followers are reluctant to engage him in conversation. Apparently little counseling takes place at this church, its followers tending to treat its minister with the distance given a shrine priest. In this case the shrine, the more imposing establishment of the two, sets the tone of the relationship.

[6] Laymen's Meetings are called by different terms in different areas, Tenshinkō being a favorite; often the name of the place where the meeting is convened is attached, for example, the Awai Tenshinkō.

Much the same situation seems to have prevailed when the Munetada Jinja in Okayama, informally known as the Ōmoto 大元, also housed the headquarters of Kurozumikyō. During the tenure of the Fifth Patriarch, the followers of Munekazu 宗和, a very warm and rather more charismatic individual than his successor, sought counseling regularly in combination with a visit to the shrine, located on the premises; but now the headquarters has been moved a distance of perhaps ten miles to a hill called Shintōzan 神道山. The shrine is still visited by members and local people, especially during its annual festivals, and an official shrine priest (*Gūji*) appointed by Kurozumikyō is installed there. Now, however, except for Kurozumikyō ceremonial occasions, it functions mostly as a tutelary shrine of the area,[7] a situation discussed more fully in chapter six.

The branch churches funnel monies received from the followers to the headquarters, retaining enough to guarantee their own maintenance. The branch churches receive fees for performing a variety of services including House Purification and Grounds Purification and special prayers requested by the followers (*kinen* 祈念); in addition a follower visiting the church generally makes a small offering in cash or produce. More rarely the branch church may relay a request from the headquarters for contributions to a special project such as the construction of the new headquarters. In the latter case all funds collected by the branch church are delivered to the headquarters as are the membership dues paid by some of the followers. For the entire Church these dues amount to some $250,000 annually. Out of the funds remaining the branch churches manage all their own expenses; they do not receive financial support from the headquarters. In rare cases, a church may be censured for not contributing enough to the upkeep of the organization.[8]

One problem encountered in the attempt to describe the role of Kurozumikyō branch churches in their local communities is the fact that it is often difficult to determine who is a member and who

[7] A comparison of shrine- and church-visit statistics reveals that more people visit middle-sized branch churches and the new headquarters Shintōzan at New Year's than visit the Munetada Jinja.

[8] Information on revenues was collected through consulting the headquarters staff and ministers of branch churches.

is not. A church established over a century ago may have such a strong hold in local society that everyone assumes that all residents are automatically affiliated with the church. The ministers themselves tend to adopt this view, especially in rural areas, and to be unconcerned with maintaining distinctions among those crossing the threshhold.[9]

Membership Categories

There are three categories of lay affiliation with Kurozumikyō. The first is that of "believer" (shinja 信者). This category is the broadest of the three and includes the other two. It is not a formal, administrative designation and can be used to indicate any person who maintains an affiliation with the church in the form of visiting the church, paying dues, having House Purification performed regularly, or attending Laymen's Meetings. The second category, "follower" (michizure 道連), can be used interchangeably with "believer," but in addition it has the more restricted, administrative sense of a dues-paying member. A subdivision of the followers is the third category, kyōto 教徒, indicating individuals or households who habitually have ancestral and funeral rites performed by Kurozumikyō, on the model of the traditional parish affiliation of households with Buddhist temples. The ministers are rather casual about the collection of dues, and although they have lists of the kyōto and followers, no special honor or privilege accrues to the status of kyōto above that of follower or believer.[10]

KUROZUMIKYŌ AND SHRINE SHINTŌ

In rural areas Kurozumikyō churches are so firmly entrenched in local society that they are perceived along the lines of a village tutelary (ujigami) shrine. Except for the signpost proclaiming that

[9] This is particularly true of rural churches.
[10] Branch churches generally maintain lists of the kyōto for the purpose of performing periodic ritual, and they have (but seem not to use systematically) lists of some of the followers, those who are regular contributing members of Laymen's Meetings. Other than these, no records on the michizure or shinja are maintained.

the building is a church (*kyōkai*), not a shrine (*jinja*), there is little to distinguish the church building from a shrine to the unpracticed eye. The entrance gate (though not a *torii* 鳥居, the gate of Shintō shrines), is hung with a sacred rope (*shimenawa* 標縄) and paper streamers (*gohei* 御幣), and a collection box stands at the door. Unlike in many small village shrines, there is a large, straw-matted room between the door and the altar in which followers may assemble. From a distance the altar itself looks like that of an ordinary shrine, the difference being the generally better condition of repair and cleanliness in the case of the Kurozumikyō church. Flowers and fresh produce offerings are replaced daily. Closer inspection reveals that the altar is divided into two sections, a large one in which three objects of worship (*shintai* 神体) are placed, and a smaller area for the ancestors of the church, represented by a single object of worship. The objects of worship are round, polished metal mirrors set in wooden stands. In the larger altar space, the central mirror is larger than the other two and represents the Sun Goddess, Amaterasu Ōmikami. On the left hand (from the worshiper's point of view) of the central mirror is a smaller one representing the Founder. To the right of the central mirror is a smaller one representing the eight million gods (*yaoyorozu no kami*). This arrangement of objects of worship is constant in all Kurozumikyō branch churches, but the decoration and offerings are left to the discretion of the branch church ministers.[11]

The dress of Kurozumikyō ministers is also so reminiscent of that of shrine priests that there is no way to tell the two apart. Purchased from manufacturers of shrine priests' attire, Kurozumikyō dress calls for a white robe (*hakui* 白衣) under a divided skirt (*hakama* 袴) and loose jacket (*haori* 羽織). More elaborate dress is used for the performance of public ritual, but this also may be seen at shrines. The major fact distinguishing the dress of Shrine Shintō from Kurozumikyō is that so many women are wearing it in the latter case.[12]

[11] This arrangement is constant, but as for the architecture of the buildings, there is great variety, some being almost indistinguishable from ordinary houses.

[12] Various branch churches seem to adopt their own style in vestments for the performance of various rites, but a standard variation of color denotes subtleties of rank.

The worship service of Kurozumikyō is also much like that of Shrine Shintō. Recitation of the Great Purification Prayer, in use in all varieties of Shrine Shintō, is the centerpiece of all Kurozumikyō worship. This is followed by ministers' reading of *norito*, prayers, again indistinguishable by the ordinary person from those of Shrine Shintō. In both cases special prayers requested by an individual (*kinen*) are performed, and routine rites of car blessing (for traffic safety), baby blessing, Grounds Purification, House Purification, and weddings are performed. Whereas Kurozumikyō performs funerals, Shrine Shintō does not, except in rare cases. Both shrines and Kurozumikyō churches are visited by those living nearby at New Year's.[13]

Not only is there a superficial resemblance in the appearance of Kurozumikyō and Shrine Shintō but in many cases there are important connections at the local level between shrine and church. Many Kurozumikyō ministers were actually born into the homes of Shintō priests, as was the Founder, and later joined Kurozumikyō. Especially in the case of women, when it was not given them to succeed to the headship of a shrine, the transition to Kurozumikyō was a natural one. Kurozumikyō ministers frequently are in charge of local shrines as well as managing their churches, a phenomenon that arises when there is no priest to manage shrine affairs. Women ministers are very often called upon by shrine priests to perform Kibigaku (吉備楽 music and dance; see below) at festivals of village shrines, and as a result there is also the custom of shrine priests sending their own children to Kurozumikyō churches to learn Kibigaku from the women. Kurozumikyō ministers sometimes take a period of training at larger shrines such as the Sumiyoshi Taisha 住吉大社 or the Grand Shrine of Ise 伊勢神宮, and there are also cases of shrine priests who have taken a course of study at Kurozumikyō. All these examples show the close connections on the local level between Kurozumikyō and Shrine Shintō.[14]

---

[13] The Great Purification Prayer (*ōharai no kotoba*) is the same in substance as its source in the *Engi shiki*. It differs in minor points from the version of the prayer currently endorsed by the Jinja Honchō.

[14] Through interviews I observed and collected many cases of such interaction between Kurozumikyō and Shrine Shintō.

Kibigaku

Kibigaku is Kurozumikyō's official music and dance for ritual, adopted by the group in 1883. It was founded by the *gagaku* 雅楽 musician Kishimoto Yoshihide 岸本芳秀 and taken over by Kurozumikyō's first musical director Ono Gempan 小野元範. Kishimoto's motive in establishing this new music was to invent a music appropriate for modern Japan. As a recent dissertation on the subject says, "Inherent in his thinking was the idea that while Gagaku was the only music having the power to fully evoke and express the Japanese spirit, it was too austere for the tastes of the general population."[15] Kibigaku was performed in Tokyo several times during the Meiji period (1868–1912), attended mainly by elite or group members and never attaining a popular following. It declined in the 1920s and now is used mainly by Kurozumikyō. Formerly it was also used by Konkokyō 金光教, a new religion founded in Okayama in 1859, but it has been superseded in that group by other forms of music and dance.

There are three types of Kibigaku, for entertainment, home use, and ritual. The first mainly dramatizes historical tales about warrior exploits. The second is for personal pleasure, and the third accompanies all Kurozumikyō public rites. It is a vocal genre accompanied by *biwa* 琵琶, *koto* 琴, *ryūteki* 竜笛 (a flute), *hichiriki* 篳篥 (a double reed instrument), and *shō* 笙 (a mouth organ with seventeen pipes and multiple reeds). Drums are also added in some rites. A number of songs are composed on the basis of five fixed melodies, and dances for both men and women were added, though now it is only the women who dance. There used to be an elaborate system for licensing and grading Kurozumikyō performers of Kibigaku, but this has fallen into disuse. Now Kibigaku is mainly performed as an apprenticeship of sorts to the Ono house, though there is a move afoot to get things back on a firmer basis and revive the practice of Kibigaku as a semi-spiritual discipline for women in Kurozumikyō.[16]

Kurozumikyō branch churches often perform dance and music

---

[15] Larry V. Shumway, "Kibigaku: An Analysis of a Modern Japanese Ritual Music" (Ph.D. dissertation, University of Washington, 1974), p. 1.

[16] Ibid., pp. 1–2.

from Kibigaku in Shintō shrines, and there is considerable informal intercourse between church and shrine centering on Kibigaku. The younger priests at the Kibitsu Jinja 吉備津神社, a very large and venerable shrine in Okayama, not infrequently visit the Ōi Church to trade tips on music and dance, and Ōi ministers and members of the family of that church have performed Kibigaku for the annual festivals of the Hiraoka Jinja 枚岡神社 in Osaka. Thus Kibigaku is an important avenue for interaction between Kurozumikyō and Shrine Shintō.[17] See Illustration 4.

The Kannami Church

A branch church that is an especially apt illustration of the local connections that often exist between shrines and Kurozumikyō churches is the Kannami Church of Awaji Island, Hyōgo Prefecture. See Map 2. Since its establishment in 1875, the Kannami Church has always maintained close ties with the village shrine, the Kawakami Temmangū. Everyone living in a radius of several miles of this shrine is automatically counted a parishioner of it and can, in accord with local tradition, be prevailed upon to contribute to its upkeep. At some point in the past, the notion arose that the Kannami Church, adjacent to the shrine, is in fact a formal extension or branch (*bunsha* 分社) of the shrine. Even tour buses visiting the shrine swing by the Kannami Church and unload passengers for brief worship at the church's altar, thus strengthening the idea that the two are somehow joined. Actually there is no official tie, but the informal connection helps channel local residents to the church and tacitly suggests that shrine parishioners have a responsibility for the maintenance of the church as well.

On this basis the followers of the Kannami Church appealed to 220 households of the area, only a third of whom previously had any direct connection with the church, to contribute to rebuilding it after it burned to the ground in 1980. None of the 220 households gave less than twenty-five dollars, and the average was $250 each. Thus the Kannami Church is but dimly distinguished from the

[17] Ibid. pp. iv–v, 2–12.

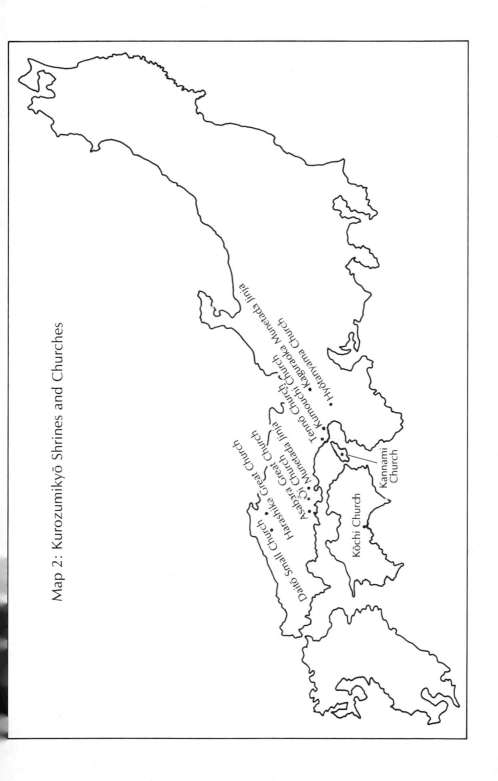

Map 2: Kurozumikyō Shrines and Churches

Hyōtanyama Church

Kaguraoka Muneoka Jinja

Kunōchi Church

Daiji Church

Taenō Church

Munenaga Jinja

Asahina Great Church

Asahina Church

Haraeshike Great Church

Daiō Small Church

Kōchi Church

Kannami Church

village shrine, and affiliation with the latter can be used to assert financial obligation toward the former.[18]

The Observances and Schedule of Branch Churches

Kurozumikyō churches are set apart from Shrine Shintō by their full schedule of lay activities. Shrines usually have seasonal festivals organized in large part by the laity, and priests offer prayer performances upon request; but shrines do not usually have periodic lay meetings for sermons or doctrinal instruction of any kind. Furthermore, shrine priests do not generally offer personal consultation to their parishioners on personal problems. Finally, shrines seldom involve women on a regular basis either as priests or in lay capacities.[19]

The church schedule is quite different from that of shrines, including daily, monthly, annual, and occasional activities. The ritual most important to Kurozumikyō is daily worship of the sun, *nippai*, performed at sunrise by ministers and any followers who care to attend. The practice of going to the church daily for *nippai* or at some other time of day to recite the Great Purification Prayer is called *nissan* 日参, "daily worship." Those who desire to visit the church daily but who are unable to do so have one of the ministers pray for them by including their names in a prayer before the altar, a custom called *nikku* 日公. Typically a small number of followers attend *nippai*, a slightly larger number perform *nissan*, and a very large number request *nikku*. Absolute numbers vary greatly according to the size of the branch church, but at the Ōi Church, a church of the middle grade, around ten come for *nippai*, twenty to thirty for *nissan*, and over 1,200 are entered in the *nikku* register, a service for which they pay about ten dollars annually.[20]

[18] This information was collected at the church through interviewing its ministers and followers on July 14 and 15, 1981.

[19] Meiji law prohibited women holding many Shintō ranks, but since the establishment of the Jinja Honchō in 1946 they have been allowed to fill priestly ranks on an equal footing with men, largely because of the shortage of male priests after the war. Ono Sokyō, *Shintō no kiso chishiki to kiso mondai* (Tokyo: Jinja shimpōsha, 1963), pp. 477, 497.

[20] These figures were compiled from an examination of records at the Ōi Church in Okayama.

1. Kurozumi Munetada, Founder of Kurozumikyō

2. Father and Daughter Ministers Preaching at an Izumo Laymen's Meeting

3. *Majinai* at the Ōi Church

4. *Kibigaku* at the Ōi Church

5. The Sixth Patriarch, Kurozumi Muneharu, After Preaching at the Harashika Great Church

6. Shingōzan at New Year's

7. Purification of the Congregation at the Yoshikawa Laymen's Meeting

8. Women's Group Members Helping Out in the Kitchen of the Ōi Church

9. The Fukumitsu Ministers (bottom row: Fukumitsu Sarō and Fukumitsu Hiroe; standing, left to right: Yamauchi Sachio and son Kazumasa, Yamauchi Hisashi, Nanjō Sen'ichi, Nanjō Mayumi, son Masakazu and daughter Hiroko, Fukumitsu Sukeyasu and Fukumitsu Katsue)

10. Grounds Purification in Ōi Town

11. *Mizuko Kuyō* at the Ōi Church

12. Distributing Reeds at the Great Purification Festival

13. Funeral Ritual for Mizote Miki

Monthly observances at the churches are locally termed *kaijitsu*, or *kaiunsai* 開運祭. The substance of these is identical, and they may be held once or three times per month. At these, followers assemble for recitation of the Great Purification Prayer, a common meal, and a sermon. Sometimes testimonies are given by the followers before the altar. The schedule of these observances has no relation to the work week, so in practice, of those attending, around 80 percent are women.[21]

Annual observances include a New Year's visit, *hatsumōde* 初詣 (see Illustration 6), identical to the shrine practice of the same name, and a pair of rites separated by six months, the *tōji taisai* 冬至大祭, "Winter Solstice Festival," and the *ōbarai taisai* 大祓大祭, "Great Purification Festival." The latter two, to be considered in greater detail in chapter six, have as their purpose the purification of the pollution of the body and mind accumulated in the previous half-year. Generally speaking, the entire following of a church, as well as many of the local residents otherwise unaffiliated with it, assembles for these rites.[22]

In addition to regularly scheduled activities, followers ask ministers to offer special prayers (*kinen*) for them in return for an offering in cash or produce. For example, a youngster going on a school trip may be brought to the church by mother or grandmother for a prayer for safety on the trip. A minister leads them in the Great Purification prayer, reads a *norito* for safety in travel, and then chats with them informally. Other examples of *kinen* are the case of a woman who brings her pregnant daughter-in-law to the church to pray for safe childbirth; a person requesting prayer for the recovery from illness of a relative, friend, or oneself; and a prayer for success in school examinations. There are as many types of *kinen* as there are hopes of the followers.[23]

Counseling and healing are natural extensions of *kinen* visits. After the formal praying, the minister or ministers join the fol-

---

[21] The activities of *kaijitsu* are identical in both urban and rural churches.

[22] Many more local residents attend these observances in rural areas than in urban ones.

[23] These consultations often require a minister to compose a *norito* for the occasion, which is an important means by which the minister can keep informed of developments in family lives.

lowers who have requested the prayer to talk with them. It often becomes apparent that the request for prayer was in reality a pretext to request counseling naturally and without embarrassment. Once talk of a personal nature begins, ministers and followers may move to one of the rooms of the ministers' residence, often directly attached to the church by a corridor, for more private conversation. Then the follower may seek advice on family or business problems, not only on a single occasion but often over long periods of time. When, as is often the case, the matter on which the follower requests counseling concerns sickness, counseling may give way to healing.

RURAL AND URBAN CHURCHES

The rural churches of Kurozumikyō are generally more active than the urban ones, having been founded earlier, and their activities set the standard of performance for the entire Church, a fact that is illustrated by their being chosen most often as the training ground for ministers newly graduated from the seminary. New graduates serve a sort of apprenticeship of varying length (nine months to several years) in churches particularly known for their minister's skill in spiritual training. The apprentices participate in ritual, are given practice in sermons, and are trained in the details of liturgy and church management. Branch churches are frequently so short-handed that they genuinely need the services of these ministers-in training.[24]

The Harashika Great Church

A rural branch church particularly famed for the passion of its Chief Minister in his devotion to the training of young ministers is the Harashika Great Church of Izumo in Shimane Prefecture, not far from the Great Shrine of Izumo 出雲大社. This church is the center of all area activities, dominating the other five churches in

[24] Frequently a minister just graduated from the seminary will have to be placed immediately in charge of a church for lack of more experienced personnel, without the benefit of an apprenticeship.

the area, partly by the forceful personality of Chief Minister Katsube, undiminished by a bout with throat cancer resulting in his having to use a speaking tube for all speech, including his powerful sermons. See Illustration 2. The followers of the Harashika Great Church almost all live in the rural area surrounding the church and grow rice, usually pursuing a secondary job or trade as well. As many as eight hundred assemble for annual festivals.

The work of the church is carried out by Chief Minister Katsube, his daughter Akiko, also a powerful preacher, and an unrelated female minister. Their division of labor is such that father and daughter spend all day every day, and most evenings as well, managing the fifty Laymen's Meetings attached to the church, while the other woman remains in the church to receive followers there, numbering twenty on a weekday and fifty to sixty per day on the weekends. Father and daughter are generally driven to meetings by the daughter's husband, who is not a minister.

The daughter's marriage represents a type often seen in rural Kurozumikyō churches: a female minister in line to succeed a parent to the headship of a branch church, married to a man whose major role is to assist her, whether or not he is himself a minister. He and their children may take the woman's maiden name, as in this case. He becomes in effect an "adopted husband," *mukoyōshi* 婿養子.

The Harashika Great Church is administered by the Katsube family, but once father and daughter don their ritual white (*hakui*), they are no longer parent and child but colleagues in the ministry and address each other as such. They maintain also a strict separation between the church area, always open to the followers, and their private living quarters, where followers enter only upon invitation.[25]

The Daitō Small Church

While the Harashika Great Church exemplifies the height of branch church activity, the other extreme in branch church style of

[25] Information on this church is based on interviewing and observation of ministers and followers on June 21–23 and July 11, 12, and 13, 1981.

ministry can be illustrated by another Izumo church, the Daitō Small Church. This church is about a forty minutes' drive from the Harashika Great Church, where its part-time minister was trained. The church building itself is extremely small, perhaps twenty feet by fifteen feet, and since Chief Minister Yamamoto Yutaka has another job in addition to the ministry, the church operates in effect only on the occasion of periodic ritual. His other occupation, however, is as an employee of a national organization to aid victims of the atomic bomb, of whom there are some two thousand in the prefecture. His work in this organization gives him a significant role in the community, and some of the respect for his position accrues to Kurozumikyō as well, even if his service at the church is limited to festival occasions.

Followers desiring consultation or prayer call at the minister's home, some distance from the church. There is at present only Chief Minister Yamamoto serving in this church (since his son married the incumbent of the Ōi Church, discussed below), and there is no active Women's or Youth Group. Several generations ago, however, this church gave birth to a powerful minister, Kurokawa Omatsu. Among the present-day followers of this church are the descendants of Kurokawa and of her closest followers, including families who moved from the area decades ago but who continue to attend annual festivals out of affection for other followers and for this church's tradition. The Daitō Small Church exemplifies the tenacity of Kurozumikyō followers in their devotion to a church even when its current level of activity is quite low.[26]

A major factor strengthening rural churches is the fact that in most cases the followers are connected by ties of residential proximity and cooperative labor in addition to their membership in the Church. Since the followers are already accustomed to cooperating with each other, for example in harvesting and other agricultural tasks, on the basis of semi-economic bonds, this habit of association easily carries over into church activity and reinforces membership. In the case of urban churches, however, membership is rarely if

[26] Information on this church was gathered through interviewing and observation of ministers and followers on June 22 and July 12, 1981.

ever so reinforced. Followers are neither concentrated in a certain quarter of any city, nor do they often work together. Moreover, they may live too far from the church to visit often, and the result is that in a number of cases urban churches stand empty except on the occasion of festivals. Urban churches thus must try to compensate for the lack of secondary bonds among the followers and must develop techniques to maintain firm links from the church to the followers.

The Kumauchi Church of Kobe

The Kumauchi Church of Kobe is a good example of both the stresses and the strengths of urban Kurozumikyō churches. Until 1974 the main technique used by Chief Minister Motoki Toshikazu and his grandfather before him to forge a bond between the church and the followers was the custom of House Purification, in which the minister visited the follower's house and conducted recitation of the Great Purification Prayer and a ritual purification of each room. Afterward minister and follower talked informally, and this more than the rite itself created an ongoing relationship. The minister performed this service for each of the 120 households of followers of the church on a monthly basis, and as a result he was seldom in the church building except to sleep. Besides the ritual of purifying followers' residences, House Purification afforded the Kumauchi minister monthly contact at close quarters with each household, reassuring the followers of his continuing concern for their welfare as well as providing the church with up-to-date information on each household's affairs. Although Chief Minister Motoki's wife is trained for the ministry, she has taken no full-time, active role in counseling the followers since she has young children. Thus the followers have seldom come to the church, relying on Chief Minister Motoki to come to them. Then in 1974 as a result of consultations with the Patriarch, Motoki resolved to reverse the situation: to cease House Purification and instead to shift the center of activity to the church itself.

The Chief Minister reports that his policy has met with mixed success over the past seven years since its inception. There is considerable reaction against this change in time-honored custom, and

117

a number of followers have been lost. The followers looked forward to the minister's visits, often staying home from work to receive him. They saw in the occasion a benefit to the spirits of their ancestors, before whose memorial tablets the minister intoned his prayers. At the same time it requires a certain amount of adjustment to accustom followers to the newly established rhythms of monthly meetings in the church. Since these are not attuned to the work week, in practice they host only those who are not employed. In addition, meetings in the church are not, in the case of this church, accompanied by Laymen's Meetings, which could bolster the ties among followers.[27]

In spite of the difficulties encountered by this and other urban churches, however, in one respect urban churches are free of an element that hinders the growth of rural Kurozumikyō. In rural areas Kurozumikyō followers are in a majority of cases also affiliated with a Buddhist temple, and the usual arrangement is that the temple is expected to perform all funerals and ancestral rites of the household. Even individuals who desire to have their own funeral conducted by Kurozumikyō typically encounter serious opposition from other family members if the household maintains, as most rural families do, a hereditary affiliation with a temple. It is understood that funeral and ancestral rites are a household, not an individual, matter. It is very difficult for rural followers, especially first sons, to cut the tie with Buddhism, no matter how strong their desire to do so.[28]

This matter is greatly simplified in the urban setting. At the Kumauchi Church all the followers are committed to performing household funeral and ancestral rites in the Kurozumikyō style, with no relation to Buddhism. Most of the follower's households became affiliated with Kurozumikyō generations ago and were at that time located in Okayama or some other part of western Japan. Then a second or third son took up residence in Kobe and retained the link to Kurozumikyō. He could assume that the family's ancestors were being cared for back in his home town by a temple, and

---

[27] It is probable that from the followers' point of view the main significance of House Purification is as a type of ancestor worship.

[28] This is true regardless of a family's sectarian affiliation.

this freed him to entrust his own funeral rites to Kurozumikyō. Thus urban followers are more able to commit themselves to Kurozumikyō than are those in rural areas.[29]

The Kobe Women's Group

Another Kobe development, the Women's Group drawn from all four of the churches in the city, illustrates strategies for coping with problems faced by urban churches. Headed by Vice Chief Minister Hirano, of the Tennō Church, wife of its Chief Minister, this Women's Group has 140 active members and nineteen officers. Of these officers, sixteen have taken Kurozumikyō correspondence courses, giving them a certain authority and confidence, as well as formal qualification to preach, proselytize, and heal. Thirteen of the nineteen were born in Kurozumikyō households, mainly in western Japan, and only five were actually born in Kobe. Thus they retain strong ties to the traditions of rural Kurozumikyō. They are united in the view that the time has passed when urban churches can rely solely on House Purification for contact with followers. Instead, followers themselves should take initiative in making new converts, adapting their approach to the urban setting. They publish monthly magazines and newsletters to keep others informed of their activities.[30]

Vice Minister Yamaguchi of the group, a single woman hoping to establish her own church in Kobe, described the situation as one in which prospective urban followers have generally already had some negative experience at the hands of a religious group. They are wary of straightforward attempts at proselytization, and thus one cannot expect to convert them overnight. Yamaguchi researched the situation by traveling to the Ōi Church to observe its Laymen's Meetings and as a result adopted for her Laymen's Meetings a policy of estimating that a true conversion will take two to three years. It is possible to persuade someone quickly to take out

[29] Most Kobe followers I interviewed reported that their families originated in rural western Japan.

[30] I interviewed the members of the Kobe Women's Group as a group on July 6, 1981.

119

membership by sustained discussion and pleading, but this sort of convert soon drops out. More reliable is the process of maintaining contact patiently, showing consideration and respect for the wishes of the candidate, teaching Kurozumikyō's way of life by example rather than by frontal assault. Yamaguchi has collected some thirty-six households, whom she visits for House Purification on the memorial days of their ancestors and to whom she administers healing rites when they are sick. Vice Minister Yamaguchi's example portrays the dedication of the Kobe Women's Group as well as its greater concern for the depth of relation between church and follower than for increases in membership figures per se. The presence of active ministers in this Women's Group ensures strong ties between church and followers.[31]

The Hyōtanyama Church

The Hyōtanyama Church of Osaka City represents an urban church where House Purification is still heavily relied upon. This strategy presents a problem when it empties the church itself of ministers to counsel the followers, but in the case of Hyōtanyama the wife of Vice Minister Nanjō Sen'ichi, Mayumi, is also a Vice Minister, and she fulfills the role of counselor. The area around the church, at the city's edge, is frequented by ascetics who perform various austerities in the waterfalls of nearby forests. There are also a large number of temples, shrines, and churches of various new religions, in addition to the temples of Korean residents. The generally high level of religious activity in the area has probably helped this church grow to a considerable size given its very short history (founded 1966). The ministers are also assisted by an active Women's Group, many of whom were instrumental in persuading Bishop Fukumitsu Sarō, the titular Chief Minister of this church, to open it and then to pass its daily operation on to his eldest daughter Mayumi and son-in-law, the present Vice Ministers. The church is unusual in having attracted a significant number of young men and women as active followers.[32]

[31] There is no comparable group of male ministers and followers.

[32] The male minister of this church finished seminary in 1980, having entered it at about the age of forty, after a business failure. Prior to that time, his wife and her father alone had charge of the church.

WOMEN'S ROLES

Having examined these several rural and urban branch churches, we can now inquire about the factors determining whether a church is bright and clean from lack of use or its mats torn and faded from the constant comings and goings of the followers. The presence or absence of female ministers is the key.

Perhaps more than anything else, the followers seek counseling from their ministers; many of the other services that the churches provide, such as House Purification, could be found at an ordinary shrine. Parishioners of a village shrine, however, would not seek advice of a personal nature from a shrine priest. On the contrary, Kurozumikyō ministers, especially the women, expend a great deal of energy listening to the followers' problems, thinking out possible solutions, and encouraging followers as they try to enact those solutions. This advice and counsel interact with general cultural expectations that hold that women are more sensitive to emotional nuance and the details of personal situations and thus are more desirable as counselors. Furthermore, there seems to be a belief that women are somehow closer to the spirit world than men.[33]

When in the case of some urban churches there is no active female minister, followers perceive the situation as somehow anomalous, a departure from the practice of the rural churches. Even if a male minister is present for consultation, the fact remains that the followers most often prefer to consult a woman and are frustrated when this is impossible.

Therefore, a sense of something missing prevails when women are unavailable for counseling, and by contrast there exists also the positive expectation that when women *are* present, extraordinary events such as miraculous healings are liable to occur. Legends about inspiring female ministers abound, and these tales feed the fires of the idea that women are somehow more capable of spiritual feats than men.

Women are unquestionably the center of activity in branch churches. They are the ones who come to the churches on a daily basis to chat with the ministers, request a prayer, or talk over a

---

[33] All the followers I interviewed expressed a preference for counseling by women.

problem. Women followers, especially those of middle age, often have a great deal of energy and motivation to work for the church, and since they are less often employed at nine-to-five jobs, they are generally freer than the men to devote time to the church. Women frequently initiate new church projects and carry them out, but before retirement, men are much less often committed to the church in this way. A men's group exists only in name, and men of any age come to the church much more rarely than their wives, the understanding being that since men "have work to do" they are justified in delegating the family's religious concerns to women.[34]

The Kōchi Women's Group

Projects undertaken at the initiative of the Women's Group are of great benefit to the Church. One example of activities initiated by the Women's Group is the proselytization of the Kobe churches' Women's Group, discussed above. Another example is provided by the Women's Group of the Kōchi Great Church in Shikoku. While a member of the council of Women's Groups of Kurozumikyō, Yamazaki Aiko became aware that in the Kōchi area a number of churches had entirely fallen into disuse. Although persons holding the title of Chief Minister were nominally in charge, the church doors were closed, the altars dark and dirty, and no one was caring for the followers. Shocked at this sorry state of affairs, Yamazaki decided to marshal the Women's Group of the Kōchi Great Church to revive the churches. They went into one such church after another, with bucket and broom in hand, cleaned the buildings, and decorated the altars. They also approached the local followers and the Chief Minister, involving them in the process, encouraging them to contribute money and labor to their branch church. The Women's Group then arranged for ministers of the Kōchi Great Church to give sermons and to conduct ritual in these newly refurbished churches. They remained active in the area until local ministers and followers were sufficiently roused to manage for themselves. Projects like Yamazaki's are of tremendous value to

---

[34] This attitude seems to be quite general, not limited to Kurozumikyō.

Kurozumikyō, and they illustrate clearly the crucial role of women in the church.[35]

Wherever one observes Kurozumikyō ministers, the impression that its women are more able than the men, at least among the generations under about fifty years of age, is unmistakable, and the reasons for this state of affairs are not far to seek. The custom of women joining in the Kurozumikyō ministry arose during the Meiji period, the most conspicuous examples having been born in the late 1880s. They seem to have come from former commoner households for the most part, the informal taboo on upper class women engaging in a public career greatly constraining those from a higher stratum. There are many legends of charismatic female ministers, and often those gifted male ministers one encounters today in fact trained under those women. Female ministers today come from strong ministerial households or from shrine families, in either case growing up with models before them. This seems less often true of male ministers, although this admittedly is an impression rather than a judgment based on statistical evidence.

While female ministers take charge of local affairs with little hesitation and are more or less content to leave the administration of Kurozumikyō as a whole to their male colleagues, the men are less able to deal with the counseling desired by the followers, and at present they are not able to substitute for this an involvement in group administration. They seem to suffer from a lack of leadership. The generation of male ministers now forty-five and older had the example of the Fifth Patriarch, a strong and much-loved leader. The present generation of young male minsters, however, looks to the Sixth Patriarch for its leadership (see Illustration 5), and the Sixth Patriarch is concerned to distinguish himself in rather different terms from his father.[36]

The Sixth Patriarch is very active in Okayama civic and charitable affairs and is a patron of the arts, especially pottery. He has made several overseas tours to donate pottery to foreign museums and seems to be inclined to increase the time he devotes to this sort

[35] I interviewed Yamazaki and the ministers at the Kōchi Church on July 27–29, 1981.

[36] Older followers express a very different sort of regard for the Fifth and Sixth Patriarchs.

of extramural activity. He has urged his young male ministers to give up the practice of House Purification as the principal bond between church and followers, but neither he nor they have arrived at a more satisfying use of ministers' time. He tends to reinforce young male ministers' inclination to prevent their wives, most of whom they met in seminary, from taking an active role in the ministry, and the result is that their churches stand empty. These men do not get out to the followers, and the followers are prevented from access to the one they would most like to see in a branch church, an active female minister. Thus the present generation of young male ministers either subtly opposes the present Patriarch and carries on House Purification while their wives receive and counsel followers, in which case their churches prosper and thrive, or they sit waiting for followers who seldom come and tend a church immaculate for lack of use.[37]

VARIETIES OF LAYMEN'S MEETINGS

The Laymen's Meetings of rural Kurozumikyō provide a powerful forum of proselytization and of fellowship among the followers. Held biannually, quarterly, or monthly, some Laymen's Meetings have been in existence for over a century, rotating among the households of a hamlet, with membership passed from generation to generation. On the occasion of Laymen's Meetings, ministers from the branch church to which the meeting is attached attend, conduct ritual, and deliver a sermon. The occasion is one in which meeting members invite friends and others as yet unaffiliated with Kurozumikyō, and this becomes a first step in proselytization, though no pressure to join is exerted on newcomers. The absence of Laymen's Meetings in urban churches forces them to try by various means to compensate for the lack.

Laymen's Meetings may be understood as a modern adaptation of the "confraternities" (kō, kōsha) of laymen meeting to strengthen their faith and renew their association with temple or shrine. Before

---

[37] I interviewed the Patriarch numerous times, and it was clear that a major part of his energies are largely directed to such extramural pursuits.

the Kurozumikyō ministers arrive, the followers assemble and entrust individual offerings and requests for prayers to the sponsoring household, whose representative places the former on the altar and makes a list of the latter. The "altar" generally is the *tokonoma* 床の間 (alcove) of the main room and is hung with a scroll picturing the Founder and bearing the names of the Sun Goddess, the eight million gods, and the Founder, written in the hand of the Patriarch. This scroll is the property of the Laymen's Meeting and is moved when the meeting rotates to a new household. When the ministers arrive, they lead the group in recitation of the Great Purification Prayer and read a *norito* into which the prayer requests previously gathered are incorporated. These rituals take roughly thirty minutes. Next come one or two hymns, a sermon, and possibly a testimony, followed by a communal meal, and the performance of *majinai* for anyone desiring it, usually the whole group.[38]

The Yoshikawa Laymen's Meeting

Often Laymen's Meetings show a concentration of a stratum of rural society, a phenomenon that can be illustrated by two examples from among the thirteen Laymen's Meetings attached to the Ōi Church. (See Illustration 7.) The Yoshikawa Laymen's Meeting, the Yoshikawa Tenshinkō, named after the hamlet where it is held, is hosted by the main house (*honke* 本家) of the Kawauchis, an old, wealthy family, formerly major landlords of the area. The meeting is generally attended by ten to fifteen people, four or five of whom are men, mostly representing branch houses (*bunke* 分家) of the Kawauchi line. Before the war this Meeting was much larger, because then the Kawauchis had tenant farmers upon whom they could prevail to attend. Now, however, this form of leverage has disappeared, and the meeting has become largely a family affair. Moreover, the fact that the hamlet is fourteen kilometers from the church up steep mountain roads also tends to attenuate the relation between church and meeting.[39]

---

[38] This order of events is common to all rural churches.
[39] I participated in the Yoshikawa Laymen's Meeting on June 25, 1981.

The Awai Laymen's Meeting

In sharp contrast to the Yoshikawa Meeting is the Awai Meeting, the Awai Tenshinkō, located only two kilometers from the Ōi Church. This meeting is the most active of those attached to the Ōi Church, and its members regularly attend church functions and come often to volunteer help in the church's kitchen or garden, as well as to schedule their monthly meetings. Whereas the Yoshi-kawa Meeting members meet only once or twice a year, and contribute five to ten dollars each to the church at that time, the Awai members make individual offerings of produce each month while the sponsoring household contributes about fifty dollars monthly. Since this meeting rotates among hamlet households, the financial burden evens out over the years. The members of the Awai Meeting number forty to fifty and are mostly small-scale farmers or descendants of tenant farmers. The Awai Meeting members are almost entirely women, and their common religious association is underwritten by living near each other and by ties of long friendship. The relation between ministers and followers is much more warm and informal in the case of the Awai Meeting.[40]

The rural membership of Kurozumikyō was originally as-sembled in part by the Founder's and early disciples' use of the mediation of village headmen. Once having secured the allegiance and protection of a headman, early disciples were often able to enlist large portions of the village population through his influence. Many of these Tokugawa headmen's families became the landlords of late nineteenth- and twentieth-century rural Japan. In that con-text they seem to have frequently prevailed upon their tenant farmers to follow Kurozumikyō. Though the postwar land reform has eroded the economic base of former landlords' power in rural society, there is an acture awareness of which families held power under former orders, and in Kurozumikyō these relationships are very plain. The former landlords' Laymen's Meetings are more formal, less frequent, and are fewer in number than those Laymen's Meetings composed mainly of the landlords' former tenants. The latter meetings tend to be less formal, to be held more frequently,

---

[40] I participated in the Awai Laymen's Meeting twice in 1981 and once in July 1980.

and to feature a warm, communal atmosphere. The two seldom mix, and they hold no common observances. The former landlords prefer to call the ministers to them; they seldom appear at the church. This bifurcation of the rural constituency is part of the heritage of Kurozumikyō's Tokugawa proselytization strategy. There is no such readily observable division among the membership of urban churches.[41]

The Yakane Laymen's Meeting

A final example from among the Laymen's Meetings of the Ōi Church illustrates the importance of healing and the contrast between modes of operation of Kurozumikyō and Konkōkyō. First, it is important to bear in mind that virtually every follower attending a Laymen's Meeting has experienced a cure, more often many cures, over a period of decades, the average age of followers being between fifty-five and sixty.

Yakane is a hamlet in the mountains about seventeen kilometers from the Ōi Church where peach and grape orchards produce the main cash crops. Up until 1965 everyone in the hamlet belonged to Konkōkyō, but some residents were directly affiliated with the headquarters while others belonged to a branch church of Konkōkyō two or three kilometers from the Ōi Church. The only time the entire hamlet hosted a common religious activity was the occasion of the annual visit of a Konkōkyō minister who gave a sermon and then visited each house of the hamlet for House Purification over a ten-day period. This was the only visit by Konkōkyō ministers to the hamlet. An employee of the Konkōkyō headquarters, Minister Endō, resided in Yakane, but his wife was entirely uninterested and uninvolved, and so their house did not become in any sense a Konkōkyō center.

Then in 1965, when Minister Endō was already quite elderly, his son was stricken with a kidney disease that dumbfounded the doctors. At that time an acquaintance encouraged him to go to the Ōi Kurozumikyō Church, and when he did so, he was healed. This

[41] See chapter two for an account of Kurozumikyō's use of the mediation of village headmen and landlords in the Tokugawa period.

event became the talk of Yakane, but soon after that an even more striking event occurred. A woman of the hamlet became ill and was on the point of death. So certain was her demise in the eyes of the hamlet that people were already beginning to discuss funeral preparations. The younger Endō, however, did not give up hope and resolved instead to take her to the Ōi Church, and when he bore her there on his back, she was cured. That two cures should happen in such quick succession in a tiny hamlet of fourteen houses seemed nothing short of miraculous, especially after years of inactivity under Konkōkyō.

While the hamlet was still in this state of shock, Vice Chief Minister Fukumitsu Hiroe of the Ōi Church asked the younger Endō to gather all the hamlet together to hear a sermon. She went to the hamlet, and every resident came to listen to her. After the sermon explaining the doctrine and practice of Kurozumikyō she invited them to come to the church, which they promptly did. Once they had seen for themselves what goes on in a branch church, Vice Chief Minister Fukumitsu then asked Endō to arrange an occasion in which the hamlet could gather again for another sermon, in this case with enough time to have a meal together and with provisions for child care so the women could attend fully to what was said. In effect this occasion was a trial Laymen's Meeting. After this meeting she and Bishop Fukumitsu went on foot to each house for House Purification and thereby became acquainted with each resident. In subsequent years they took with them apprentices from the seminary at the headquarters, thereby creating ties not only to the branch church but to the headquarters as well, in such a way that the two ties strengthen and complement each other. A regular Laymen's Meeting was established at Yakane, which now is among the most active of those of the Ōi Church.

Later, when Endō's father, the Konkōkyō minister, died, his funeral was conducted by Kurozumikyō, and from then on the Endōs became *kyōto*. Endō has taken two years of correspondence courses from the seminary and now is licensed as a minister.

The contrast between the approaches of the two Churches to affairs in Yakane is striking. Konkōkyō activities revolve much more exclusively around their branch churches. It is expected that followers will come to the Konkōkyō churches, and conversely, ministers do not for the most part expect to go out to the followers. Further, those in the hamlet most closely related to Minister Endō felt obliged to journey to the headquarters rather than to the nearby branch church, and this also confused the hamlet's tie to Konkōkyō. In any case, Konkōkyō ministers visited Yakane only once a year rather than monthly, as is the present schedule of the Yakane Laymen's meeting of Kurozumikyō. Finally, Kurozumikyō would not easily permit a minister's funeral to be performed by another religion, whereas Konkōkyō seems to have been entirely uninvolved in the last rites of the elder Endō. At present, thirteen of the fourteen hamlet households have converted to Kurozumikyō.[42]

PROBLEMS AND SUMMARY

We have seen that the branch churches of Kurozumikyō are distinguished in various ways from Shrine Shintō on the one hand and from Konkōkyō on the other. The most decisive distinguishing factor in either case is the closeness of the ties between minister and follower in Kurozumikyō, whether the follower visits the minister at the church, or whether the minister goes to the follower, as in Laymen's Meetings. In either case the followers can rely on the ministers for advice, counsel, and continuing concern, and these seem to be the elements ensuring the followers' repeated return. Further, Kurozumikyō churches are able to provide this warm atmosphere for counseling precisely because the branch churches are operated by families and involve all adult members of a minister's family in some capacity. This total involvement of a branch church family is attractive to the followers on the one hand and sets limits to the growth of Kurozumikyō on the other.

Most of the fifteen men and women presently studying for the ministry in Kurozumikyō's seminary will succeed their parents in managing a branch church or will marry someone who inherits the church. Every year two or three students whose parents are not

[42] I participated in the Yakane Laymen's Meeting on July 3, 1981, and interviewed the Mr. Endō of the hamlet whose cure precipitated the conversion of the hamlet to Kurozumikyō on July 4, 1981.

129

ministers are admitted, but on the whole the central administration prefers not to encourage them. The reason given is that they are more liable to drop out when discouraged by the difficult regimen, whereas the son or daughter of a branch church, even if attending the seminary with extreme reluctance, will probably become devoted to the ministry through seminary training. The result of this policy not to encourage those outside the hereditary line of succession to branch church leadership is that the branch churches are significantly understaffed.[43]

The fact of understaffing is recognized by the headquarters, and the system of dispatching new seminary graduates to help out in branch churches relieves some of the burden. The emphasis, however, is decidedly upon maintaining the status quo. This applies to the number of followers as well as the number of ministers, because the ministry as presently organized is hard pressed to care adequately for even the present number of followers. Any large increase would be beyond its capacity and would require radical restructuring. The only way to expand would be to increase the number of ministers, but in order to do so, the principle of family management would have to be sacrificed.

Branch churches are operated on the model of family farms or businesses in which there is a core of consanguines and affines, with an outer circle of apprentices. An individual who is not related to the inner core by blood or marriage cannot be given the title of Chief Minister or Vice Chief Minister of that branch church unless adopted or unless he or she marries someone in the inner circle.

If the churches were staffed according to need and their management decided without reference to the hereditary principle, then the character of family business and the atmosphere of familial warmth so important to the followers would be lost. Thus the churches cannot satisfy staffing needs without coming into conflict with the family principle, and the only solution to this quandary is to try to maintain the status quo rather than to attempt to reach the phenomenal size associated with many new religions. Thus Kurozumikyō continues to manage branch churches much as it always has and refrains from media and proselytization campaigns, typical

---

[43] I interviewed students currently enrolled in the seminary on July 1, 1981.

of the new religions, which would swell the ranks beyond the capacity of a family-centered ministry.[44]

At present Kurozumikyō aims to maintain the status quo, and although there are some who find this a regrettable state of affairs, no one is willing to undertake the radical changes that would have to occur to mount a more activist campaign. The branch churches are understaffed as it is. Those that are active in the counseling of their followers and that have a substantial number of Laymen's Meetings attached to them are scarcely able to attend to all the demands on their time from the present constituency. Even involving all the members of a family and relying on the assistance of a minister-in-training, they barely manage to respond to the requests of the followers. There is no time left to go into the wider community to proselytize or to make the practices and beliefs of Kurozumikyō better known. This they can only leave to the informal activities of followers on the local level and to the central administration on the wider scale. The administration itself, however, is understaffed, and there is presently no one but the Patriarch who habitually represents the group to the public.

As outlined above, the present Patriarch is involved in civic affairs of a nonreligious nature, and he does not proselytize or otherwise actively promote an increase in numbers. The group lacks the resources to ensure the replacement of its aging generation of ministers and followers, except by relying on the habit of hereditary affiliation, and this is a means that is increasingly unreliable in contemporary Japanese society.

The branch churches of Kurozumikyō continue to embody many characteristic features of the practice of religion from earlier eras of Japanese religious history, especially those of its own Tokugawa heritage. Reliance on the habit of hereditary affiliation by household units continues to be the major means of recruitment, and there is correspondingly little if any emphasis now on proselytization or religious education. It is assumed that followers will instruct their children unassisted by the ministers.

---

[44] In this way a tacit decision has been reached not to take the measures that would propel Kurozumikyō irrevocably into the ranks of the new religions. These trends suggest that Kurozumikyō is not likely to grow markedly in the near future.

Kurozumikyō observances continue to be scheduled according to the month, on days ending in two, seven, and so forth, a device that takes no account of the seven-day week, which for both rural and urban members is the more relevant unit of time. The result is that those working at salaried jobs find it difficult to attend regularly.

The obvious bifurcation of the rural constituency according to its class consciousness regarding origins in landlord or nonlandlord groups began with early Kurozumikyō proselytization practices that relied heavily upon the authority of power-holders in rural society. All these factors have contributed to the general difficulty this group has now in initiating new growth or invigorating the present membership. These factors are, however, counterbalanced at the local level in the tight organization within individual branch churches.

Both rural and urban churches have been most successful in meeting the several challenges they face when they have made full use of the talents and energies of women followers and ministers. Rural churches set the standard of performance for the whole, but they are hindered by the difficulty of breaking hereditary ties to Buddhism. Urban churches, by contrast, have reached a stalemate by the Patriarch's policy of abolishing House Purification and by the absence of Laymen's Meetings. In both cases organization is bound by the family principle, and Kurozumikyō has been unable to adapt this principle to meet staffing needs. Therefore, it shows little evidence of new growth. Nevertheless, the allegiance of present followers is quite tenacious, and the Women's Groups of both urban and rural churches presently seems the agency most capable of innovation to meet changing circumstances.

The ministry is committed as a whole, but women seem more able than men. Women are easily cast in the roles of counselor and healer by the followers and by Japanese religions' general perceptions about women. Though they have trouble meeting all the followers' demands for these services simply because of understaffing, they seem capable in their performance of these roles. Men, however, at least those forty-five and younger, do not seem to function well in counseling. They seldom seem to be gifted with a deep faith or firm rapport with followers or with insight into followers' problems to the degree these faculties are possessed by their wives. Moreover, unlike women who have the tradition of Women's Groups in Kurozumikyō, men have no formal channels designed to help them exchange information or to pool resources to meet common problems. When male ministers prevent their wives, nearly all of whom have been trained for the ministry, from taking an active role in counseling the followers, the result is a decline in the branch church. When this is further combined with a policy of abolishing the practice of House Purification, the male ministers are out of a job; neither they nor the central administration has yet conceived of an alternative mission of the ministry. These churches seem unlikely to prosper until such an alternative is found.

CHAPTER FIVE

Ministers and Followers

INTRODUCTION

Following the last chapter's examination of how Kurozumikyō's
branch chruches range along the spectrum of "new" and "old,"
this chapter returns to the question of world view to show how
world view is enacted and implemented in the activities of a single
branch church. It begins with the setting and early history of the Ōi
Church in rural Okayama, so named after the hamlet where it is
located. The church's daily activities and the social characteristics of
its followers are discussed, turning then to three rites frequently
performed by this church for followers and members of the community. These rituals publicize the symbolism of purification and
make known the accessibility through Kurozumikyō of pathways
of self-cultivation.

A central focus of the chapter is the question of "this-worldly-
benefits" (*genze riyaku* 現世利益), a standard interpretative category
in studies on the new religions. A substantial body of scholarship
holds that blessings in this life or boons are the be-all and end-all of
the new religions. I believe that this contention rests on a failure to
grasp what *kokoro naoshi*, "curing the heart," a complete reorientation of self, is. This chapter offers a sustained case study of counseling
to illustrate the new religions' reorientation of self, with interpretation intended to undermine the rather prejudicial tone often
associated with the notion of "this-worldly-benefits." Since the
idea of a complete reorientation and fulfillment of self as the goal of
world view is central to the new religions as a whole, one may
apply the results of this examination of Kurozumikyō to the new
religions generally.

Studies of the new religions that take them to task as debasements
of historical religious tradition are numerous. Although there are

many versions of the claim, the central point is that in their eagerness to use religion to secure the good things in life, the new religions have appropriated bits and pieces of Japanese religious history eclectically and assembled them *ad hoc*. The result is a hodgepodge that defies rational attempts to unify and systematize doctrine and practice. This eclecticism cheerfully ignores the inconsistencies and contradictions produced by uninformed borrowings, and it is no surprise to find people browsing among the many new and innovative (if bizarre) concoctions with the attitude of a consumer in a supermarket.[1]

The rush to apply a negative judgment to the entire spectrum of the new religions is, however, rooted rather shallowly in academic concerns and is better understood when subjected to historical inquiry. Since a number of those who have arrived at such negative judgments are former or present Buddhist priests with academic appointments, and whose parishioners are not seldom inveigled by the new religions, a positive reading of the perpetrators by the victims would have been more surprising. Other writers are journalists whose main concern is to produce a good story, and since 1945 the press has reacted negatively to the new religions almost as a matter of principle, as it sees its own role as champion of other gods: rationality, science, and progress, however superficially conceived.[2] The legacy of prewar administrative judgments about the new religions that relegated all of them to the status of "pseudo-religions" (*ruiji shūkyō* 類似宗教) may also play a role in the thinking of these writers.[3] A final factor is a rather easy psychologizing, reasoning that defeat in the war led to many frustrations and bankrupted the prewar system of values so that people sought

---

[1] Ikado Fujio, "Genze riyaku—sono ronri to shinri," *Nihon Bukkyō* 34 (February 1972): 1–23; Fujii Masao, "Genze riyaku," pp. 179–238, in *Girei no kōzō*, ed. Tamaru Noriyoshi, vol. 2 of *Nihonjin no shūkyō*, 4 vols. (Tokyo: Kōsei shuppansha, 1972); Fujii Masao, *Gendaijin no shinkō kōzō*, Nihonjin no kōdō to shisō 32 (Tokyo: Hyōronsha, 1974), p. 214. See also the bibliography on "this-worldly-benefits" in Japanese religions in Miyake Hitoshi, "Genze riyaku kankei bunken mokuroku," *Nihon Bukkyō* 34 (February 1972): pp. 46–47.

[2] Inoue Nobutaka, *Shinshūkyō kenkyū chōsa handobukku* (Tokyo: Yūzankaku, 1981), pp. 7–10.

[3] Ibid.

quick religious answers to all their problems. With any of the above considerations in mind, a number of writers have held that the new religions have impoverished Japanese religious tradition by seeking only this-worldly-benefits.[4]

It is undoubtedly true that the new religions positively embrace the idea of benefits in this life for the faithful devotee. By contrast, they are little interested in the next life. Their concern is with the here and now. More to the point than simplistic normative evaluations, however, is an account of this phenomenon showing how it operates in a specific group and how it is derived from the world view of the new religions. Kurozumikyō provides a case study of this general problem.

THE BRANCH CHURCH AT ŌI

Detailed records of the Ōi Church's history, preserved by past and present ministers, show changing patterns in ministerial and lay activities that reflect changing trends in employment and residence in the area. A study of this church can help put the problem of "this-worldly-benefits" in a fresh perspective. Ōi is a hamlet located about an hour's drive from the center of Okayama City, at the confluence of two small rivers. Officially, Ōi is on the northern border of the city's metropolitan area, but in the minds of local residents it is less a part of the city than the countryside, and as they describe it, Ōi is definitely *inaka* 田舎: "the sticks." The people of Ōi grow rice and *igusa* 藺草, the plant used in the manufacture of straw mats. There are perhaps ten stores in Ōi, including groceries, a fish market, an oculist, a druggist, and a small restaurant or two. See Map 3. A primary school, bus depot, and agricultural cooperative are also located there. Few families farm full time because these days farming alone will not support a family at a very comfortable level. Therefore, in most three-generation families, the middle generation goes out to work at salaried jobs in the city while the grandparents remain in Ōi to care for the grandchildren.

The Ōi Church of Kurozumikyō is the only religious organization with a building in the hamlet. At some remove there is a village

---

[4] The works cited in note 1 above are typical of this approach.

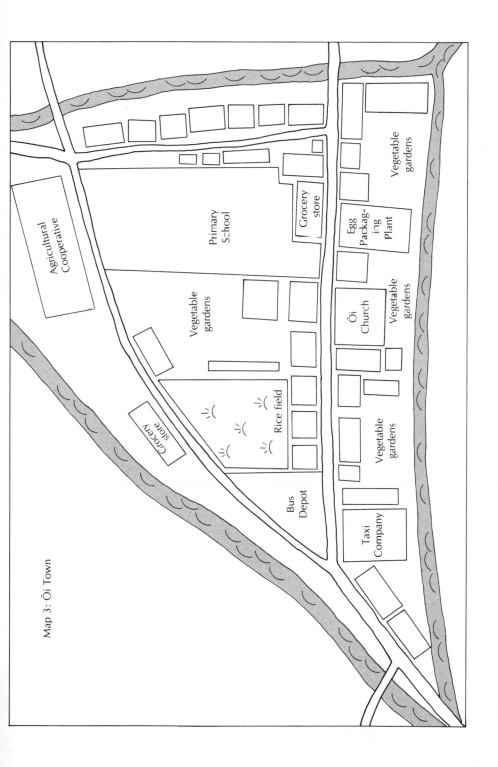

Map 3: Ōi Town

Agricultural Cooperative

Grocery Store

Bus Depot

Rice field

Vegetable gardens

Primary School

Grocery store

Taxi Company

Vegetable gardens

Ōi Church

Vegetable gardens

Egg Packaging Plant

Vegetable gardens

shrine (*ujigami*) that has no resident priest, and about a kilometer away is a temple of the Fujufuse 不受不施 sect of Nichiren 日蓮 Buddhism. The doors are shut, and because the priest has become a full-time mailman, the temple is not a vital center of religious activity. Ashimori 足守, the neighboring hamlet, about two kilometers distant, has a Konkōkyō Church.

The Ōi Church is the closest church to the headquarters of Kurozumikyō, a distance of about ten kilometers. It was founded at the rank of Small Church in 1875 in the time of the Third Patriarch, Muneatsu 宗篤. It grew out of a Laymen's Meeting originally established by Chibara Tōzaemon, a landowner who had been cured of tuberculosis by the Founder. He proselytized widely among the landowning class in Ōi and in Ashimori. The present Chief Minister, Bishop Fukumitsu Sarō, is the church's seventh Chief Minister. No exact records exist of the terms of service of the previous six, but the descendants of two of them still live in the area and serve as *sōdai* 総代, "deacons," of the church.[5]

The church rests on a site of sixty-eight *tsubo* 坪 (one *tsubo* equals 3.3 square meters) of which the building itself occupies fifty-seven *tsubo*. In 1955, on the occasion of the eightieth anniversary of the church's founding, there was a huge celebration, which all the hamlet residents attended, contributing labor, money, and produce. In 1963 the church was promoted to the Middle grade. The church's hundredth anniversary celebration was held in 1975, and laymen donated land to enlarge the site. At that time rooms were also added to the church building. Recently some of the more active laymen have initiated a plan to enlarge the site by purchasing more land and to rebuild the church.

Reviving the Church

At present the Ōi Church is active and prosperous, but this has not always been the case. In 1949 the Ōi Church was about to be

[5] Data on the history of the Ōi Church was gained through interviewing its present ministers and through consultation of unpublished historical manuscripts held by the church. The two that yield the most historical information are titled "Ōi kyōkai nisshi," 4 vols. (1949–1954, 1958), and "Kurozumikyō Ōi chūkyōka-isho enkakushi" (1875–1949).

closed. The sixth Chief Minister was unable to assemble enough followers to support the church, and he was forced to abandon its ministry. At that time Fukumitsu Sarō and his wife Hiroe, who were serving at the Asabara Great Church 浅原大教会, the largest in the area (located on the outskirts of Kurashiki 倉敷), were dispatched to revive the Ōi Church. (Parts of this story are related in Hiroe's life story, in chapter six.)

Fukumitsu Sarō, born in 1905 into the family of an Okayama Shintō priest, trained in the doctrine and practice of Kurozumikyō at the Asabara Great Church under the famous minister Muroyama Moto Sensei, a charismatic woman active early in this century in Okayama. He was one of her closest disciples and married her eldest daughter. But this first wife died. His second wife, Hiroe, presently the Vice Chief Minister of the Ōi Church, was also born into a Shintō priest's household, in 1915. Though they came to the Ōi Church with four young children, with Sarō's aged father, and with high hopes, the sight that first greeted them was a shock and a disappointment.[6]

When the Fukumitsus first set foot in the Ōi Church, the plaster had fallen away from the walls, the doors were broken, the straw mats had been removed, the dishes were full of mold, and there was only enough bedding for a single person. At first, while there were still no followers, they were very poor and hard pressed to feed the children and pay their school fees. Sometimes husband and wife would return cold and exhausted, late on a winter's night, having bicycled high into the mountains to lead a Laymen's Meeting or visit the sick, only to find their children alone and so hungry they could only fall asleep and dream of an adequate meal. Soon, however, the two ministers acquired a substantial reputation as preachers and healers, and by the end of 1949 the church received a daily average of thirty believers calling for prayer and consultation. On festival days so many followers came to the church that it was impossible for all of them to enter the building at once.

---

[6] Information on the postwar history of the Ōi Church and on its ministers' personal histories was gained through interviews with them and from the unpublished autobiography included in chapter six titled "Nan ari, arigataki."

Establishing Laymen's Meetings

The Fukumitsus increased the number of followers by several means, all of which depended on *okage*: "blessings." A term in general use in Japanese religions, *okage* denotes visible or tangible rewards for faithful self-cultivation and may include healings, improved familial relations or economic circumstances, and miscellaneous boons such as recovery of lost articles. In Kurozumikyō followers speak of "receiving blessings," *okage o itadaku* 御陰を頂く.

Rumors of blessings received can lead to the founding of new Laymen's Meetings. People healed of sickness became a topic of conversation at the church and in their own hamlet. The new follower would then invite the Fukumitsus to that hamlet to preach, and eventually a regular Laymen's Meeting would be established. In order to cement relations with each resident of the hamlet, the Fukumitsus would visit every house and perform House Purification. This afforded them an opportunity to talk individually with every hamlet member, form an adequate idea of the circumstances of each household, and personally invite everyone to come to the church. Thus House Purification established channels of communication between the church and every hamlet household. Laymen's Meetings were formed by this process in thirty-one locations, a substantial achievement for two ministers working alone.

While the Fukumitsus were pouring all their energies into rebuilding the Ōi Church, their children were reared in the care of women followers who came daily to the church and relieved Hiroe of all a housewife's duties, taking charge of cooking, cleaning, and child care. The four children took it as a matter of course that they would all become Kurozumikyō ministers. As the church gradually gained stability, however, the Fukumitsu's growing happiness was shattered by the death of their son. This left three daughters to succeed their parents in the ministry.

Once the Ōi Church's survival seemed certain, Fukumitsu Sarō was dispatched in 1959 to Ōsaka, where in 1966 he established the Hyōtanyama Church. Only one Kurozumikyō church was left standing in that city after the war, of a previous total of thirteen. There again he set about reviving the followers, this time taking with him his eldest daughter, Mayumi. Thus began a long period of separation for the Fukumitsus, lasting until 1982 as Hiroe remained in Ōi to manage the church there. By the time of Sarō's departure, however, changes were occurring in Okayama that were to affect the church.

SOCIAL CHANGE AND THE ŌI CHURCH

In 1955 the balance of urban and rural populations in Japan tipped in favor of the former. The farms began to be emptied of their sons and daughters as they left the land for salaried jobs in the city. Simultaneously a period of high economic growth began. Since 1955 the population of agricultural areas has decreased steadily as has the proportion of the work force engaged in agriculture.[7]

This nationwide trend also holds true in Okayama, where from 1955 to 1975 the number of persons engaged in agriculture dropped by half, and the population of the prefecture as a whole began to decline. This vast change affects both men and women, and the current trend is that both young men and women are taking salaried jobs and leaving children in the care of grandparents, who live either with the younger couple or nearby.

Large numbers of Okayama women do piecework of various kinds at home, at a rate four times that of the national average. There is also a conspicuous trend for women to seek employment on a day-labor, seasonal, or temporary basis, at a rate double the national average. Although 40 percent of Okayama women are employed (about 3 percent more than the national average), an even greater number is seeking employment but is unable to find it.

These facts all indicate the desire for a greater cash income than can be obtained through agriculture alone. Nowadays the majority of farming families must have at least one income, and increasingly often two adults work at salaried jobs; the proportion of household income deriving from agriculture is on the decline. Whereas formerly workplace and residence were identical, now they are more

---

[7] For thorough discussion of the continuing trend to the decline of agriculture see Robert J. Smith, *Kurusu: The Price of Progress in a Japanese Village, 1951–1975* (Stanford: Stanford University Press, 1978), chap. 3.

141

frequently separated. This intensifies the influence upon young children of those adults who remain at home.[8]

Predictably, these changes in the structure of rural society have affected the Ōi Church. Whereas daily church attendance by those followers seeking prayer and consultation reached a high in 1950 and 1951 of about thirty persons per day and around a hundred on each of the three monthly meetings in the church, this number declined to about twenty per day by 1979. Simultaneously, whereas in the early 1950s the church had thirty-one Laymen's Meetings, this number had by 1980 declined to thirteen. These changes came about as a result of social changes and of the departure of Fukumitsu Sarō for Osaka.[9]

The Church Schedule

The church's schedule calls for meetings on the tenth, twentieth, and thirtieth of each month, dates that take no account of the work week. Thus as more people leave the land for nine-to-five, Monday-through-Saturday jobs, they become unable to adjust their work schedules to that of the church. Also, when Fukumitsu Sarō left for Osaka, Hiroe was unable to attend to all the church's business alone, and the headquarters was too understaffed to dispatch an assistant.

In those days Hiroe had no one to drive her to evening meetings, and it was neither socially acceptable nor safe for a woman alone to pedal ten or twenty kilometers up a mountain road on a bicycle at night to Laymen's Meetings. Thus she was forced to give up those meetings that were held at night, but of course these night meetings were precisely the ones that could not be held in the daytime because their followers were working at salaried jobs. Yet although these setbacks appear quite formidable, when we view them in the light of the larger shifts in population and changes in work patterns, the general impression is of maintenance of the status quo, if not a slight gain.

---

[8] Okayama Keizai kenkyūjo, *Okayama ken no sangyō kōzō* (Okayama: Okayama-ken, 1980), pp. 112–36.

[9] These data were compiled from attendance records at the Ōi Church and interviews with the ministers.

The Women's Group

The Women's Group was the salvation of the Ōi Church. (See Illustration 8.) Once her husband was called to Osaka, Hiroe was left with the care of two young daughters and her father-in-law in addition to full responsibility for managing the church. She was able to manage because the Women's Group went to her aid and relieved her of all duties not directly a part of her ministry. They took charge of the children, planted a garden, came daily to cook and clean the church, and encouraged Hiroe to devote herself entirely to the ministry. Since this represented significant sacrifices on their part, we musk ask why they were so moved by Hiroe.

The women who were of most help to Hiroe at this time did not wait to be interviewed to tell this researcher why they helped Hiroe when she needed them. They say they were drawn to her because of her concern for them and for anyone in trouble. Since she began her ministry at Ōi thirty-odd years ago, Hiroe has taken in nearly fifty women who came to the church in distress. She took in young widows and their children, fed and clothed them out of the little she had for her own faimily, and sent the children to school. She cared for the retarded and the handicapped when relatives deposited them on her doorstep, having them share the same living quarters with her and her chileren. She took in orphans, women who had been discarded by their husbands or families, and women who were poor and had no place to go. In short, any woman in Ōi in any sort of trouble could count on a bed and a share of the meager board at the Ōi Church. Since the women of Ōi had received such kindness at Hiroe's church, they were quick to support her when she needed their help.[10]

Succession

All three Fukumitsu daughters went to seminary and became Kurozumikyō ministers, but eventually it was decided that Katsue, the youngest, would succeed her parents in the leadership of the Ōi Church. (See Illustration 9 and Figure 3.) Katsue was raised in the

---

[10] Many women taken in by the church live now in the vicinity and are some of its strongest supporters.

Figure 3: Kinship Relations of the Ōi Church

Ōi Church

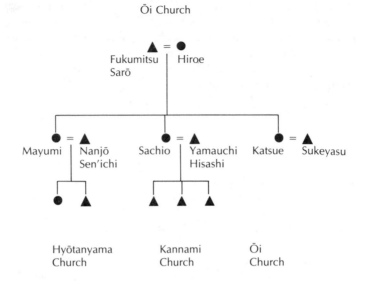

church from birth. Some of the followers cut their ties with Buddhism entirely when her succession was decided. She is responsible in large part for the daily training of the women who were apprentice ministers in residence at Ōi (always one to three are there), and she has certificates to teach them flower arranging, calligraphy, *koto*, the other instuments and dance of Kibigaku, as well as ritual and management of the church's affairs. She performed her first cure as a child, and while still in her twenties, together with her elder sister, she cured a woman who had been unable to walk for years. She is much sought after for consultation by elderly followers as well as younger ones, and she is known as a powerful preacher. At thirty-seven her accomplishments are those of a much older minister.[11]

Katsue and her husband Kōichi met when he was working in Okayama City and worshiping daily at the Ōi Church. Because she

---

[11] This information was compiled through interviews and constant association during June and July 1981.

is three years older than he, and because as the first son he was expected to succeed to the ministry of his father's Daitō Small Church (see chapter four), there was tremendous opposition to their marriage on both sides. In the end they were able to marry, after persevering against parental opposition for six years, only when it was agreed that they would live at the Ōi Church and that Katsue would succeed to its leadership. After several years of marriage, Kōichi was adopted into his wife's family and changed his name to Fukumitsu Sukeyasu. Sukeyasu, because he is younger and because his rank in the ministry is lower than Katsue's, is officially her junior, and his position in the Fukumitsu household is that of an adopted husband.

THE ŌI CHURCH AND RURAL SOCIETY

Rural Followers

The situation at the Ōi Church as of 1983 is that Fukumitsu Sarō has been named Bishop of Kurozumikyō and resides at the headquarters, commuting once a week or so to Ōi. Thus the resident ministers are Vice Chief Minister Fukumitsu Hiroe and her daughter and son-in-law Fukumitsu Katsue and Fukumitsu Sukeyasu. In addition there are always an apprentice minister or two in residence and usually at least one or two women who have come in distress to the church. Women's Group members and other followers are constantly in and out, from 5 A.M. to midnight. The Ōi Church is a pillar of local society, and hamlet residents otherwise unaffiliated as followers regularly drop in to exchange information and to enjoy the friendly atmosphere. There are three male deacons and twenty-five "helpers" (*sewanin* 世話人) who can be called on for help and advice, as well as several men and women who are qualified to assist in ritual when necessary. During fieldwork in 1981, in addition to one apprentice minister, there were two women who had come there in distress and were being counseled by Vice Chief Minister Fukumitsu Hiroe, and two others who resided elsewhere but spent many hours in the church each day. The apprentice minister came to the church in June of 1981 for a stay of indefinite duration. She

145

graduated from the seminary's introductory course (lasting one hundred days) and is considering whether to enter the two-year course as she assists the Ōi ministers in daily and periodic rites and lay activities of the church. Minister Fukumitsu Katsue gives her instruction in sermon delivery.

One young woman in distress in residence married very young and was divorced after having a child and being forced to leave the child in the husband's care. The other, a woman of thirty-three, has been in the church for half a year, whereas the divorced woman has arrived only recently. They both spend most of the day occupied with housecleaning and cooking, also participating in morning worship as well as their own devotions of prayer and doctrinal study. These activities are of their own invention and are not specially required as part of their residence. The divorced woman has resolved to enter the seminary and study for the ministry, a plan strongly supported by the Ōi ministers.

The cooking at the Ōi Church is mainly done by a woman living nearby who arrives around 8 A.M. and returns home around 4 P.M. Years ago Fukumitsu Hiroe helped her through a marital crisis, and ever since then she has come to the church daily to cook, gratis. About forty years old, she is childless and thus can donate her time to the church freely. Every evening around 8 P.M. another unmarried woman in her early forties arrives. She lives across the street with her parents, but for years she has slept at the church, a habit she began when Hiroe was first left alone by her husband's departure for Osaka. At that time she came to help with the cooking and to keep Hiroe company, but even after the need had passed, she continued with the new purpose of advancing her own spiritual development through close contact with the ministers.[12]

About one-third of the most active followers of the Ōi Church are descended from the prewar landlord class, and women outnumber men by a margin of three to one. The average age is sixty, and only one in five households is committed to having Kurozumikyō perform funeral and ancestral rites. Each household con-

---

[12] I collected this information on the women of the inner circle at the Ōi Church through many interviews and informal conversation through living with them daily.

tributes an average of seventy-five dollars in cash annually, but followers living nearby generally supplement this donation with produce and volunteer labor. This is especially true of the Awai followers. All of them live in rural areas and farm small parcels of land. Most live with their married children and in a majority of cases are responsible for part of the care of grandchildren while the parents' work takes them away from home.

The Ōi Church has lists of the dues-paying members, numbering 474 households residing in thirty-one hamlets (those where Fukumitsu Sarō and Hiroe originally opened Laymen's Meetings). Assuming a minimum of four persons per household, there are thus roughly 1,900 followers attached to the church in an official way.[13] This figure, however, does not take account of the more informal ties linking the church to the community.

The Role of the Elderly

The influence of the elderly in Kurozumikyō is considerable, and the great majority of the followers present in the Ōi Church, or any other Kurozumikyō branch church, are in late middle age or old age. This observation, however, is deceiving to some extent and should not be taken to mean either that the followers are too old to be active or that Kurozumikyō is of no concern to anyone but the elderly.

The followers are quite active even into their seventies, and in Kurozumikyō it is assumed that the elderly have more interest in religion than do the young, partly because they have more leisure to pursue it. All concerned are fairly satisfied with the arrangement in which the older generation is given charge of daily observances, on the understanding that the young will take over from them when the time comes. This parallels the notion that women of any age can be entrusted by men with the conduct of the family's religious life. Both notions derive from the tendency to perceive religion as a matter of the household, not of individual commitment.

[13] This information is based on a survey carried out at Awai, Yoshikawa, and Yakane in July 1981, and on a manuscript of Ōi Church records titled "Michizure kaiin meibo" (1976–1980).

The heritage of hereditary temple and shrine affiliation has bequeathed the habit of a household delegating religious affairs to a specified individual, who is usually a woman of its most senior generation. This arrangement is a statement of the intent of the household to maintain an affiliation with Kurozumikyō. The older generation, since it plays such an important part in childrearing now that so many younger women work, has a great influence on the religious education of children. In addition, if daughters-in-law are not employed outside the home, they also come under the influence of Kurozumikyō through their parents-in-law.[14]

RITES AND THE PUBLIC SYMBOLISM OF SELF-CULTIVATION

There are three rites frequently performed by the Ōi Church for rural followers that become means to display publicly the symbolism of purity and purification discussed in chapter one. This symbolism is associated with the goal of achieving sincerity, and these rites are public expressions of self-cultivation, advertisements of the availability in Kurozumikyō of pathways of self-cultivation and guidance along the way.

Grounds Purification

The local residents frequently call upon the church to perform Grounds Purification before any new construction, regardless of whether they hold official membership in the church. The amount of money paid for this service is left to the discretion of the household concerned, but on an average the ministers generally receive about fifty dollars. (See Illustration 10.)

Also performed by Shintō shrines, Grounds Purification is an occasion for Kurozumikyō to appropriate Shintō's prestigious symbolism of purity discussed in chapter one and to extend self-cultivation into the sphere of public, communal rites. Grounds Purification has as its object the purification of new building sites

---

[14] This tendency to leave religion to the elderly women as part of their family role is probably stronger in rural churches such as Ōi than in urban churches.

and the pacification of the earth god (*tochigami* 土地神), widely worshiped in this area. Kurozumikyō Grounds Purification is distinguished from that of Shrine Shintō and Konkōkyō by the greater number of ministers participating (four or five as opposed to one or two) and by the inclusion of Kibigaku.

At the four corners of the site, bamboo poles are set up, topped with *sakaki* 榊 branches (the tree always used as a Shintō offering), and hung with sacred rope (*shimenawa*) of braided straw, thus roping off the area and establishing a sacred space. Inside the enclosure an altar is set up with offerings of fruit, fish, vegetables, dried foods, and sake. After purification of ministers the family undertaking the construction, and a representative of the construction firm with salt water and a large wand (*ōnusa* 大幣) hung with paper streamers, the ministers recite the Great Purification Prayer. Then while all stand with bowed head the presiding minister reads a *norito* announcing the commencement of construction and asking for the god's protection. The presiding minister, one of the family members, and a construction company representative offer *tamagushi* 玉串 (*sakaki* branches decorated with paper streamers) at the altar while the assisting ministers play "Tamagushi" on flute, *hichiriki*, and *shō*.

The minister entrusts the family with a small packet (*shizume-mono* 鎮物) to be buried under the main pillar; the packet contains sand from the Grand Shrine of Ise, a few grains of rice, salt, and bits of paper in seven colors. These are wrapped in a *majinai* paper for protection and placed between two inverted sake cups tied together. Then a mixture of the same items is cast to the four corners of the site, and the bamboo poles are sprinkled with sake. The ceremony ends with the minister's informal congratulations to those assembled. Grounds Purification is unhesitatingly requested by anyone in Ōi or surrounding hamlets. They are most numerous in May and June, when the ministers may perform two or three in a day.[15] This colorful, musical rite makes Kurozumikyō highly visible in local communities and serves as a sort of advertisement of benefits available through affiliation.

---

[15] During June-July 1981, I observed five Grounds Purification ceremonies and interviewed church ministers several times on the fine points of ritual practice.

House Purification

House Purification is another service for which local residents frequently call on the church. Less public than Grounds Purification, House Purification brings the purity symbolism of self-cultivation within a dwelling, into the private realm, into the sphere of the *ie*.

There seems to be a general notion in the area that houses should have a ritual purification every so often, and this is linked to old folk practices of the area. Troupes of masked dancers from the Ise Shrine and dancers representing the Bitchū Kagura 備中神楽, a masked dance declared an Intangible National Treasure, visit area households annually and perform a dance and intone prayers that have as their object the purification of the dwelling.[16] This practice supports the Kurozumikyō practice in which ministers go to a home, recite the Great Purification Prayer, and then say shorter prayers before each altar in the home. This includes in most cases the Buddhist ancestral altar (*butsudan* 仏壇), the Shintō gods' altar (*kamidana* 神棚), and the altar of the kitchen gods (*dokkusama* 土公様). These rites are believed to benefit ancestral spirits in some way, much like regular recitation before the Buddhist altar of sutras by a Buddhist priest. Besides the message that living members of an *ie* require purification, House Purification suggests that Kurozumikyō's rites extend to deceased members, hence superseding the role of Buddhist priests.

Area residents request House Purification after any inauspicious event, such as a fire or even when some previously unknown inauspicious event of the past comes to light. One such case was that of a woman who recently discovered that her grandfather had ill-treated his concubine and had not made proper provision for the care of her spirit after death. The granddaughter, now in her sixties, decided to try to make things right by having Kurozumikyō perform House Purification, particularly before a small altar she had dedicated to the spirit of the concubine.[17]

---

[16] On Bitchū Kagura see Yamane Ken'ichi, *Bitchū Kagura*, Okayama bunko 49 (Okayama: Nihon bunkyō shuppan kabushiki kaisha, n.d.).

[17] House Purification is one of the most common rites performed by ministers. At Ōi I observed it perhaps ten times, June–July 1981.

Mizuko Kuyō

A final example of the services requested of the Ōi Church by nonmembers is services to pacify and console the spirits of the unborn, *mizuko kuyō* 水子供養. (See Illustration 11.) This custom is enjoying a minor boom in contemporary Japan, due to the notion that the easy availability of abortion encourages women to terminate pregnancy, thus preventing the spirits of unborn children from coming into the world. Generally the *mizuko kuyō* ceremony is performed in a Buddhist mode, but it is also carried out in Kurozumikyō churches as well. *Mizuko kuyō* purifies the soul of the unborn, which in abortion or miscarriage was polluted by contact with blood, and is believed to comfort the spirit. The mother is urged to rededicate herself to self-cultivation. The rite confronts the individual with the symbolism of purity and presents the urgency of entering Kurozumikyō's pathways of self-cultivation.

The woman making the request, invariably the one who would have been the mother of the child, comes to the church, and a minister prepares an ancestral tablet (*mitama bashira* 御霊柱) for each aborted or miscarried child, writing a name and approximate date on each slip of white wood. Initially this is placed on a small movable altar adjacent to the ancestral altar of the church. The church's ancestral altar is decorated with particularly colorful flowers and food offerings and with a large red and white paper streamer, representing a symbolic offering of clothes for the child. Before the ancestral altar, the ministers recite the Great Purification Prayer and read a *norito* to console the child's spirit, directing it to enter the ancestral tablet previously prepared. The officiating minister, who has donned a paper mask covering the mouth, and an assistant then move to a temporary altar on which the tablet rests. The officiating minister directs the spirit of the child to enter the tablet as the assistant intones a long "Ooooo" indicating the spirit's passage into the tablet. Then the tablet is removed to the ancestral altar, and all assembled offer *tamagushi* before it while music is played.[18]

In addition to Grounds Purification, House Purification, and

---

[18] I observed this ceremony at the Ōi Church on July 14, 1981.

mizuko kuyō, residents also consult the church about the location and orientation of graves, horoscopy (lucky and unlucky days), and names for their children. They feel free to do so because they know they will not be pressured to join Kurozumikyō, and because the church has the reputation of being reliable in these matters. Thus the Ōi Church has assumed the role of the tutelary shrine of the area and provides local residents with all the services they expect from a shrine, in addition to the counseling, healing, and lay activities that define it as a Kurozumikyō establishment.[19]

BLESSINGS IN THIS LIFE

When asked why they keep coming back to the Ōi Church, the followers report that they have received many blessings, *okage*, through the church and that they return to express gratitude. These blessings take the form of healing, of solving a problem in human relations, or of escaping a disaster. Virtually any adult Kurozumikyō follower can describe numerous larger and smaller blessings received. They are eager to recount these vivid experiences and point to them as proof of the truth of Kurozumikyō's doctrine and the spiritual power of its ministers.[20]

Scholars of the new religions, however, have seen in these blessings the distinguishing mark of the new religions (sometimes of modern religious consciousness as a whole) and have implied that this orientation is superficial by comparison with the "established" religions. Employing such slogans as "Coca-cola consciousness," some have relegated the new religions to the ephemera of mass culture. On this view, an individual comes to one of the new religions when sick or in trouble, receives a cure or advice, and then leaves, terminating the relationship. Since little of this scholarship is based on fieldwork, its authors seldom have had the

---

[19] Horoscopy seems to be performed on a walk-in basis by Fukumitsu Hiroe for anyone in the community who wishes it. It seems to be performed for a nominal offering. The younger ministers express mild disapproval of this practice, saying that human life is not ruled by such fatalistic principles but by the *kokoro*.

[20] Most followers spontaneously report many stories of blessings, *okage banashi* 御陰話, including healing stories.

opportunity to observe the process of reorientation of life set in motion by the cure or counseling. It is also important to distinguish religionists of the *ogamiya* 拝み屋, "occultist," variety from the new religions.

In contemporary Japan the number of *ogamiya* is legion. These are individuals or small groups who practice prayer healing, fortune telling, horoscopy, grave geomancy, palm reading, astrology, and other arts of the occult. They receive clients for a fee and perform a ritual to heal sickness, change or predict fate, divine the future, contact spirits or ancestors and divine their will, or diagnose a family problem as due to a mistaken arrangement of the family plot.

Much as a patient consults a doctor and pays for treatment, an untold number of people consult *ogamiya* on the same "cash on the barrelhead" basis. If they do not care for the result, they are free to go elsewhere, just as a dissatisfied patient may find another doctor. In neither case is the practitioner purveying a comprehensive doctrine or guidelines on how to live. What the client does after the transaction is of no concern to him, and he is entirely uninterested in the ethical or moral dimension of the client's life. This commercial mode of interaction is different from the new religions in general and from Kurozumikyō in particular.[21]

Blessings are the starting point, the "doorway," as the followers express it, to the religious life, which for them is a process of reorientation of life around Kurozumikyō doctrine. That not all go beyond this stage does not alter the fact that the blessing is only a single moment in a longer process in which the ministers support the followers in their attempt to restructure their way of life.

The first stage comes in the form of a problem followers have, sickness or some difficulty in personal relationships, which they bring to the church. The ministers counsel them with advice and sermons. Generally they tell them to pray the Great Purification Prayer as often as possible, to pray at the church daily, and to believe they can return to the original state of joy and happiness. There may be several consultations at this point.

The second stage is entered when clients begin to reorient their

[21] *Ogamiya* establishments are found in virtually any neighborhood of Japanese cities.

life around praying and going to the church. This is the beginning of the change of heart without which blessings cannot be received. It is the ideal of a change of heart that is most crucial in distinguishing the religious consciousness of Kurozumikyō from the *ogamiya* type. In Kurozumikyō, though, the real blessing is this change of heart (*kokoro naoshi*), not the actual benefit received in the form of healing or reconciliation.[22]

The third stage is the blessing: a healing or breakthrough in a personal problem. The fourth stage commences when followers return to the church to express gratitude; this visit is called *orei mairi* 御礼参り. The ministers congratulate them on their faith and encourage them. From the ministers' point of view, the purpose of the entire transaction is to change the heart, to take joy in life, to be thankful, and to develop sincerity. These stages, with variations, are characteristic of the new religions as a whole. This reorientation is the meaning of *kokoro naoshi* and constitutes the major goal of self-cultivation. It can be assumed that self is being brought into harmony with the body, the family, society, and the cosmos through this reorientation. These stages in the reorientation of life can be clarified by a case study of counseling.

The Case of the Abes

The Abes (the name is fictitious) are a family that have been Kurozumikyō *kyōto* since 1833. The members of the family are represented in the following diagram.

The oldest person in this four-generation household is Sanae, mother of Yoshio. She has been a firm believer since childhood, as has her son, who is a mason. His wife Reiko manages a small factory producing women's clothing and employing six persons. Reiko and Yoshio adopted Kazuo as their son because they had no children of their own. Machiko, Kazuo's wife, gave birth to triplets ten years ago.

This pregnancy was the occasion of a consultation at the Ōi

---

[22] Kurozumikyō ministers spontaneously volunteer the idea that *okage* are just the starting point (*omichi no iriguchi* 御道の入口), whereas the real goal is changing the *kokoro*.

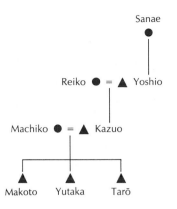

Sanae

Reiko ● = ▲ Yoshio

Machiko ● = ▲ Kazuo

Makoto   Yutaka   Tarō

Church. Reiko and Machiko had been informed that three babies were on the way and were considering whether to abort. Hiroe, however, urged them not to do so, and eventually Machiko had a safe delivery. The birth represented three distinct blessings besides the triplets themselves. First, the fact that the birth was a safe one; second, the birth of three sons assured the family of an heir for the next generation; and third, their births broke the family's long history of having to adopt sons.

Reiko and Machiko paid a visit to the Ōi Church on June 8, 1981, ostensibly for the purpose of having this researcher record the story of the blessing their family received in the birth of the triplets.[23] But just as the interview was completed and tape recorder stowed away, the real story came out. Recently Kazuo had been drinking heavily and staying out nights. Both Hiroe and Katsue began to counsel the two:

HIROE: (to Machiko) How are you two getting along? [no answer]

HIROE: He may be an alcoholic. You should pray for him to be cured.

KATSUE: You should talk things over with him.

REIKO: He won't stop, or if he does, it will only last a week or two.

[23] I was present at all the consultations of the Abes reported hereinafter.

HIROE: Does he have a lover?

MACHIKO: No.

KATSUE: Are you sure?

MACHIKO: I think he doesn't.

KATSUE: Drinking can turn into a bad habit. How is the atmosphere at home?

REIKO: It could be that's the problem.

HIROE: Where does he drink?

REIKO: In his car, sometimes in bars. We don't really know. The doctor told him he's got a liver problem and that he won't get well if he doesn't stop drinking.

HIROE: Have you thought of hospitalizing him?

KATSUE: Don't do that.

MACHIKO: I've heard that there are medicines to stop it.

KATSUE: There must be a problem between you and your husband.

HIROE: (to Machiko) You should ask him what's wrong.

REIKO: If she does, he'll hit her.

HIROE: (to Reiko) Do you give him money to drink?

REIKO: No, there would be no end to it. He skips work, and we don't know where he is.

HIROE: If he is playing around with women, there will be a bad influence on the children. It will be hard to cure him unless he will listen to and heed our sermons. (to Machiko) Get him to come to the church. You've got to pray for him. (to Reiko) Do you fuss at him?

REIKO: No, not unless he's really awful.
The children ask him why he doesn't come home.

HIROE: Don't let the children look down on their father. They have to respect him. (to Reiko) Do you pray for him? [no answer] (to Machiko) How about you?

MACHIKO: No.

HIROE: You have to pray for him to be a good father to his children.

KATSUE: You mustn't will yourself to unhappiness. You should go forward with confidence that the situation will improve. You must have faith. This is a trial sent to test you. Didn't he start drinking outside the home because

156

he felt he couldn't drink at home? Doesn't that mean that
all of you are responsible for this? You've got to return to
the time when you first fell in love, and the way to do
that is worship. Don't just clap your hands before the
altar; really put your heart into it. Look for his good
points. What he really wants is the love of the family.
You have to pray for him to return to his original spirit as
a child of God. Don't just pray for him to stop drinking.
You can't do it without religion.

After this part of the consultation, it came out that Kazuo's real
mother died of uterine cancer and that he had been raised by a very
harsh and unloving stepmother before the Abes adopted him. This
information suggested to the ministers that Kazuo's real problem
was lack of love from an early age. This consultation lasted two
hours and ended with Katsue and Hiroe encouraging the two to
believe that they can bring Kazuo back to his senses, through faith
in Kurozumikyō.

That night Reiko telephoned the church, and Katsue urged her
to pray to God and her ancestors, and to believe Kazuo would
return. The next day Katsue telephoned the family in the morning,
and Reiko announced that Kazuo had been found. The whole
family promised to come to the church in the afternoon. This
second consultation was very different from the first.

At around 4 P.M. Yoshio, Reiko, Kazuo, and Machiko arrived
and sat kneeling before the altar. Katsue seated herself on the
sermon dais and began to speak in a powerful voice. She reminded
them of the love of the Founder for his wife, Iku, speaking in the
formal *sōrōbun* 候文 style,[24] telling them that they, like the Founder, must make the teaching live in their daily lives. After three or
four minutes all were in tears. They must join their hearts together
and come to the church whenever they have a problem.

Next, they all prayed together the Great Purification Prayer, and
then Hiroe ascended the sermon dais. Katsue handed her a scroll of
the Seven Household Principles, which she unfurled and read while

---

[24] This is a formal, semi-classical form of Japanese used in the Founder's lifetime
but not now.

157

everyone else bowed low. After this recitation she addressed them in an especially formal but not *sōrōbun* style, telling them they must all accept a share of the blame for the situation. She gave several examples of followers who had righted derailed relations within the family by faith. The examples gradually became more pointed as Hiroe turned the focus of attention to Kazuo. Suddenly, after perhaps twenty minutes of preaching in this manner, Hiroe shouted at Kazuo, striking her fan on the dais, saying he must become a good father to his children. Still speaking quite loudly, she said to him, "Do you understand?" to which he could only whisper an answer in the affirmative. Hiroe then turned to Machiko, saying that for the children's sake the couple must make up and must pray daily with the children. Both husband and wife must reflect on their past conduct and resolve to make a new start. They must serve their family and work for a better world. Again beating the dais with her fan, she ordered them to apologize to each other, interspersing this command with quotations of the Founder, as all continued to cry.

Gradually her voice softened, and she began to encourage them again, assuring them that they absolutely would recover their original happiness. Just then Fukumitsu Sarō returned, and he, Katsue, and Hiroe began to give *majinai* to the four.

The climax of the scene came when Hiroe joined the hands of Kazuo and Yoshio. Kazuo then threw himself at Yoshio's feet in tears, and everyone apologized to each other, still in floods of tears. The ministers, who were crying as hard as the Abes, began to congratulate them on their breakthrough.

When everyone had regained calm, the Abes were escorted into the living quarters of the ministers where they shared a meal, complete with festival rice, *sekihan* 赤飯, to commemorate the breakthrough, and the Abes went home in high spirits.

There was no further news from the Abes until the eighteenth of June, when Reiko brought flowers to the church as an expression of gratitude and reported that the family's reconciliation was still holding.

Then, on the twenty-fifth, on the way back to the church from an afternoon Laymen's Meeting, Sukeyasu decided quite suddenly to drop in on the Abes. The house was a fright. The triplets were running about while Yoshio was in bed asleep. Reiko and Machiko appeared from the back of the house and broke into tears. Kazuo had had a fight with Yoshio and stormed out of the house. He was arrested for drunken driving, and his license was suspended. To make matters worse, he had become involved with another woman. He threatened to leave home and have the triplets placed in an orphanage. This unnecessary touch of cruelty particularly infuriated Yoshio, especially now that Machiko was pregnant again.

All these remarks were addressed to Katsue, who noted that the torn Kurozumikyō family scroll hanging forlornly in the alcove seemed symbolic of the family's state of mind. They must pray, morning and night, she said, assembling the entire family before the altar, including the children so that all would unite in the purpose of bringing harmony and happiness back to their lives. Then when Kazuo eventually does come home, Machiko must greet him warmly, keeping food, sake, and a hot bath ready for him. At this point the older couple must stay out of the way. On nights when he does not return home, Machiko should place his photo next to her pillow, explaining when he returns that she loves him and is lonely without him. After an hour and a half, the family was considerably encouraged.

On the twenty-eighth a call came to the church from the Abes, reporting that they had reached another reconciliation and resolved to persevere. On the thirtieth, Machiko and Kazuo appeared all smiles and attended the church's monthly meeting together to give thanks for their reconciliation. After the service Katsue took them into the ministers' living quarters and again encouraged them to persevere. They had a meal together, and the young couple stated that this time, for sure, they had reached a lasting understanding. This consultation lasted about three hours.

In all, these consultations spanned a period of three weeks and included perhaps ten hours of intensive counseling over four occasions. In addition, a number of telephone calls to and from the church kept the ministers informed of the current state of affairs in the Abe household.

Redefining the Problem

During the first consultation at the church, Machiko and Reiko presented their problem to Katsue and Hiroe: Kazuo was drinking and staying away from home for days at a time. The ministers asked questions to discover all dimensions of the problem and quickly reformulated it. Whereas Machiko and Reiko wanted a simple prescription to keep Kazuo away from the bottle, the ministers informed them that this understanding of the situation was mistaken. Katsue in particular was adamant that all members in the family must accept a share of the responsibility. In other words, whereas Machiko and Reiko had laid all the blame on Kazuo, Katsue asserted that all concerned had a responsibility for maintaining an atmosphere in the home that would not drive any of its members away. The ministers also told them that they must not think of Kazuo as sick or bad but as a child of God who could be returned to his original state of happiness and joy.

Kurozumikyō's notion of the sort of love that should exist between husband and wife calls for the two to be on an equal footing but with a clear division of labor. The woman is entrusted with the "inside," the *ura*, everything that relates to intrafamilial relations, while the man should manage everything on the "outside," the *omote*, anything concerning the family's relations with the rest of society. While it is accepted that the man will have no share in cooking or cleaning, he has a significant responsibility for rearing the children, as Katsue and Hiroe emphasized by saying that by all means Kazuo must become a good father to his children. While the man is allowed the prerogative of expecting a clean house, a hot meal, and a bath, violence between husband and wife is completely beyond the pale and is not tolerable behavior for any reason. The expression most often used to convey the spirit that should obtain between husband and wife is "mutual reverence," *ogami-ai*, like the worshipful attitude of the Founder for Iku. The husband–wife relation idealized by Kurozumikyō is less hierarchical and the husband's position invested with less authority than is the case in many new religions. Whereas other groups, such as Risshōkōseikai 立正佼正会, an offshoot of Reiyūkai, make a point of preaching male superiority as an item of doctrine, this notion is not found in Kurozumikyō and is generally less prevalent in Shintō-derived groups.

The counseling offered by the Ōi church to the Abes was based on the world view of the new religions. Humanity is originally in harmony with the cosmos. Problems in human relations arise when people depart from this original condition, becoming preoccupied with self. Thus the Abes' problem is one of the whole family becoming preoccupied with self, and to return to their original happiness, they must rise above egotism (*ware o hanare*) and work for the good of the family. To do that, they must adopt a religious conception of marriage as the union of two children of God joined by a spirit of mutual love and respect (*ogami-ai*). Finally, Machiko must act on the basis of her duty and role in the marriage, again rising above self and her own injured feelings, believing it only natural that Kazuo return to his proper role in their marriage, as a responsible husband and father. All of them must find the strength to solve the problem through worship.

The counseling the Abes received through Kurozumikyō is vastly different from that offered by *ogamiya*. First and most obvious, no money changed hands; there was no expectation on either side that the ministers would receive money for their counsel. Second, there was not one but many consultations, some of which were initiated not by the Abes but by the ministers. *Ogamiya*, like physicians, wait for clients to come to them. Third and most important, while the Abes approached the church with a problem of a son/husband who drank too much, the ministers recast this problem in a larger framework and called for a comprehensive solution requiring change not only in the son's behavior but in the religious life of the whole family.

In short, the ministers told the Abes that the blessing they sought (i.e., an end to Kazuo's drinking) was only a part of the real goal: a reorientation of the family's life around Kurozumikyō thought. This approach certainly includes the notion of "this-worldly-benefits," but it is by no means limited to it. The blessings of Kurozumikyō are neither easily gained nor quickly forgotten by the followers. Although in isolation a blessing may appear superficial, when viewed in the context of the prolonged process of counseling by which it is obtained it becomes clear that a comprehensive

161

reorientation of life in accord with a coherent world view is at the heart of the matter. The fact that they are benefited in the process is less an indication of the debasement of tradition than one of the *vitality* of tradition, of its successful appropriation and adaptation in contemporary society. Though this treatment has spoken only to the case of Kurozumikyō, a similar demonstration could be made in the case of other new religions as well.

Seen in this light, it is apparent that the emphasis in the new religions upon "this-worldly-benefits" is a much more complicated phenomenon than has been recognized so far. The seriousness behind this orientation should not be denigrated but should be understood in the context of its applications in contemporary society and of its derivation from the world view of the new religions.

CHAPTER SIX

Space, Time, and
the Human Life

INTRODUCTION

In addition to its doctrine, articulated with clarity in texts and
sermons, another part of Kurozumikyō's distinctiveness within the
world view of the new religions takes an unarticulated form, in
concepts of sacred time, sacred space, and thought on the human
life cycle. Based on its pathways of self-cultivation, Kurozumikyō
establishes different ideals, periodicities, and compartments in the
course of a human life than does secular society. In a consideration
of sacred space, this chapter includes a discussion of Kurozumikyō's
relationship to the Grand Shrines of Ise, with an examination of the
significance for this new religion of maintaining strong ties to the
center of Shrine Shintō. Another sector of Kurozumikyō's spatial
orientation is fixed in relation to the city of Okayama. The annual
"Procession of the Gods" constitutes a symbolic statement of the
group's identity as providing the tutelary shrine of the city and
suppresses its identity as a "new religion." Sacred time is discussed
in terms of Kurozumikyō's annual calendar, which divides the year
in accord with the movement of the sun and moves in an oscillation
among pure, impure, and ordinary states. Ideas of purity are further
examined through a study of funeral ritual. A certain ambivalence
on the question of death pollution supports the idea, introduced in
chapter four, that typologically as well as historically Kurozumikyō stands on the border between old and new in Japanese
religions. Kurozumikyō's thought on the human life span emphasizes patterns of gratitude and the repayment of benefice and the role
of suffering in self-cultivation. These themes are vividly mirrored
in the life history of Fukumitsu Hiroe of the Ōi Church.

Chapter Six

SACRED SPACE

The Founder initiated the custom of making a pilgrimage to the Ise Shrine, and he himself made the trip six times.[1] For Kurozumi, Ise represented the original site of the worship of Amaterasu Ōmikami. During his lifetime, hundreds of thousands were caught up in waves of enthusiasm for Ise pilgrimage, and great numbers passed through the castle-town of Okayama on the way to Ise. In his letters the Founder spoke approvingly of these mass pilgrimages, and after his death, his disciples and successors began taking groups of followers to Ise. The Second Patriarch in particular used Ise pilgrimage as a means of proselytization, carrying out his evangelistic campaign all along the route. Riding the wave of Ise pilgrimage, disciples increased the membership greatly by presenting Kurozumi's teaching as an expression of the faith in Amaterasu Ōmikami.[2]

The Ise Shrines are the main shrines of the Japanese imperial family, who worship Amaterasu Ōmikami as their ancestral deity. The import of this fact for contemporary Kurozumikyō pilgrimage to Ise is not entirely clear. The present Patriarch reverences the emperor and regards him as a living *kami*. His attitude is complex but seems at bottom to express a general conservatism and preference for the mores of the past. It also expresses a wish to create a symbolic connection between a small, rural religious group and the political realm. The deity worshiped is, however, the only real connection between the two.

This attitude resonates with the venerable theme in Japanese religious history of the unity of government and religion, which found its classical expression in early Japan's *ritsuryō* 律令 state. During the eighth and ninth centuries, government was largely conducted through activity we would now think of as "ritual," a union of rites and administration, *saisei itchi* 祭政一致, *matsurigoto* 政.

Although the Patriarch is quite explicit on the subject of the Emperor's divinity, this matter probably is not uppermost in the

---

[1] A fragment of the Founder's diary of one of his own Ise pilgrimages is reproduced in Kurozumi Muneshi, ed., *Kurozumikyō kyōtensho* (Okayama: Kurozumikyō nisshinsha, 1974), pp. 279–82.

[2] On the Second Patriarch's Ise pilgrimage see Kurozumikyō Ōmoto Gakuin, *Seikintoku kenroku* 17 (n.d.): 5–6.

minds of most Kurozumikyō followers on the Ise pilgrimage. They tend instead to regard the pilgrimage as an opportunity to go to the main seat of the deity, Amaterasu Ōmikami. At Ise they can worship deity in an old, beautiful, solemn shrine that they know has existed since long before the founding of their religion. To go to Ise is to place oneself at the site of origin of all worship of Amaterasu Ōmikani. Thus Ise is proof to followers that their Founder's religion was not "merely" his personal invention but sprang from a deeper, more ancient well. The fact of a common worship in Kurozumikyō and at Ise demonstrates in a new way the purity of the teaching of Kurozumikyō.

Not being historians, followers are little interested in the vicissitudes of Shintō history. They neither know nor care to be told about those eras in which imperial rites at Ise fell into desuetude and empty coffers precluded the rebuilding of the shrines at twenty-year intervals.[3] Followers look upon Ise as the source of Japanese culture and as an unmoving center defining the pure and timeless in a period of rapid and pervasive change. Going to Ise, they reaffirm what they regard as the unchanging, always-relevant teachings of their Founder, symbolically expressed in Ise. Viewed from a slightly different perspective, the fact that a Kurozumikyō follower may go to Ise shows again that the Founder's teaching stands like a rock in a sea of change. The pilgrim has in Kurozumikyō an unbreakable bond to an unchanging source of purity, order, and goodness.

Presently Kurozumikyō makes large donations to the Ise Shrines for annual and occasional pilgrimages. These contributions entitle the Patriarch to be allowed inside the palisade beyond which ordinary worshipers may not pass. The Patriarch leads groups of a thousand followers on a pilgrimage to Ise several times a year, and occasionally groups as large as ten thousand make the trip. Pilgrims no longer proselytize along the route, but participation is considered an important part of membership.

At Ise Kurozumikyō pilgrims approach the shrines by the same route as any worshiper or group. They bear flags with the Kurozumikyō seal and smaller banners inscribed with the name of their

---

[3] On this dark period of Shintō history see Ono Sokyō, *Jinja Shintō no kiso chishiki to kiso mondai*, pp. 702ff.

165

branch church. Unlike secular pilgrims, they touch no alcohol from beginning to end. The approved attire is a dark suit for men, formal kimono or a black dress for women. Approaching Inner and Outer shrines, the group chants the Great Purification Prayer, and they may be lectured by the Patriarch on the significance of Ise.

Although the movement of the Ise pilgrimage is from the periphery to the center, other observances show a movement of Ise symbolism from the center outward. In the new headquarters, Shintōzan, two pillars from Ise were used in the main worship hall. These pillars were obtained on the occasion of the rebuilding of the Ise shrines. Thus a bit of Ise has been built into the symbolic center of Kurozumikyō. Of a different order is the practice of including a few grains of sand from Ise in the *shizumemono* used in Grounds Purification (described in chapter five). Placed between two shallow sake cups tied together to form a shell-shaped packet, the Ise sand is then buried beneath the central pillar of followers' houses. This symbolic act deposits a portion of Ise at the center of the dwelling, orienting the inhabitants and all their activities toward Ise, through the mediation of Kurozumikyō.

Kurozumikyō stands in the role of mediating a member's relation to Ise. Providing these mediating services creates one of the obligations of followers to the group. Thus Ise is an important element in the relation between Kurozumikyō and its followers.

Kurozumikyō's relation to Ise usefully illustrates a parameter dividing the new and the old in Japanese religions. We may imagine a spectrum, one end defined by a shrine that is a branch of one of the venerable and nationally important shrines such as Kasuga, Fushimi Inari 伏見稲荷, Izumo, and so forth. At the other end of the spectrum would be a religious group, the paradigmatic "new religion," that acknowledges no sacred center save those of its own creation. The branch shrine has as part of its *raison d'etre* the channeling of monies and believers to the main shrine. This role is performed by hundreds of branch shrines of those named above.[4] Ōmotokyō and Tenrikyō serve as good examples of new religions that have established their own sacred centers and pay no special veneration to Ise or other shrines. One could illustrate a similar

---

[4] On the origins and classification of branch shrines see ibid., pp. 86–110.

spectrum on the Buddhist side. For example, there are more than ten thousand branch temples of Nishi 西 and Higashi Honganji 東本願寺 of the Jōdo Shinshū 浄土真宗 School, and each sends contributions and pilgrims to the head temple.[5] At the other end of the spectrum are groups like Reiyūkai and Risshōkōseikai, which have broken entirely with established Buddhism and ignore its sacred centers.

Along such a spectrum as this, Kurozumikyō is located toward the middle. On the one hand, it maintains its own headquarters as a pilgrimage site and can function quite independently in this regard. On the other hand, however, it continues to accord Ise a priority above its own headquarters as a sacred center. Its Patriarch likes to assert that Kurozumikyō is a branch of Shintō, with Ise standing at its head. There is, however, no reciprocal, organizational arrangement imbuing the Patriarch's vision with reality, and it is doubtful whether the Ise Shrines are eager to accept from the new religions tokens of respect other than money. Kurozumikyō, however, continues to send its pilgrims to Ise and thus to acknowledge Ise as the primordial center of the cult of Amaterasu Ōmikami.

Whereas observances related to Ise situate Kurozumikyō in relation to the national mythology embodied in Ise, the rite called *Jinkō* 神幸, "Procession of the Gods," carried out in March, establishes a relation to the city of Okayama. The role defined by the ritual is that of the city's tutelary shrine. Kurozumikyō's focus here is on Kurozumikyō the sponsor of the Munetada Jinja rather than on Kurozumikyō the new religion.[6]

The Procession of the Gods is a festival in which the mirrors representing Amaterasu Ōmikami and the deified spirit of the Founder are paraded in palanquins in solemn procession from the Munetada Jinja through the streets of Okayama to the Okayama castle and back. The palanquins are accompanied by the Patriarch and officials of Kurozumikyō, and by the Head Priest of the Munetada Jinja, installed in that office by Kurozumikyō. All wear priestly vestments and ride in *rikshas* or on horseback. If a boy of about twelve

[5] On the origins and classification of branch temples see Kuroda Toshio, *Jisha seiryoku*, Iwanami shinsho 117 (Tokyo: Iwanami shoten, 1980), chap. 5.
[6] See chapter two herein on the establishment of the Munetada Jinja.

can be found among the sons of the Patriarch or officials, he also rides a horse near the head of the procession and is made up with cosmetics in the Heian style as a *chigo* 稚児, or divine child. The palanquins are shouldered by male ministers in white robes, long-tailed black hats, and black, wooden Chinese shoes. Behind them comes a group of ministers to draw up the rear. Since the Procession of the Gods has become a major annual observance of Okayama City, the route of march is lined with spectators, and most of them have no formal relation to Kurozumikyō. When the procession returns to the Munetada Jinja, Kibigaku dances are performed to honor the deities. These dances are attended by the Okayama citizenry, and none of the observances contain any specific mention of Kurozumikyō. Instead, they are patterned on the rites of a large tutelary shrine and seek to define the Munetada Jinja as such.

The significance of the Procession of the Gods is largely contained in the fact that Kurozumikyō is never mentioned by name. In treating the observance exactly as the festival of an ordinary shrine, Kurozumikyō seeks to define itself as the city's protector, thus assuming the tutelary function associated with Shrine Shintō.

Any Shintō shrine large enough to be attended by a priest and sufficiently vital to command a group of parishioners holds at least one annual festival.[7] Of the many forms these festivals (*matsuri* 祭) may take, among the most common is the *shinkōsai* or *jinkōsai* 神幸祭, in which the shrine's object of worship (*shintai*) is transferred to a portable shrine (*mikoshi* 御輿) or palanquin and paraded through the territory over which the deity presides and which it is believed to protect spiritually. The general name for such tutelary gods is *ujigami*, and the people living in the *ujigami's* territory are its "children," *ujiko*. Thus residence in the area under the deity's aegis automatically makes one a parishioner. Being a parishioner of a local shrine is not a matter of personal belief. Instead, living within the *ujigami's* territory means one receives divine protection, and therefore one has an obligation to support the shrine and its ob-

[7] On *matsuri* and their several forms see Ono Sokyō, *Shinto, The Kami Way* (Rutland, Vt.: Charles E. Tuttle, 1962), pp. 63–71.

servances as a parishioner.[8] This entire scheme of ideas is communicated in Kurozumikyō's Procession of the Gods, more powerfully for the fact that Kurozumikyō the new religion is never mentioned.

Kurozumikyō's presentation of itself in the Procession of the Gods takes a form recognizable by anyone as a *jinkō* type of *matsuri*. Unless informed that the rite is sponsored by a new religion, the average person coming upon the *Jinkō* unawares would simply assume it to be purely a shrine festival. Of course this result is not unintended. The *Jinkō* is a self-conscious assertion that in a certain sense Kurozumikyō is *not* "new." That is, Kurozumikyō is concerned to avoid those connotations of the idea of a new thing that suggest novelty, eccentricity, or adulteration of something more pure and original. It does not seek to be "new" in that sense. Instead, it uses the Procession of the Gods to equate itself with the original, the unadulterated, the unchanging, and the pure

It is not accidental that the Procession leads to the Okayama Castle. The castle was the seat of government during the Founder's lifetime, and symbolically it represents secular rule even now. Joining the castle and the Munetada Jinja creates a sense that the shrine is the spiritual protector of the city, just as the castle protects its civic order. Thus the conjunction of the two constitutes a symbolic assertion of the unity of religion and government. That Kurozumikyō should revive this ancient theme both with respect to Ise and with respect to Okayama City shows how it symbolically puts itself on a par with secular authority as a peer and counterpart in the spiritual realm.[9]

Finally, the Procession of the Gods embodies a message for the

[8] On the Shintō parish system see Gorai Shigeru et al., eds., *Minzoku shūkyō to shakai*, vol. 5 of their *Kōza Nihon no minzoku shūkyō*, 7 vols. (Tokyo: Kōbundō, 1980), chap. 2.

[9] The idea of a perfect union between religion and government has been identified as one of the most important themes in Japanese religious history. It has been formulated in a Buddhist idiom as well as in Shintō terms and has been prominent from the eighth-century mythic chronicles to the present-day Buddhist group Sōka Gakkai 創価学会. Thus in no way is Kurozumikyō eccentric in idealizing the combination of sacred and civil rule. See Byron Earhart, *Japanese Religion: Unity and Diversity*, 3d ed., Religious Life of Man series (Belmont, Calif.: Wadsworth Publishing Co., 1982), p. 16 and passim.

169

people of Okayama. By defining the Munetada Jinja as the tutelary shrine of the city, the citizenry are automatically defined as parishioners. That is, the symbolic role defined for the shrine carries the implication that those living within its territory receive its protection and thus are obligated in some unspecified way. This notion of obligation is never spelled out, and Kurozumikyō does not push the point beyond the symbolic import of the rite itself. Kurozumikyō, however, takes pride in this tutelary function, and the Procession gives it a status locally that it would not enjoy in its capacity as a new religion.

SACRED TIME

Kurozumikyō maintains an annual calendar of festivals (see below), and of these the two most important are those held on the solstices. Their basic significance is marking the extremes of the solar year: its longest and shortest days. In addition, both are occasions to renew purity and reaffirm group membership. The winter solstice was the day on which the Founder experienced the Direct Receipt of the Heavenly Mission, and now Kurozumikyō remembers that occasion as well as celebrating the movement of the sun. The summer solstice coincides with that time of year when festivals to exorcise vermin and disease were traditionally performed.[10]

Annual Calendar of Kurozumikyō Ritual

New Years   *January 1–3*
Setsubun   *February*
Procession of the Gods   *March*
Great Purification Festival   *Mid-summer*
Tōji Taisai   *Winter Solstice*

The winter solstice, or *tōji*, has a long history in Chinese and Japanese religions stemming from its significance as the point from which the days become longer and the sun's rays stronger. Put

---

[10] On folk rites of expulsion of vermin see Ōtsuka minzoku gakkai, ed., *Nihon minzoku jiten* (Tokyo: Kōbundō, 1975), p. 720.

another way, *tōji* marks the time from which *yang* begins to rise, dominating *yin*. Starting with the winter solstice, the sun's vital essence, *yōki*, starts to increase. The summer solstice is the mirror image of *tōji*. It is the point from which the days begin to shorten, when *yin* starts to overshadow *yang*, and the sun's strength weakens. Both are occasions for purification.[11]

At the summer solstice rituals Kurozumikyō assembles symbols and rites of purification. A large circle of reeds (*kaya* 茅), called a *chinowa* 茅輪, is constructed in the gateway of each branch church, and followers step through this to purify themselves, following a folk custom found widely in Japan. They write their names and year of birth on paper dolls, in a space left after the printed phrase, "The pollution of ————." These dolls, called *hitogata* 人形, are hung on a large branch of bamboo and buried or set adrift in water at the conclusion of the ceremony. After communal recitation of the Great Purification Prayer, followers are handed a single reed of *kaya*, and with this they ceremonially brush from their bodies the pollution (*kegare*) accumulated during the past half year.[12] (See Illustration 12.)

Purity and Pollution

The observances at summer and winter solstices show how Kurozumikyō defines the passage of the year as an oscillation between *hare* はれ (the state of intense purity represented by periodic ritual) and *ke* け (the ordinary state between *hare* and the polluted state of *kegare*). Kurozumikyō's appropriation of these concepts is not unique, because notions of pollution and purity are central to all Japanese religious traditions.[13] Kurozumikyō's use of

[11] On the history of rites on the winter solstice in China and Japan see Suzuki Tōzō, *Nihon nenjū gyōji jiten* (Tokyo: Kadokawa shoten, 1977), pp. 641–42.

[12] Rites utilizing *hitogata* and *kaya* are widespread in Japan. See Ōtsuka minzoku gakkai, *Nihon minzoku jiten*, p. 597. See also Suzuki Tōzō, *Nihon nenjū gyōji jiten*, pp. 470–72.

[13] Namihira Emiko, "Nihon minkan shinkō to sono kōzō," *Minzokugaku kenkyū* 38, nos. 3 and 4 (December 1974): 230–56. Namihira delineates a model of varying relations among *hare*, *ke*, and *kegare* that allows us to see how they are emphasized differently in various rites. Whereas *ke* is the realm of the profane, both *hare* and *kegare* can, depending upon the ritual context, become sacred.

this complex of ideas, however, is distinctive. Kurozumikyō combines notions of *hare* and *ke* with natural symbolism inherent in reeds used in the rites and the focus upon the sun. Defining time as the movement between *hare* and *ke*, Kurozumikyō's temporal orientation is quite different from that of secular society, which is attuned most immediately to the seven-day week and then to the calendar of annual national holidays. Kurozumikyō does not proscribe these time periods, but neither does it alter its own rhythms to accommodate them.[14]

Kurozumikyō's most distinctive feature with respect to traditional notions of purity lies in its concept of pollution: *kegare*. No Japanese religious tradition has a more acute sensitivity to pollution than Shintō.[15] Although a Shintō form of funeral rite exists, Buddhism has for the most part been entrusted with these rites to prevent the pollution of death from contacting the *kami*. In addition to death (the greatest source of pollution), menstruation, childbirth, and sexual intercourse have also been regarded as pollution, leading to requirements that priests officiating in shrine ritual undergo a period of abstinence before serving the gods. Pollution notions have also restricted women from officiating in shrine rites.[16] In Kurozumikyō, however, most such ideas have been reinterpreted in line with the world view's assertion of the primacy of self-cultivation.

In Kurozumikyō neither death nor menstruation, childbirth, or sexual intercourse is considered a source of *kegare*. There are no

[14] In *Kami no minzokushi* (Tokyo: Iwanami shoten, 1979), Miyata Noboru shows how in traditional folk conception rites of passage make of the life cycle an alteration among *hare*, *ke*, and *kegare*. See pp. 160ff.

[15] On Shintō's classification of pollutions see Ono Sokyō, *Jinja Shintō*, pp. 312–19. To emphasize Shintō's preoccupation with purity and pollution is not to say, however, that Japanese Buddhism is unconcerned with pollution. Quite the contrary—Japanese Buddhist clerics have produced voluminous writings on the pollution of women. See Kasahara Kazuo, *Nyonin ōjō shisō no keifu* (Tokyo: Yoshikawa kōbunkan, 1975).

[16] For a useful compendium of pollution notions, see Miyata, *Kami no minzokushi*. Miyata's study shows how concepts of death pollution were radically changed in early Japanese history through Buddhist influence (pp. 79ff.). Pollution concepts attached to menstruation are treated in several sections. See especially pp. 60ff. and 80–95.

requirements of abstinence before rites, and female ministers may perform rites during menstruation and as soon after childbirth as they like.[17] Ministers who have conducted funerals are not required to undergo purification. Kurozumikyō does not deny the existence of *kegare*, but it does deny that *kegare* originates in physical, material existence. Instead, it holds that *kegare* originates in the withering or atrophy of *ki*, the vital essence pervading the human being and uniting it with divinity: *kegare wa ki ga kareru koto desu* 穢 は気が枯れる事です. "*Kegare* is the withering of *ki*." Thus the way to remain in a state of purity is to maintain *yōki*, optimism and joy in harmony with deity.[18]

Funeral Ritual

This understanding of purity and pollution is given symbolic expression in Kurozumikyō funerals. During my field work, I observed a large-scale funeral and subsequent memorial rites for a family of Okayama followers named Mizote. The grandmother of the family, Mizote Miki, died at eighty-eight on June 9, 1981.

Prior to 1945, the Mizote family was one of the largest landholders in the area immediately adjacent to Okayama City. The family house stands at the top of a range of precipitous mountains, commanding a view of a long valley terraced from top to bottom. On the night of the wake and main funeral rite, the fifty or so persons in attendance were composed of about thirty members of the main and branch Mizote families and about twenty others who remained outside the house. (See Illustration 13.) These latter persons were former tenants of the Mizote family under the prewar landholding system and their descendants. They came to help with funeral preparations and to assist in the odd jobs inevitably involved in a large gathering. Although no explicit rule dictated their attendance, their evident willingness to assist at the funeral and subsequent rites testifies to the strength of bonds between former

---

[17] On traditional taboos surrounding pregnancy and childbirth see Takenaka Shinjō, *Nihon no tabū* (Tokyo: Kōdansha, 1971), pp. 136ff.

[18] In denying that *kegare* is an inevitable accompaniment of human life, Kurozumikyō is significantly different from folk conceptions as outlined by Namihira, Miyata, and others. It is also radically different from the established religions.

tenant and landlord in Kurozumikyō, though these were officially dissolved forty years ago.

Funeral ritual in Kurozumikyō has four phases. Following preparation of food offerings and their arrangement on two altars comes the most important act: transferring the soul of the deceased to an ancestral tablet. Then comes recitation of the Great Purification Prayer before the tablet, and finally all offer a *tamagushi* before the altar. Food offerings are identical to those fruit and vegetable offerings presented at any Kurozumikyō ritual. For its funeral rites Kurozumikyō utilizes a red and white paper streamer, indicating that the occasion is to be regarded as joyous. The rationale for this attitude is that the dead are believed to become one of the myriad *kami: yaoyorozu no kami no hitohashira* 八百万神の一柱. The larger altar houses the red and white paper wand, and a picture of the deceased and the ancestral tablet are placed on the smaller. The wooden tablet (*mitama bashira*) is hollow and contains a slip of white wood, upon which is written the posthumous name (*mitama gō* 霊号). The name is composed by the presiding minister, and the form differs slightly according to age and sex. Once placed inside the pillar, the whole is wrapped with white paper and set upon the smaller altar. Funeral *norito* are read, but unlike *norito* performed on other occasions, the claps (*kashiwade*) preceding and following funeral *norito* must not make any sound. To the accompaniment of music on the *hichiriki*, the lights are extinguished, and the two presiding ministers don white masks and carry the *mitama bashira* to the adjoining room where the body is laid out in a coffin. After several minutes of prayer, a long, drawn-out "Oooo," uttered by the minister holding the tablet, signals the movement of the spirit of the deceased from her body into the tablet. Still in total darkness, the tablet is carried back to the main room, and the lights are lit. Following this transfer of the soul, those assembled recite the Great Purification Prayer and offer *tamagushi* in the order of degree of kinship relation to the deceased, beginning with her son and his wife.

In the ritual I observed the ministers eulogized the dead woman in a short speech and congratulated those assembled on their ancestor's certain achievement of a high seat in heaven. They spoke of the occasion as auspicious (*arigatai*) and greeted the bereaved with congratulations: *Omedetō gozaimasu* お目出度うございます. In this and by the symbolism of the rite, they denied that death is pollution or a defeat of *kokoro*. Instead, they regard death almost as a victory of *kokoro*, which begins a new existence in heaven. In this denial of the pollution of death, Kurozumikyō distinguishes itself from Shrine Shintō, which for the most part finds death a form of pollution.

When directly questioned, ministers do not deny the existence of hell, but generally they assume that everyone becomes a *kami* after death. The major distinction is between high and not-so-high places in heaven, *Takama no hara* 高天原, the "High Fields of Heaven." Mizote Miki, for example, lived to a ripe old age as a devout follower, and she had a reputation for virtue. Thus she can be expected to achieve a high place (*takama no hara no takai tokoro* 高天原の高い所). There is little speculation in Kurozumikyō upon the causes for achieving a higher or lower place, nor is there any clear sense that more benefit or advantage accrues to a high place. When someone dies, there is little comment on the person's probable fate, since everyone assumes it will be good unless there is very strong reason for doubt.

Kurozumikyō affirms the idea of ancestors and makes provisions for ancestral tablets to be enshrined in branch churches. Some followers who elect to keep the tablets at home regard the performance of House Purification as beneficial to ancestral spirits. Memorial services are performed ten, twenty, and one hundred days after the death, and at each of the five-year intervals after death until the fiftieth. After that time the ancestor is believed to be so firmly established in the world of the *kami* that it becomes indistinguishable from the general collectivity. This final transition is called *kami-agari* 神上り, becoming a *kami*. At each of the memorial services, as many relatives as possible assemble to recite the Great Purification Prayer, offer *tamagushi* on an altar of food for the deceased, and have a communal meal. Kurozumikyō ministers officiate at the memorial services by reading auspicious *norito* proclaiming that the dead has become a *kami* and is grateful for the continuing regard of family members. Kurozumikyō followers

175

practice cremation, and they make graves at Buddhist temple grounds, or on privately owned land, or in public cemeteries. Some followers have a portion of the ashes interred in a special mound-covered crypt on Shintōzan.

In the process of a Japanese new religion attaining independence from an older tradition, funerals and memorial services are always an obstacle. Because of the long period in which these functions were nearly universally performed by Buddhist temples, breaking out of this mold is difficult. In previous chapters we have seen how hereditary temple affiliations remain so strong in rural areas that followers are prevented from having funerals performed by Kurozumikyō. They could do so much more readily if in Kurozumikyō there were provisions for graves either at the branch churches or at the headquarters. The purchase of a large tract of land at Shintōzan makes this possible, and the Patriarch's advisers have urged him to create a cemetery there. He resists, however, and says that such a move would turn Kurozumikyō into an undertaking business. Although a cemetery would surely attract badly needed revenue, it would also become a major preoccupation, requiring hiring and training new staff, acquiring special licenses, and achieving a consensus of the administration on the proper allocation of land and other resources. Finally, creating a cemetery on Shintōzan would establish a continuous contiguity between death and the deities enshrined there. Cemeteries on the lands of Shintō new religions are not unheard of; Ōmotokyō, for example, has one. Given the origins of so many ministers in shrine priests' families, however, there would probably be considerable resistance within the ranks.

In fact, although Kurozumikyō requires no special purification of ministers after a funeral, many have assistants purify them with *nusa* 幣 and salt water while they stand at the church door with a *sakaki* leaf between their lips. At the end of the purification, they rip the leaf in two, throwing half over their left shoulder. Younger ministers dislike this sort of practice, and there is considerable discussion about whether to abolish it. Thus the preoccupations of Shrine Shintō have not disappeared from Kurozumikyō. This ambivalence about death pollution constitutes a hindrance to the group's complete self-sufficiency and illustrates the way it stands with a foot in both old and new religious patterns.

THE LIFE CYCLE

A major component of Kurozumikyō's orientation is provided by
its thinking on the course of human life, how things tend to happen
from cradle to grave. Its thinking is not entirely independent, nor is
it unrelated to other sources of ideas on the subject. For example,
Kurozumikyō ministers dislike television and define their own
ideals, at least in part, in contrast to media portrayals. To formulate
their own images of the life worth emulating, Kurozumikyō ministers draw upon the Founder's life and upon events in their own
lives. The life histories of revered ministers are made known to
followers in a number of ways.

In general, popular culture evaluates success in life and to a
certain extent the moral worth of a person in terms of achievements
in the workplace and in the family.[19] Early education is regarded as
playing a determining role, and thus parents are justified in exact-
ing great sacrifices from themselves and their children to achieve
academic success. The trials the child faces are to be overcome
through an exercise of the will and the help of supportive parents.[20]
Religious faith plays no significant role. For the most part television
avoids any portrayal of religious sentiment other than occasional,
ecumenical scenes of the elderly praying before domestic altars for
the Buddhas and ancestors, the *butsudan* 仏壇, or of the *kami*, the
kamidana 神棚.

When Kurozumikyō searches for an exemplary life, it looks first
to the Founder. Besides the personal qualities of faith and filial
piety, followers identify the deciding factor in the Founder's experience as his suffering in youth. As a young man, his parent's deaths
caused him great suffering, and sickness nearly took his life. Ministers and followers alike believe that suffering and hardship experienced in youth strengthen character and serve as preparation
for the tests of maturity. As discussed in chapter one, this pattern of
action, thought, and emotion is common to the world view of the

[19] George DeVos, *Socialization for Achievement* (Berkeley: University of California Press, 1973), part 2.

[20] Harumi Befu, *Japan, An Anthropological Introduction* (San Francisco: Chandler
Publishing Co., 1971), pp. 143–49.

new religions. Only suffering gives strength and the ability to endure. Further, a person who has never experienced hardship remains forever immature and lacks mercy and compassion. With no depth of insight into human experience, his accomplishments will be few and shallow.

Thus Kurozumikyō looks to those who have suffered to produce real and lasting achievements. The pattern of life they most admire is found in those ministers known as *ikimono sensei* 活物先生, "charismatic teachers." One present-day charismatic teacher is the Vice Chief Minister of the Ōi Church, Fukumitsu Hiroe. During my fieldwork, I asked her to write her life story, and she consented. In this work we can see how an *ikimono sensei* views her own life and interprets her past. This work is a remarkable document that presents the optimistic ethos of Kurozumikyō clearly and illustrates the ideal of rejecting self-pity and refusing to think of oneself as victimized.

From Sorrow Comes Joy

I was born on the thirtieth of July 1915, daughter of the seventeenth-generation head priest of the Kameishi Hachiman Shrine, located in western Okayama Prefecture, in Kawakami County. Until I was seven and my brother was twelve, I was raised with loving care by my parents, but suddenly my father fell ill, and all my mother's nursing was in vain. He died, leaving the three of us behind. After that, my mother struggled hard to make a living and raise her two children, but was it that she was exhausted by the strain? As if to follow my father, she left this world two years later. Having lost both our parents, my brother and I were separated, one taken to our aunt's house and the other to our uncle's.

As the saying goes, "When a child loses his parents, life changes drastically." Everything changed completely from what life had been before, and I, with a child's heart, was lonesome, sad, and afraid. All the proverbs about parents are true: "Their light illumines the universe"; "An orphaned child cries the tears of a thousand cranes on a desolate beach"; "No mother in ten million can surpass one's own." Truly, there is no greater blessing than parents; they are the hearts of God.

My brother and I endured unimaginable hardship, and we were

lucky to live until today. I believe that the reason we were able to endure is that the souls of our parents who had served God, were always inside us as well, and thus no matter what the hardship, we were not broken, nor were we warped, nor were we bowed low; whatever the trial, we found courage to fight against hardship.

My student days were especially painful. All my friends received allowances from their parents and were able to study without wanting for anything. But for me, it was impossible to live on the pittance my uncle sent me, so I scrimped on food, or worked at odd jobs. As for my study time, I practiced writing characters on the steamy window of the bath, I ciphered numbers in the toilet, and my only place to study was in the bus or train.

One day I finally collapsed of exhaustion and was carried to a sickbed. When I awoke, and the doctor told me I was suffering from malnutrition, I felt keenly how such a thing would never have happened if only I had had money, and the blessing and precious value of money really came home to me.

Another time my body felt weighed down and heavy; feverish and in pain, I was examined by a doctor and told that I was having an attack of pleurisy, and that I absolutely *must* rest. Hearing that, I prayed constantly to God, saying, "If there is any use for me in this world, let me live, but if there is not, then let me die now." Praying desperately, I performed cold water austerities to find out the truth.

About a month later, both body and spirit seemed to be recovering, and when I was examined by a doctor, I had recovered completely. My illness had vanished like the melting snows. I felt deeply grateful to God and humble for the great blessing I had received.

I hoped that the next year would pass quickly. The dates I wrote in the corner of each page of my notebook seemed to go by in a blur, though the six years to graduation seemed very far away. But even in my painful student days, "Time passed like an arrow of light and shadow," and the days and months flowed by like a dream until finally I received my diploma, with joy and tears, and a feeling of victory surpassing all description filled my heart with delight.

After that I was finally an adult and able to take my place in society enthusiastically. I went to work as a clerk in a large company, and then at the year's end I took the position of Instructor in

Sewing at the Seika Women's Technical School. Four years later I had a proposal of marriage from a priest of a Shingon 真言 temple, and we married. I was blessed with a son, but this happiness vanished in an instant as my husband died of illness. My husband's elder sister had no children, and when she asked for my son to raise as her own, I pondered long and hard, but for the sake of the child's future and in sympathy with my sister-in-law and her husband, I gave up my child. It pained me as if blood would run, and I cried out to God. Not a day passed that I haven't thought of my beloved child as if my heart would break. Within half a year he died of diptheria. Thus my pain at leaving him was redoubled.

After that I returned home, but I couldn't stand being dependent on my brother and his wife, so finally I made up my mind to return to the Youth School (*seinen gakkō* 青年学校) and devote myself exclusively to education. While I was working there, I had a proposal from my present husband,[21] and we married on October 10, 1943 at the Asabara Great Church.

Previously my husband had been married to the eldest daughter of the Chief Minister of the Asabara Great Church, and they had two sons. The older boy, however, had died, and then the remaining son had been left motherless at the age of four. When my husband came to me, leading the little boy by the hand, and we married, that was the beginning of a happy time, although we were poor.

When World War II was at its height, in March of 1944 my husband was drafted to supervise the women's dormitory of the Mizushima Armaments Factory. I returned to live with my husband's father and younger sister. There I opened a school for the study of sewing, flower arrangement, cooking, etiquette, and spiritual training as the days of living apart from my husband flowed by.

Then in 1949, out of the blue came a messenger from the headquarters and the Ōi Church. The church had rapidly gone downhill, and now like a lamp before the wind the doors were

---

[21] Fukumitsu Sarō, already a minister of Kurozumikyō at that time, serving in the Asabara Great Church [of Kurozumikyō]. He is presently Bishop of the entire Church.

about to be shut. The messengers asked us, for the sake of Kurozu-mikyō and for the sake of this fine church our forebears had built, to end our twenty years' training[22] at Asabara and take over the Ōi Church. We took this as a great mission and felt we must respond to the sincerity of this call, now issued repeatedly, which seemed to be a path beckoning us. Thus, as if in a war we were departing for the front, on January 25, 1949 we took over the Ōi Church, taking with us our seven-year-old son, our five-year-old eldest daughter, our second daughter of three, and our third daughter of one.

When we stepped inside the door, the sight awaiting us was a rude shock. The walls were falling down, the sliding doors were broken and torn. The *tatami* 畳 had almost all been taken up. For a time we just stood there looking at this place that no one could imagine a human being inhabiting. Shards of broken cups were rolling about on the floor, and there were only two dirty, smelly blankets.

Just to look at it, it seemed a hopeless task to try to revive such a church, and for a moment I was at a loss to think what a trial it would be. But when I looked back on my childhood, I thought to myself that it couldn't be as bad as all that. Just the fact that the church existed at all was a precious thing, and I realized that it would be wrong to complain or to be dissatisfied. Instead, as husband and wife we should look upon it with joy and courage, as an opportunity for service and spiritual training. With that thought in mind, I firmly resolved to set myself to the task.

At the end of the war, however, food was still rationed, and we had to make sacrifices in order to make ends meet for our growing children. We had a terrible time paying their school fees. But as it says in our Founder's teaching, "Work with sincerity. Those who exert themselves sincerely will neither be defeated nor be in want. They will have no difficulties." I strongly believed these words, and I also put my trust in the proverb that says that "The wind brings more than enough flying leaves to burn." So I decided to leave it up to nature, believing that if you devote yourself wholeheartedly to your work, nothing can defeat sincerity. Thus I put all of myself into my work.

In the midst of all this, there was much to be grateful for. Many

---

[22] That is, the husband had been in residence at Asabara for a total of twenty years.

works of God appeared, and the number of people who received blessings increased day by day. Many came daily to the church, and it began to recover its former stature. Soon there were so many followers that not all could enter the church at the same time. We had to hold all our ceremonies twice, morning and evening, so that everyone could come and receive a great blessing. Otherwise they could not all be seated at one time. As the Founder's poem goes, "Swords, arrows, fire, and water are powerless in the face of sincerity."

Another saying holds, however, that as soon as one trouble is banished, another appears. Our eldest son,[23] who had grown up healthy since the age of four, became critically ill. We took him to the hospital and did everything humanly possible. I nursed him myself, but medicine proved useless. He died at the age of seventeen, clutching to his chest the certificate showing that he had passed an examination qualifying him to enter the Prefectural High School. His last words were to thank us quietly as he closed his eyes as if in sleep.

The sorrow of the loss of my son can be compared to nothing else in human life. It was harder to bear than anything. I cried and grieved myself into a stupor. I had no sense of whether it was breakfast or lunch that appeared on the table.

After that we received the order from headquarters that my husband was to take up a post at the Osaka Great Church. He left his aged father, three children, and me behind. On October 12, 1959, he took up his post in Osaka. He also had to bear the loneliness of being without a family for the sake of Kurozumikyō and the sake of our mission. He gave himself over entirely to the Church.

I wondered what I should do to show my sincerity toward my husband, and I decided that the first thing would be to pray for his health, for his well-being, and for the success of the Church. It was in this spirit that I began cold water austerities. I have continued daily without a break for twenty-three years. Thanks be to God, my husband and family have been healthy and have had no problems in life. It is truly due to God's virtue that they have been able to

[23] The son of Fukumitsu Sarō and his first wife.

work vigorously every day. I am deeply filled with gratitude to God when I think of our good fortune.

At first I was quite at a loss when all the rites of our church fell to me: Laymen's Meetings, House Purification, Memorial Services, weddings, funerals, and Grounds Purification ceremonies. At first I consulted my husband by letter and telephone, even asking someone else to teach me when necessary. By now finally I am able to carry on by myself, and every day is so very busy that I feel only gratitude and humility for being able to work without any great difficulty.

Later my husband opened the Hyōtanyama Church,[24] and on May 8, 1966 we held the church's Founding Celebration. Although the church is a small one, it was built with the contributions of each and every sincere follower. The gathering of these pure and sincere followers was truly a precious moment for us. Now the Hyōtanyama Church is led by my eldest daughter and her husband, following after her father, and they are working with joy and gladness.

In March of 1974 my husband received the order from headquarters that he was to become Bishop. Now he begins each day at Shintōzan with worship of the sun. This will be his final spiritual training, and he is blessed daily and filled with gratitude and humility.

Having finished their schooling, my three daughters all attended the Kurozumikyō seminary at the headquarters, where they learned the most profound parts of the teaching. Now each is married and has been assigned to a church, at Ōi, on Awajishima, and in Osaka. Now they devote themselves to proselytization for the betterment of humanity and the world in the service of God. I cannot imagine a more joyous peak of achievement.

As for myself, when I look back on the past and think of how I suffered in childhood, I am reminded of the proverb that says, "The

---

[24] This church, described in chapter four, began as a group of followers living in the Hyōtanyama section of Osaka who were originally attached to the Osaka Great Church after the war, when ten of the eleven Kurozumikyō churches in that city were destroyed. They were able to form their own church in Hyōtanyama with Fukumitsu Sarō as its Chief Minister.

suffering of youth is more precious than gold." That is, I realize that all the times I truly suffered have become like precious jewels to me. Now they are a source of joy.

I may occupy only a humble position in the Church, but I feel grateful to those who tried and tempered me in youth. There were times when my trials were like storms and swords, when my suffering was more than I could endure, and at times my heart rose in anger and hatred. But all of this pain made my spirit stronger, more courageous and brave, more able to endure. Those who made me suffer trained my spirit in mercy and gratitude. To those who made me suffer I owe more than I can repay, and when I think of my debt to them, I am filled with the spirit of repentance and gratitude. Looking back, my life has been like that of the nameless grasses along the roadside.

"Even trodden upon, the roadside
grasses grow strong.
Finally the spring comes, and they will bloom.
Torn by storms, frozen in snow,
Only later to attain the height of a pine."

And as our Founder has taught, "From sorrow comes joy."

For me, now is the time when the flower has bloomed; now every day is joyful. Every day is full of thanks to the teaching, thanks for the grace of God, and gratitude to the ancestors.

This autobiographical sketch offers important insights into Kurozumikyō's ethos. As a summary of sixty-seven years, it is of course selective in its emphasis and interprets the past with an eye toward the contribution of any single event to the present. Its overall theme is the transformation of suffering to joy, and of the importance of past hardship for present and future happiness. It identifies religious faith as that quality that enables one to overcome adversity.

A strong sense of mission decrees that there is no division of time into the separate spheres of work and leisure seen in popular culture. Neither is there any strong distinction between being "on duty" and "off duty." Whereas popular culture generally makes a strong distinction between "work" and "home," these are identical in this account. Neither do we find the "work-versus-marriage" dichotomy in force. Finally, whereas popular culture usually makes "motherhood" and "career" opposing alternatives, in this account the two are continuous rather than alternative choices.

This autobiography exemplifies self-cultivation through the pattern of gratitude and repayment of benefice. It represents a recasting of personal history in terms of this pattern. Characters such as the stingy foster parents become benefactors to whom one must express gratitude. Although in other conversations Hiroe described her mother-in-law Moto Sensei as having never missed a chance to humiliate Hiroe, this figure has dropped out of the story entirely. In shaping personal history to conform to the pattern of gratitude, suffering is transformed through the flow of gratitude that allows the individual to extend self to the service of others.

Kurozumikyō's orientations toward the progress of life and its internal compartments are made known to followers in several ways. First, ministers frequently describe events from their own lives when they counsel followers. This is a means of showing how a strategy for solving a problem grows out of a more comprehensive orientation. At the Ōi Church Hiroe's life story has several times been dramatized by members of the Women's Group for the instruction and entertainment of church followers. Presenting their own orientations by these means, Kurozumikyō ministers watch television infrequently and say they dislike the portrayals they see there. What they seem to object to most is television's tendency to glorify morbid obsessions with onself and other people under the banners of profundity or passion. This tendency Kurozumikyō finds vacuous in the extreme and detrimental to emotional health and spiritual development.

CONCLUSION

This chapter has portrayed the orientation of Kurozumikyō through its conceptions of space, time, and the human life cycle. Although doctrine provides a self-conscious, intellectual framework of ideas, these orientations are unarticulated, a tacit frame of reference seldom subjected to direct inquiry or examination. Few elements are unique, since they draw on folk religion, Shrine

Shintō, and prewar social mores, but their combination is distinctive. The new religions share Kurozumikyō's evaluation of suffering, and this idea is also present in the established religions.

Examination of Kurozumikyō revealed several areas in which the group seems to adopt the identity of an established religion rather than a new one, orienting itself to the sacred center of Ise and acting as the tutelary shrine of Okayama City. Its maintenance of two shrines in addition to the branch churches allows it to act in this way. Establishing the Munetada Jinja early in its history was an important element in the survival of Kurozumikyō under Tokugawa and Meiji religious law, and this shrine was the original headquarters of the group. The shrine marks the recognition granted Kurozumikyō by the Yoshida house and confers upon it an authority that is different from new religions not so recognized. This allows it to assume tutelary functions like Shrine Shintō. Continuing this pattern, and thus crossing the line between new and established religions, is to Kurozumikyō's benefit in linking it to a fount of religious truth and a pattern of mediating between followers and a sacred center of an antiquity far outdistancing the Founder of the group.

Kurozumikyō's spatial orientation toward Ise takes several forms. Ise pilgrimage serves to vouchsafe the purity and truth of Kurozumikyō teaching, and the centrality of Ise is given symbolic expression within a family dwelling through the Grounds Purification rite. In taking a subordinate role toward Ise, the leadership of Kurozumikyō acts as a mediator between its followers and this ancient shrine while continuing the Founder's self-understanding of his teaching as simply a new enunciation of truth that finds its symbolic center at Ise. This "understanding", however, is one-sided, inasmuch as the Ise hierarchy does not acknowledge the relationship. While with regard to Ise Kurozumikyō regards itself as a branch of an "old" religion, its partner regards it as a "new" one. Similarly, the identity of Kurozumikyō as a new religion is suppressed in the Procession of the Gods. Reviving the theme of the unity of religion and government, Kurozumikyō symbolically proclaims itself the spiritual peer of Okayama's secular rule and in the process names itself the tutelary shrine of the city and the citizens its parishioners.

The temporal orientation of Kurozumikyō focuses upon solar movement as central to the division of the year. Since the sun is the symbol of divinity, this orientation amounts to an attempt—in a temporal mode—to maintain congruence and harmony with Amaterasu Ōmikami. The festivals of the solstices are times of special purity; establishing them as the major punctuations of the year underlines the centrality of Amaterasu Ōmikami. Time itself becomes an oscillation between *hare* and *ke*. *Kegare*, the third partner, receives a novel interpretation. Death is not *kegare*, and *kegare* is a matter of *kokoro*, not a question of external cleanliness. The denial of traditional pollution notions is a hallmark of the new religions, but ambivalence in Kurozumikyō on this point shows its continuing dependence on the world view of Shrine Shintō.

With respect to its views on the life cycle, Kurozumikyō values suffering above all else as the *sine qua non* in building character, and it sees in suffering a potential for transformation to joy, through the mediation of faith and cultivation of *kokoro*. It regards a sense of mission as central to adult life and considers this an all-embracing orientation, requiring none of the further compartmentalization seen in popular culture.

Concepts of space, time, and the human life in Kurozumikyō orient members' thought and action in a general, pervasive way. These concepts constitute important sectors of a world view. It is probable that not all members share this orientation equally, and that few are guided by it alone. Nor does it seem likely that all are immersed in it all the time. Making allowances for these qualifications, however, does not invalidate the composite as a general frame of reference and orientation. This characteristic orientation, no less than doctrine, is part of the distinctive quality of Kurozumikyō and definitive of its place within Japanese society. Upon the contemporary religious scene it typifies the world view of the new religions yet also illustrates the tensions that exist in the practical application of that world view, showing how both new and old can coexist side by side.

The Unity of
The New Religions

The new religions grew out of the world view that emerged as a general religious orientation late in the Tokugawa period. Kurozumi Munetada clothed this world view in the garb of a henotheism and breathed life into it through intense religious experience. He communicated his doctrine and demonstrated his power through meetings for preaching and healing. Only when he left the Imamura Shrine and delegated power to his ministers was his teaching perceived as a "new religion." Lack of organizational connection to the established religions as required by contemporary law was the source of this perception more than ritual or doctrinal elements.

A consideration of contemporary Kurozumikyō's preaching and healing shows that modern ministers have altered their Founder's teaching in order to draw from it what they see as a timeless creed. Central to the group's present orientation is a spirit of activism and individual ethical responsibility. When these qualities are seen in terms of the world view of the new religions, they serve as keys to the interpretation of many features of organization that characterize the new religions as a whole.

This study has identified a vitalist, spiritualist world view as the most fundamental factor unifying the new religions. Whereas prior studies have recognized a rather standardized list of traits as shared by a number of the new religions, this study has tried to show how those traits are unified in originating from a particular conceptualization of self in relation to other levels of existence coupled with regular patterns of thought, action, and emotion. The kingpin of the system is the idea that the self-cultivation of the individual determines destiny. The religious life consists of such cultivation and of repaying the benefice of deity. Textual erudition, esoteric ritual, and the observance of abstinences will not serve as a basis for elevating the religious status of priests above that of the laity. The laity therefore tend to be central. Since individual self-cultivation is the primary determiner of all affairs, fatalistic notions and ideas of pollution must be recast. Unhindered (or less hindered) by notions of pollution, women play key roles. Because all problems can be traced to insufficient cultivation of the self, one cannot expect fundamental social change to occur through political action. Similarly, attempting to cure disease through medical therapies alone can produce only a shallow healing.

The code of ethics seen in Kurozumikyō is not solely its own invention but is generally shared by both new and established religions. It rests on principles of family solidarity, authority of elders, and a clear-cut division of labor between the sexes. We have seen that when Kurozumikyō ministers counsel followers on family problems, they begin by relating events from the Founder's life that stress his love for his wife, and they urge troubled family members to renew the love among themselves. Problems in the family are to be solved through each member reaffirming the core values and uniting in Kurozumikyō worship. Where these strategies succeed in alleviating followers' problems, the fact that goals, roles, and lines of authority are so clear-cut reduces doubt and self-questioning, enabling action to proceed unhindered.

This family-centered ethic is found in established Buddhism and Shrine Shintō, and no new religion denies it. Some in fact go much further than Kurozumikyō to articulate it plainly and to implement it with a vengeance. The main difference in the familistic ethic between the established religions and the new lies in the sustained attention, systematic socialization, and organizational support available to the follower in the new religions. Specifically, counseling helps followers implement the world view's patterns of thought, action, and emotion, and rewards them for doing so.

The question why this world view of the new religions arose as a pervasive orientation at the end of the Tokugawa period is beyond the scope of this study, but its strength since that time is quite remarkable. In large part the new religions themselves are responsible for its propagation. In addition, however, it harmonized well with social institutions and mores prevalent before 1945. The autobiographical sketch presented in chapter six, for example, clearly drew upon the mores of the early twentieth century. The family system as codified in the Meiji Civil Code of 1898 embodied a familistic ethic closely resembling that of the new religions. No doubt these religions were greatly supported by the promulgation of this ethic by the pre-1945 educational system. Even when compulsory education dropped morality courses (*shūshin kyōiku* 修身教育) from the curriculum, the new religions continued to preach much the same content, shorn of chauvinistic rhetoric about the divinity of the emperor and the sacrality of the Japanese nation. As in Kurozumikyō, fragments of that rhetoric remain in other groups as well, no longer integrated into a larger vision.

In all the new religions, persons over about fifty years of age occupy most positions of leadership, and the consequences of this fact are weighty. These individuals were educated under the prewar system, and they have received as part of their primary education a view of the family as a microcosm of the nation, of its roles as pervaded with a sacred character, paralleling a view of Japan as a divine nation. They tend to see the family in terms of the *ie* rather than in terms of the nuclear family, and to regard its organizational principles as sharing the quality of sacredness. Thus it is not simply efficient or proprietous to obey elders, for women to defer to men, or to maintain clear role distinctions between men and women. It is sacred; failure to uphold these principles is immoral and worthy of censure.

The new religions continue to think of the *ie* as the model for family relations. That is, the idea of a corporate body passed from generation to generation, engaged in a common means of subsistence, its eternality symbolically manifest in the cult of ancestors, continues to be the conceptual norm. The importance placed on perpetuating the *ie* produces a widespread concern for issues related to it. Although aware of the prevalence of the nuclear family, the new religions often deplore its spread and see in it no corresponding ethic. They find romantic attachment a poor basis for contracting a marriage and tend to favor arranged marriages, though this tendency is by no means absolute. Ancestor worship, in a variety of forms, expresses the desire to perpetuate the *ie* and is typically a major practice, though Kurozumikyō is somewhat exceptional in this regard. Filial children are considered the most reliable form of old age insurance, and a desire to have several children beyond the statistical norm of two is pervasive.

In Kurozumikyō the family is central not only in ethics but in the maintenance of the whole organization. The followers are now composed largely of families who have been members for generations. Many families can trace their affiliations back a century or more and take pride in this antiquity. Conversion is almost entirely limited to urban areas. The ministry as well is in effect limited to descendants of ministers through the policy of refusing seminary admission to others. The primacy of hereditary affiliation in recruitment conflicts with the principle of individual commitment, otherwise generally given precedence.

In the case of other new religions, routinization might account for a shift from conversion to hereditary affiliation in recruitment. As Max Weber pointed out, there is a tendency for practices begun on the basis of individual commitment to become formalized and to be performed instead through institutional prescription. At the same time it proselytized for converts, from the beginning of its history, Kurozumikyō has also recruited by households. Using the conversion of local landlords and village headmen as a springboard to enrolling all the households in their charge, Kurozumikyō used both principles at once. Nevertheless, the fact that little proselytization is to be seen now in rural Kurozumikyō suggests a tendency to adopt the practices of the established religions in recruitment. This tendency, which also represents the path of least resistance, is accurately described by the term "routinization."

The idea of women and men as hierarchical categories with men in the dominant position is only clumsily grasped by a phrase like "subordination of women." The many roles of women are essential to the new religions. Examination of Kurozumikyō has provided a wealth of examples, and in other groups as well, women's counseling and healing contribute greatly to the vitality of religious groups. There is a pervasive sense that women are somehow closer to the spiritual world, often based on the intuition that their "lot" is harder. Enduring greater suffering, they have a special depth of character, their cultivation of self is very deep. Widespread among women of the new religions is a paradox of rhetoric to the effect that women's place is in the home combined with conspicuously active roles outside the home via religious activity.

A rural group like Kurozumikyō assumes that women work. Work per se is not the issue. Women should build up their husbands and not put themselves ahead of men, especially in public. Where work is concerned, the crux of the matter is the notion that a woman's cash income should not be greater than her husband's, because that would be a blow to his ego, which it is a woman's job to support. Whether the family or the religious group, men should represent the collective to the "outside" (*omote*) while women are active on the "inside" (*ura*). As long as this "inside-outside" distinction is honored and the hierarchical principle affirmed, there is no objection to women taking active roles. This is why women are so active as counselors and healers but less often fill positions in administrative hierarchy, except where the perceived predilection for religious experience has propelled them into the positions of founders. For women as for many men, the new religions offer cherished avenues to prestige and recognition seldom open to them in secular society.

Large corporations in Japan typically screen prospective employees to eliminate members of the new religions. There is an inherent conflict between these two types of organizations, based upon a paradoxical similarity. The company at its largest and most elaborate seeks to accommodate nearly every need of its employees until the time of retirement, with a corresponding claim upon their loyalties and to a lesser extent, those of their families. Thus individuals already committed to a creed and to an organization over which the company has no control are suspect and probably unable to commit themselves to the extent of someone who has no such commitment. But it is necessary to recall that only a small proportion of the work force is employed by large corporations. The new religions provide ladders of prestige and reward for achievement, and this is a potent source of their appeal. Promotion in rank within the group is a factor of little significance in Kurozumikyō, but in larger groups, members are able to advance in rank through proselytization and doctrinal study. Much as a man rises through the ranks in a company, members of the new religions can win reward and recognition that might well be beyond their reach in secular society. Since secular success so often depends heavily upon education and personal connections, persons lacking these may find themselves barred from many opportunities.

Most conspicuous is the case of women. Restricted for the most part to the least interesting and least remunerative forms of employment, women frequently find in the new religions an extremely satisfying avenue of prestige and an outlet for talent and energy. Since there are fewer pollution restrictions to limit their participation than in established religions, women participate in great numbers and with remarkable energy. For many members the new religions provide means to achieve prestige and recognition that parallel those available to men employed by large corporations.

The attitude of the new religions toward politics is complex. On the one hand, the world view decrees a distrust for political action aimed at producing social change. For example, the student movement of the 1960s was greatly disapproved. Combined with the feeling that no problem would have arisen if all concerned had been cultivating *kokoro* was a disapproval of youth daring to criticize their elders. It is not the case, however, that the new religions entirely eschew political activity. In smaller groups, chapters canvas for slates of local candidates with emphasis on electing members of the religious group. Although this activity varies widely and has never been systematically studied, the tendency to vote in blocks is conspicuous. In 1964 the Buddhist group Sōka Gakkai 創価学会 founded the political party Kōmeitō 公明党, which now holds the third largest number of seats in the Diet; since 1980 other Buddhist groups have created political bureaus. Often these activities serve to rationalize campaign contributions, as well as to give these organizations a way to present their views on a variety of legal and political questions affecting the operation of religious organizations. So far, these activities have been carried out without widespread change in the general political conservatism of the membership.

Many groups were suppressed before 1945 or were pressured to promulgate government ideology and on this basis deplore any involvement of the state in religion. Thus with a few major exceptions, they do not favor granting official status to the Yasukuni

193

Shrine 靖国神社, previously the national shrine of the war dead. The Yasukuni question is the focus of a number of issues regarding the separation of church and state, and in general the new religions firmly uphold this principle. On the other hand, as this study showed in the case of Kurozumikyō, the ideal of perfect union between religion and government, the *matsurigoto* or *saisei itchi* theme, has an enduring appeal. There is a tendency to accept the ancient idea that religion has a role to play in "protecting the state" in spite of the view, virtually unanimous since 1945, that one of religion's most important responsibilities is to work for world peace. Demonstrated in groups uniting to fund such assemblies as the World Council on Religion and Peace and the publication of numerous works on peace-related themes, the commitment to peace is absolute and may come to provide an alternative to centuries of *matsurigoto* and "religion as protector of the state." How this stance will bear upon issues of national defense is not yet clear. Although most new religions would undoubtedly oppose repeal of Article Nine of the Constitution renouncing war, they have not yet taken a position within the rapidly changing constellation of views on other issues of defense and rearmament. When they do, however, the power of their influence will be weighty indeed.

Throughout this study we have seen that Kurozumikyō's world view entails a "this-worldly" orientation, and that benefits in this life are attained only after rigorous cultivation of self. This implies that the sarcasm with which the notion of "this-worldly-benefits" is so often employed is misplaced and requires considerable qualification. Most important, the many benefits named must be understood in the context of the world view, as natural consequences of being in harmony with the ground of being or a proper relation of reciprocity with deity. They are not simply gratuitous advertisements to lure the unwary. On this point we may generalize widely from insights gained through a study of Kurozumikyō.

If it is the case that all the new religions can be traced to the world view outlined in chapter one, why is there such variety in their doctrines, and what determines whether a group flourishes or not? Doctrine clearly depends upon a founder's religious experience, which in turn is partly a product of previous religious activity and orientation. Needless to say, the content of revelation is not altogether predictable. In a sense, creed becomes recognizable and familiar if the world view is present. In the same way that worshipers at temples and shrines are often unaware of and uninterested in the identity of the supernaturals enshrined there, in the new religions the precise identity of the pantheon is less important than the general orientation.

Numerous organizational factors guarantee the vitality of a group as well as its doctrine, but among those revealed by this study of Kurozumikyō the following are central. There must be a transition from an initial period when the group functions mainly as a healing cult or *ogamiya* to the adoption of the world view of the new religions and the consequent interpretation of healing as one outcome of a more pervasive orientation. Further, interlocking ties among followers, between followers and local chapters, and between followers and the headquarters must be created, as the case material comparing Kurozumikyō's performance and Konkōkyō's in chapter five suggested. Finally, this study has shown that failure to utilize the talents of women fully results in drastic consequences for the vitality of local churches.

This study has tried to describe the world view that binds the new religions together. The world view of the new religions has a coherence and stuctural unity that cannot be reduced to a random collection of traits. Its characteristic conceptualzation of the relation of self to the body, to the social order, and to the cosmos is linked to cultural patterns of thought, action, and emotion that are given heightened significance and that are systematically taught to members. Rewarded by these organizations for consistent implementation of the world view, members become motivated to teach the world view of the new religions to other people, perpetuating both their organizations and the world view itself. Given the strength of appeal of a world view that can incorporate between one-fourth and one-third of the entire Japanese population, the appearance of the Japanese new religions is a major development of Japanese religious history.

The Great Purification Prayer

This appendix presents the Great Purification Prayer, *Ōharai Norito*, as it is used in Kurozumikyō. This translation is adapted from Donald Philippi, *Norito*, The Institute for Japanese Culture and Classics Tokyo: Kokugakuin University, 1959), pp. 45–49.

> By the command of the Sovereign Ancestral Gods and
>   Goddesses,
> Who divinely remain in the High Heavenly Plain,
> The eight myriad deities were convoked in a divine
>   convocation,
> Consulted in divine consultation,
> And spoke these words of entrusting:
> "Our Sovereign Grandchild is to rule
> The Land of the Plentiful Reed Plains of the Fresh Ears of
>   Grain
> Tranquilly as a peaceful land."
> Having thus entrusted the land,
> They inquired with a divine inquiry
> Of the unruly deities in the land,
> And expelled them with a divine expulsion;
> They silenced to the last leaf
> The rocks and stumps of the trees,
> That had been able to speak,
> And caused him to descend from the heavens,
> Leaving the heavenly rock-seat,
> And pushing with an awesome pushing
> Through the myriad layers of heavenly clouds—
> Thus they entrusted [the land to him].
> The lands of the four quarters thus entrusted,
> Great Yamato, the Land of the Sun-Seen-on-High,
> Was pacified and made a peaceful land;
> The palace posts were firmly planted in the bedrock below,

The cross-beams soaring high toward the High Heavenly
    Plains,
And the noble palace of the Sovereign Grandchild constructed,
Where, as a heavenly shelter, as a sun-shelter, he dwells hidden,
And rules [the kingdom] tranquilly as a peaceful land.
The various sins perpetrated and committed
By the heavenly ever-increasing people to come into existence
In this land that he is to rule tranquilly as a peaceful land:
First, the heavenly sins,
The earthly sins.
When they thus appear,
By the heavenly shrine usage,
Let the tops and bottoms of heavenly narrow pieces of wood
Be cut off
And place them in abundance on a thousand tables;
And let the bottoms and tops be cut off the heavenly sedge
    reeds,
and cut them into myriad strips;
And let the solemn ritual words of the heavenly ritual be
    pronounced.
When they are thus pronounced,
The heavenly deities will push open the heavenly rock door,
And pushing with an awesome pushing
Through the myriad layers of heavenly clouds,
Will hear and receive [these words].
Then the earthly deities will climb up
To the summits of the high mountains and to the summits of
    the low mountains,
And pushing aside the mists of the high mountains and the
mists of the low mountains,
Will hear and receive [these words].
When they thus hear and receive,
Then, beginning with the court of the Sovereign Grandchild,
In the lands of the four quarters under the heavens,
Each and every sin will be gone.
As the gusty wind blows apart the myriad layers of heavenly
    clouds;
As the morning mist, the evening mist is blown away by the

morning wind, the evening wind;
As the large ship anchored in the spacious port is untied
at the prow and untied at the stern
And pushed out into the great ocean;
As the luxuriant clump of trees on yonder [hill]
Is cut way at the base with a tempered sickle, a sharp sickle—
As a result of the exorcism and the purification,
There will be no sins left.
They will be taken into the great ocean
By the goddess called Se-ori-tu-hime,
Who dwells in the rapids of the rapid-running rivers
Which fall surging perpendicular
From the summits of the high mountains and the summits
of the low mountains.
When she thus takes them,
They will be swallowed with a gulp
By the goddess called Haya-aki-tu-hime,
Who dwells in the wild brine, the myriad currents of the brine,
In the myriad meeting-place of the brine of the many briny
    currents.
When she thus swallows them with a gulp,
The deity called Ibuki-do-nusi,
Who dwells in the Ibuki-do,
Will blow them away with his breath to the land of Hades,
the underworld.
When he thus blows them away,
The deity called Haya-sasura-hime,
Who dwells in the land of Hades, the underworld,
Will wander off with them and lose them.
When she thus loses them,
In the four quarters under the heavens,
Beginning from today,
Each and every sin will be gone.
Cleanse and purify!
Cleanse and purify!

Glossary

This glossary is intended for the reader's ready reference. It does not attempt to present a full explanation of terms or to explain how these terms are used outside Kurozumikyō. Some expressions are colloquialisms.

Amaterasu Ōmikami　天照大御神　Also called Tenshō Daijin 天照大神, Tenshōkōdaijin 天照皇大神. The supreme deity of Kurozumikyō, with whom humanity is originally one and undivided. The head of the Yamato pantheon in Shintō mythology.

Arigatai　有難い　A grateful attitude.

Bunshin　分神　See *wake-mitama*.

Dokkusama　土公様　The kitchen gods revered in Okayama.

Gaman　我慢　Perserverance.

Gūji　宮司　Chief Priest of a Shintō Shrine.

Harae　祓　Purification; a prayer for purification.

Hare　はれ　Purity of body and spirit. See chapter six.

Hichiriki　篳篥　A double-reed instrument about six inches long; used in *Kibigaku*.

Hitogata　人形　A paper doll representing the pollution of an individual.

Ie　家　The traditional family system of Japan; the joint-stem family.

Ikidōshi　生通し　"Living through"; incipient doctrine of immortality.

Ikimono sensei　活物先生　Charismatic minister.

Jichinsai　地鎮祭　Grounds Purification; see chapter five.

Jinkō　神幸　Procession of the Gods; a Kurozumikyō festival held in March; see chapter six.

Kagura　神楽　Sacred dance for the *kami*.

Kaguraoka Munetada Jinja　神楽岡宗忠神社　A Kyoto shrine founded in 1858 to worship the spirit of the Founder and (later) the High Disciple Akagi Tadaharu; see chapter four.

Kagyō　家業　The hereditary occupation of a household.

Kaijitsu　会日　The meeting days scheduled for a branch church.

Kami　神　The deities of Shintō; also, the quality of divinity, the numinous.

Kamidana　神棚　The altar to the *kami*, a small altar for domestic use.

Kashiwade　拍手　Two claps made before an altar of the *kami*.

Kaya　茅　Reeds used in the Great Purification Festival.

Ke　け　Ordinary state between extreme purity and pollution.

Kegare　穢　Pollution of body or spirit; see chapter six.

Ki　気　Vital breath or essence; a vitalistic principle believed to underlie all existence.

Kibigaku　吉備楽　Music and dance developed by Kishimoto Yoshihide for Kurozumikyō; see chapter four.

Kinen　祈念　Prayer performed by a minister at a follower's request; may include *majinai* and counseling.

Kō　講
　Kōshaku　講釈　Confraternity; small groups meeting for sermons, healing, and fellowship in Kurozumikyō. Commonly called "Tenshinkō."

Kokoro　心　The heart; heart-mind. A faculty of intellection, moral judgment, and emotion. In Kurozumikyō the *kokoro* of humanity is originally one with the *kokoro* of deity.

Konkōkyō　金光教　A new religion founded in 1858 in Okayama by Kawate Bunjirō.

Kōseki　講席　Confraternity; more specifically, the place where the confraternity meets.

Kōtei　高弟　The High Disciples of the Founder; see chapter two.

Majinai　禁厭　A rite to strengthen the spirit by infusing it with *yōki* used in healing. See chapters two and three.

Makoto　誠　Sincerity; single-minded devotion and faith.

Matsuri　祭　A festival observance for the *kami*.

Matsurigoto　政　Ideal of the unification of religion and state.

Michizure　道連　General name for Kurozumikyō followers.

Mitama-bashira　御霊柱　An unpainted, hollow, wooden pillar

into which slips of wood inscribed with posthumous names
are inserted. Kurozumikyō's ancestral tablet.

Mitama-gō 御霊号 Posthumous name inscribed upon the
ancestral tablet.

Mizuko kuyō 水子供養 Ritual to pacify the spirits of aborted
or stillborn babies.

Munetada Jinja 宗忠神社 A shrine that was the former headquarters of Kurozumikyō. See chapter six.

Nikku 日公 Register of followers' names read before the altar
daily by ministers.

Nippai 日拝 Daily worship of the sun.

Nissan 日参 The practice of daily visits to a Kurozumikyō
church.

Norito 祝詞 Prayer; formal prayer offered by a minister before
the altar to deity.

Nusa, Ōnusa 幣, 大幣 A wand of paper streamers used for
purification.

Ōbarai taisai 大祓大祭 Great Purification Festival held on or
near the summer solstice; see chapter six.

Ogamiya 拝み屋 A person practicing palmistry, fortune telling, and other minor arts of the occult; see chapter five.

Ōharai norito 大祓祝詞 Great Purification Prayer; see Appendix A.

Okage お陰 Blessings or favor from deity.

Okage mairi お陰参り "Thanks pilgrimage" made to the Ise
Shrines during the Tokugawa period.

Omote 表 The "outside," the public domain.

Orei mairi お礼参り A visit of thanksgiving to a Kurozumikyō
church.

Sakaki 榊 An evergreen tree, the branches of which are used in
Shintō ritual.

Senmai 洗米 Holy rice distributed in small paper packets.

Sewanin 世話人 A "helper" at a Kurozumikyō church; generally an older man whose family has been affiliated with the
church for several generations.

Shimenawa 標縄 Sacred rope hung to demarcate a sacred space.

Shintai 神体 A symbol of deity; in Kurozumikyō, a mirror
representing deity.

Shintōzan　神道山　The headquarters of Kurozumikyō.

Shizumemono　鎮物　Packet of sand from Ise, salt, and seven-colored paper cuttings that is buried beneath the main pillar of a new building at the Grounds Purification rite.

Shō　笙　A mouth organ of vertical pipes used in *Kibigaku*.

Shōya　庄屋　Village headmen during the Tokugawa period.

Sōdai　総代　A "deacon" in Kurozumikyō; a senior man qualified to assist in ritual.

Takama no hara; Takama ga hara　高天原　Heaven; the High Fields of Heaven.

Tamagushi　玉串　A branch of *sakaki*, hung with paper streamers, which is offered to the *kami*. A symbolic offering of clothing for deity.

Tenmei Jikiju　天命直受　Direct Receipt of the Heavenly Mission; Kurozumi Munetada's original revelation.

Tenrikyō　天理教　A new religion founded in 1838 by Naka-yama Miki.

Tochigami　土地神　The earth god widely revered in Okayama.

Tōji　冬至

　Tōji taisai　冬至大祭　The Winter Solstice Festival commemorating the birth of the Founder and his revelation; see chapter six.

Ujigami　氏神　A tutelary deity.

Ujiko　氏子　People living within the territory of the *ujigami*.

Ura　裏　The "inside," the private domain.

Wake-mitama　分霊　The soul of each human being; a microcosm of deity.

Yabarai　家祓い　House Purification; see chapter five.

Yōki　陽気　Vital essence of deity inspired through daily worship of the rising sun. A cheerful, optimistic attitude.

Bibliography

Beasley, William G. *The Meiji Restoration.* Standford: Stanford University Press, 1972.

Befu, Harumi. *Japan, An Anthropological Introduction.* San Francisco: Chandler Publishing Co., 1971.

Bellah, Robert. *Tokugawa Religion.* New York: The Free Press, 1956.

Blacker, Carmen, and Michael, Lowie, eds. *Ancient Cosmologies.* London: George Allen and Unwin, 1975.

Bohm, David. "Human Nature as the Product of Our Mental Models." In *The Limits of Human Nature,* edited by J. Benthall et al. London: Allen Lane, 1973

Daniel, E. Valentine. "Conclusion: Karma, The Uses of an Idea." In *Karma, An Anthropological Inquiry,* edited by Charles F. Keyes and E. V. Daniel. Berkeley and Los Angeles: University of California Press, 1983.

De Bary, William T. *Neo-Confucian Orthodoxy and the Learning of the Mind-and-Heart.* New York: Columbia University Press, 1981.

————, and Irene Bloom, eds. *Principle and Practicality.* New York: Columbia University Press, 1979.

DeVos, George. "Afterword." In *The Quiet Therapies: Japanese Pathways to Personal Growth,* edited by David K. Reynolds. Honolulu: University of Hawaii Press, 1982.

————. "Apprenticeship and Paternalism: Psychocultural Continuities Underlying Japanese Social Organization." In *Modern Japanese Organizations and Decision Making,* edited by Ezra Vogel. Berkeley: University of California Press, 1975.

————. *Socialization for Achievement.* Berkeley: University of California Press, 1973.

Dore, Ronald P. *Education in Tokugawa Japan.* Berkeley: University of California Press, 1965.

Earhart, H. Byron. *Japanese Religion: Unity and Diversity.* 3rd ed. Religious Life of Man series. Belmont, Calif.: Wadsworth Publishing Co., 1982.

—————. *The New Religions of Japan: A Bibliography of Western-Language Materials.* Monumenta Nipponica. Tokyo: Sophia University, 1970.

Eliade, Mircea. *Myths, Dreams, and Mysteries: The Encounter between Contemporary Faiths and Archaic Rites.* Translated by Philip Mairet. New York: Harper and Row, 1960.

Fujii Masao. *Gendaijin no shinkō kōzō.* Nihonjin no kōdō to shisō 32. Tokyo: Hyōronsha, 1974.

—————. "Genze riyaku," pp. 179–238. In *Girei no kōzō,* edited by Tamaru Noriyoshi. Vol. 2 of *Nihonjin no shūkyō.* 4 vols. Tokyo: Kōsei shuppansha, 1972–1973.

Fujitani Toshio. *Shintō shinkō to minshū: Tennōsei.* Kyoto: Hōritsu bunkasha, 1980.

Fukawa Kiyoshi. *Kinsei minshū no rinriteki enerugii.* Nagoya: Fūbaisha, 1976.

Geertz, Clifford. *The Interpretation of Cultures.* New York: Basic Books, 1973.

Gorai Shigeru et al., eds. *Minzoku shūkyō to shakai.* Vol. 5 of their *Kōza Nihon no minzoku shūkyō.* 7 vols. Tokyo: Kōbundō, 1980.

Hall, John W. *Government and Local Power in Japan.* Princeton: Princeton University Press, 1966.

Hara Keigo. "Kōmei tennō to Kurozumikyō." *Kokoro* 23, no. 9 (September 1970): 65–71.

—————. *Kurozumi Munetada.* Jimbutsu Sōsho 42. Tokyo: Yoshikawa kōbunkan, 1960.

Hardacre, Helen. *Lay Buddhism in Contemporary Japan: Reiyūkai Kyōdan.* Princeton: Princeton University Press, 1984.

—————. *The Religion of Japan's Korean Minority: The Preservation of Ethnic Identity.* University of California Insititute of East Asian Studies Korean Studies Monograph 9. Berkeley: University of California, 1984.

—————. "The Transformation of Healing in the Japanese New Religions." *Journal of the History of Religions* 20 (May 1982): 45–60.

Hayashiya Tatsusaburō, ed. *Bakumatsu bunka no kenkyū.* Tokyo: Iwanami shoten, 1978.

Hepner, Charles W. *The Kurozumi Sect of Shinto.* Tokyo: Meiji

Japan Society, 1935.

Hirota Masaki. "Bakumatsu, isshin-ki no Kurozumikyō." *Oka-yama daigaku hōbungakubujutsu kiyō* (Shigaku-hen) 34 (October 1974): 13–25.

———. *Bunmei kaika to minshū ishiki.* Tokyo: Aoki shoten, 1980.

———. *Bunmei kaika to zairai shisō.* Tokyo: Aoki shoten, 1980.

Horton, Robin. "The Kalabari World-View: An Outline and Interpretation," *Africa* 32 (July 1962): 197–220.

Ikado Fujio. "Genze riyaku—sono ronri to shinri." *Nihon Bukkyō* 34 (February 1972): 1–23.

Inoue Nobutaka. "Hamamatsu ni okeru Kurozumikyō no juyō to tenkai." In *Toshi shakai no shūkyō,* edited by Tamaru Noriyoshi. Tokyo: Tokyo daigaku shūkyōgaku kenkyūshitsu, 1981.

———. *Shinshūkyō kenkyū chōsa handobukku.* Tokyo. Yūzan=kaku, 1981.

———. "Shintō-ha shūkyō undō no shisōteki keifu." In *Kindai Nihon no shūkyō shisō undō,* edited by Wakimoto Tsuneya. Tokyo: Tokyo daigaku shūkyō kenkyū shitsu, 1980.

Jansen, Marius B. *Sakamoto Ryōma and the Meiji Restoration.* Princeton: Princeton University Press, 1961.

Kasahara Kazuo. *Nyonin ōjō shisō no keifu.* Tokyo: Yoshikawa kōbunkan, 1975.

Keyes, Charles F. "Introduction: The Study of Popular Ideas of Karma." In *Karma, An Anthropological Inquiry,* edited by Charles F. Keyes and E. V. Daniel. Berkeley and Los Angeles: University of California Press, 1983.

Kishimoto Yoshio. *Kinsei Shintō kyōikushi.* Tokyo: Ōbunsha, 1962.

Kodera Motonoko. "Kurozumikyō no rekishiteki seikaku." *Okayama shigaku* 24 (September 1971): 39–64.

Kōmoto Kazunobu. *Akagi Tadaharu.* Okayama: Kurozumikyō Nisshinsha, 1980.

Kōmoto Kazushi. *Kurozumikyō tokuhon.* Okayama: Kurozumikyō Nisshinsha, 1961.

———. *Kyōsosama no oitsuwa* [*Tales of the Founder*]. Okayama: Kurozumikyō Nisshinsha, 1976.

Kondo, Dorinne K. "Work, Family, and the Self: A Cultural Analysis of Japanese Family Enterprise." Ph. D. dissertation,

Harvard University, 1982.

Kuroda Toshio. *Jisha seiryoku*. Iwanami shinsho 117. Tokyo: Iwanami shoten, 1980.

Kurozumi Muneshi, ed. *Kurozumikyō kyōsho*. Okayama: Kurozumikyō Nisshinsha, 1974.

Kurozumi Tadaaki. *Kurozumikyō kyōsoden*. 5th ed. Okayama: Kurozumikyō Nisshinsha, 1976.

Kurozumikyō kyōgaku kyoku, ed. *Nichiyō norito shū*. Okayama: Kurozumikyō Nisshinsha, 1978.

Kurozumikyō kyōhanhensan iinkai. *Kurozumikyō kyōtenshō*. Okayama: Kurozumikyō Nisshinsha, 1981.

Kurozumikyō Ōmoto Gakuin. *Seikintoku kenroku* 17 (n.d.): 1–12.

Lebra, Takie S. "Self-Reconstruction in Japanese Psychotherapy." In *Cultural Perceptions of Mental Health and Therapies*, edited by A. Marsella and G. White. Dordrecht, Holland: D. Reidel, 1982.

Lock, Andrew. "Universals in Human Nature." In *Indigenous Psychologies: The Anthropology of the Self*, edited by Lock and Paul Heelas. London: Academic Press, 1982.

Lock, Margaret. *East Asian Medicine in Urban Japan*. ed. Charles Leslie. Comparative Studies of Health Systems and Medical Care, no. 4. Berkeley: University of California Press, 1980.

McFarland, H. Neil. *The Rush Hour of the Gods*. New York: Macmillan, 1967.

Maruyama Masao. "R. N. Bellah, *Tokugawa Religion* no shōkai." *Kokka zasshi* 72 (April 1958): 437–58.

Mendelson, E. M. "World View." *International Encyclopedia of the Social Sciences*. 17 vols. New York: Macmillan and The Free Press, 1968, 17:576–79.

Minami Hiroshi. *Nihonjin no shinri*. Iwanami shinsho 149. Tokyo: Iwanami shoten, 1953; 37th printing, 1983.

Minami Kazuo. *Bakumatsu, Edo shakai no kenkyū*. Tokyo: Yoshikawa kōbunkan, 1978.

Ministry of Education. *Shūkyō nenkan*. Tokyo, 1982, 1983.

Miyagi Kimiko. "Henkaku-ki no shisō." *Kōza nihonshi*. ed. Rekishigaku kenkyūkai. 10 vols. Tokyo: Tokyo daigaku shuppankai. 1970–1971. 4:257–86.

Miyake Hitoshi et al., eds. "Genze riyaku kankei bunken mokuroku." *Nihon Bukkyō* 34 (February 1972): 46–47.

Miyata Noboru. *Kami no minzoku shi.* Tokyo: Iwanami shoten, 1979.

Murakami Shigeyoshi. *Japanese Religion in the Modern Period.* Translated by Byron Earhart. Tokyo: Tokyo University Press, 1980.

————. *Kokka Shintō.* Iwanami shinsho 770. Tokyo: Iwanami shoten, 1970.

————. *Konkō daijin no shōgai.* Tokyo: Kōdansha, 1972.

————. *Minshū shūkyō no shisō.* Nihon shisō taikei 67. Tokyo: Iwanami shoten, 2nd printing, 1973.

————. *Seimei no oshie.* Tōyō bunko 319. Tokyo: Heibonsha, 1977.

Muramatsu Yasuko. *Terebi dorama no joseigaku.* Tokyo: Sōtakusha, 1979..

Nagayama Usaburō. *Okayama-ken tsūshi.* 2 vols. Okayama: Seibundō, 1930.

Nakayama Keiichi. *Kyōha Shintō no hassei katei.* Tokyo: Moriyama shoten, 1932.

Namihira Emiko. "Nihon minkan shinkō to sono kōzō." *Minzokugaku kenkyū* 38, nos. 3 and 4 (December 1974): 230–56.

Nobuhara Taisen. *Kurozumi Munetada to sono shūkyō.* Tokyo: Meitoku shuppansha, 1976.

Norbeck, Edward. *Religion and Society in Modern Japan.* Rice University Studies, vol. 56, no. 1. Houston: Rice University, 1970.

Oguri Junko. "Kindai shakai ni okeru kyōha Shintō no hatten," *Kindai bukkyō,* pp. 9–75. Vol. 19 of *Ajia bukkyōshi.* 20 vols. Tokyo: Kōsei shuppansha, 1972.

Okayama Keizai kenkyūjo. *Okayama ken no sangyō kōzō.* Okayama: Okayama-ken. 1980.

Ōkuwa Hitoshi. *Jidan no shisō.* Kyōikusha rekishi shinsho (Nihonshi) 177. Tokyo: Kyōikusha, 1979.

Ono Sokyō. *Jinja Shintō no kiso chishiki to kiso mondai.* Tokyo: Jinja shimpōsha, 1963.

————. *Shinto, The Kami Way.* Rutland, Vt.: Charles E. Tuttle, 1962.

Ooms, Emily. "Deguchi Nao and Ōmoto-kyō: An Analysis of a

Millenarian Cult in Meiji Japan." M. A. thesis, University of Chicago, 1982.

Ōtsuka minzoku gakkai, ed. *Nihon minzoku jiten.* Tokyo: Kōbundō, 1975.

Philippi, Donald. *Norito.* Institute for Japanese Culture and Classics. Tokyo: Kokugakuin University, 1959.

Plath, David. *Long Engagements: Maturity in Modern Japan.* Stanford: Stanford University Press, 1980.

Reynolds, David K. *Morita Psychotherapy.* Berkeley and Los Angeles: University of California Press, 1976.

Robertson, Jennifer. "Rooting the Pine: Shingaku Methods of Organization." *Monumenta Nipponica* 34 (Autumn 1979): 311–32.

Saki Akio. *Shinkō shūkyō.* Tokyo: Aoki shoten, 1960.

Sakurai Tokutarō. *Nihon minkan shinkōron.* Rev. ed. Tokyo: Kōbundō, 1970.

Sasaki Junnosuke. *Bakumatsu shakairon.* Tokyo: Kōshobō, 1969.

Shibata Hajime. *Kinsei gōnō no gakumon to shisō.* Edited by Negishi Yōichi. Tokyo: Shinseisha, 1966.

Shimonaka Yasaburō, ed. *Shintō daijiten.* 3 vols. Tokyo: Heibonsha, 1940.

Shinjō Tsunezō. *Shaji to kōtsū.* Nihon rekishi shinsho. Tokyo: Chibundō, 1960.

Shōji Kichinosuke. *Kinsei minshū shisō no kenkyū.* Tokyo: Kōshobō, 1979.

Shumway, Larry V. "Kibigaku: An Analysis of a Modern Japanese Ritual Music." Ph. D. dissertation, University of Washington, 1974.

Smith, Robert J. *Kurusu: The Price of Progress in a Japanese Village, 1951–1975.* Stanford: Stanford University Press, 1978.

Suzuki Tōzō. *Nihon nenjū gyōji jiten.* Tokyo: Kadokawa shoten, 1977.

Takagi Hirō. *Nihon no shinkō shūkyō.* Tokyo: Iwanami shoten, 1959.

Takenaka Shinjō. *Nihon no tabū.* Tokyo: Kōdansha, 1971.

Tanaka Yoshito. *Kurozumikyō no kenkyū.* Tokyo: Tokyodō shoten, 1918.

Taniguchi Sumio. "Bakumatsu ni okeru Kurozumikyō ni tsuite

no ichikōsatsu." *Okayama daigaku kyōikubu kenkyū shūroku* 6 (March 1968): 65–81.

————. *Okayama-han seishi no kenkyū*. Tokyo: Kōshobō, 1964.

Taylor, Rodney L. "The Cultivation of Sagehood as a Religious Goal in Neo-Confucianism: A study of selected writings of Kao p'an-lung (1562–1626)." Ph. D. dissertation, Columbia University, 1974.

Thomsen, Harry. *The New Religions of Japan*. Rutland, Vt.: Charles E. Tuttle, 1963.

Tsurufuji Ikuta. *Kyōha Shintō no kenkyū*. Tokyo: Rinzan shoten, 1939.

Tsushima Michihito et al. "Shinshūkyō ni okeru seimeishugiteki kyūsai kan." *Shisō* 665 (November 1979): 92–115.

Tu Wei-ming. *Humanity and Self-Cultivation: Essays in Confucian Thought*. Berkeley: Asian Humanities Press, 1978.

Wessing, Robert. *Cosmology and Social Behavior in a West Javanese Settlement*. Ohio University Center for International Studies, Southeast Asia Series no. 47. Athens: Ohio University, 1978.

Wilhelm, Hellmut. *Change, Eight Lectures on the I Ching*. Translated by Cary F. Baynes. Bollingen Series 62. Princeton: Princeton University Press, 1960.

Yamane Ken'ichi. *Bitchū kagura*. Okayama bunko 49. Okayama: Nihon bunkyō shuppan kabushiki kaisha, n.d.

Yasumaru Yoshio. *Nihon no kindaika to minshū shisō*. Tokyo: Aoki shoten, 1974.

Index

Index

LIBRARY OF CONGRESS CATALOGING-IN-PUBLICATION DATA

Hardacre, Helen, 1949–
  Kurozumikyō and the new religions of Japan.

  Bibliography: p.
  Includes index.
  1. Kurozumikyō (Religious organization)
  I. Title.
  BL2222.K884H37   1986   299'.5619   85-43287
  ISBN 0-691-06675-2 (alk. paper)